MINORITIES AND POLICE IN INDIA

Minorities and Police in India

Edited by

ASGHAR ALI ENGINEER
AMARJIT S. NARANG

MANOHAR
2006

First published 2006

ISBN 81-7304-678-6

Published by
Ajay Kumar Jain for
Manohar Publishers & Distributors
4753/23 Ansari Road, Daryaganj
New Delhi 110 002

Typeset by
Kohli Print
Delhi 110 051

Printed at
Lordson Publishers Pvt. Ltd.
New Delhi 110 007

Distributed in South Asia by
FOUNDATION BOOKS
4381/4, Ansari Rorad
Daryaganj, New Delhi 110 002
and its branches at Mumbai, Hyderabad,
Bangalore, Chennai, Kolkata

Contents

Preface

The volume is a collection of selected papers presented at a seminar on 'Police and Minorities: Lessons for Human Rights Education' organized jointly by the Human Rights Education Programme of Indira Gandhi National Open University (IGNOU) and Centre for Study of Society and Secularism, Mumbai, in New Delhi. The seminar was sponsored by the Ministry of Human Resource Development, Government of India, as part of the National Action Programme for UN Decade for Human Rights Education (1995–2005). Some of the papers were specially commissioned for the volume after the seminar.

The seminar was held primarily to look into the questions and issues raised by victims of communal violence regarding the callous and prejudiced attitude of the Police during riots. The purpose of the seminar was not just to condemn the police or highlight their failures but to take note of the phenomena in a proper perspective. It is well known that the police in India is not only part of the state-structure but is also completely under political control. Therefore when we discuss the role of the police in any situation, we have to take into account the role of different organs of the state and that of the political leadership. While we expect from the police force that they should deal with law breakers, murderers and looters irrespective of whether they are Hindus, Muslims, Christians or Sikhs, we have to keep in mind how much of the departmental hierarchy in police and their political masters are actually free from communal and social biases. It is also true that most police personnel, particularly at lower level, due to their own social orientation and mindsets, themselves get swayed by communal prejudices and willingly allow themselves to be governed by the local politicians. As an observer points out, the changing nature of politics, the response of the civil services to it and the legitimacy that blatant Hinduization has provided to both politics and administration, has further complicated the problems.

The issue of police attitude and behaviour towards minorities, therefore can not be seen in isolation or be changed likewise. What is needed is a comprehensive understanding and analysis in an holistic manner and from a multidisciplinary approach. Keeping this in view the seminar was organized as an interactive dialogue among professionals concerned with the issues involved. These included academics, journalists, police officers, lawyers, human rights activists and minority right advocates. Contents of the papers in the volume reflect this multidisciplinary and societal approach. We present this volume with the hope that it will help in generating a fresh debate and demand for much needed police reforms, as also sensitize police and administration towards their social duties.

We express our sincere thanks to the Ministry of Human Resource Development, Government of India for its remove funding for the seminar under the scheme of Studies, Seminars, Evaluation, etc., for implementation of Education policy. We take this opportunity to express our sincere thanks to Prof. H.P. Dikshit, Vice-Chancellor, IGNOU and Prof. S.C. Garg, Pro Vice-Chancellor for supporting and encouraging us in holding the seminar.

We owe our grateful thanks to our contributors, who really have given shape to this book. We thank colleagues and staff members at Centre for Study of Society and Secularism, Mumbai and School of Social Sciences, IGNOU without whose help the seminar would not have been held successfully. Special mention needs to be made of Prof. Pandav Nayak, Professor of Political Science who originally conceived the idea of the seminar. We also express our appreciation for the transcribers who transformed the tapes to texts. Dr. Pankaj Bhan gave shape to the transcripts. We thank him sincerely. Our thanks are also due to Shri Ramesh Jain of Manohar for his enthusiastic interest in the publication of the volume.

Asghar Ali Engineer
Amarjit S. Narang

Introduction

AMARJIT S. NARANG

Lessons of history reiterate that diversities cannot and must not be suppressed, ignored or bypassed. To do so would give rise to resistance, conflict and ultimately withdrawal from the nation state. A keen student of history and a great visionary Jawaharlal Nehru made this point about India as early as 1930. In the *Young India* of 15 May 1930, he wrote,

> The history of India and of many of the countries of Europe has demonstrated that there can be no stable equilibrium in any country so long as an attempt is made to crush a minority or to force it to confirm to the ways of the majority. There is no surer method of rousing the resentment of the minority and keeping it apart from the rest of the nation than to make it feel that it has not got the freedom to stick to its own way. Repression and coercion can never succeed in coercing a minority. They but make it more self-conscious and more determined to value and hold fast to what it considers its very own. It matters little whether logic is on its side or whether its own particular brand of culture is worthwhile or not. The mere fear of losing it makes it dear. Freedom to keep it would itself lessen its value. . . . Therefore, we in India must make it clear to all that our policy is based on granting this freedom to the minorities and that under no circumstances will any coercion or repression of them be tolerated. There is hardly any likelihood of economic questions affecting the minorities as such, but should they do so we can also lay down as our deliberate policy that there shall be no unfair treatment of any minority. Indeed we should go further and state that it will be the business of the State to give favoured treatment to minority and backward communities.

The Constitution of India, did reflect this concern of Nehru and others committed to build a new India based on principles of equality and justice. The Constitution projected an India based on not only provisions of liberty, equality and fraternity but also promised justice: social, economic and political. Thus backward classes including scheduled castes and tribes, and minorities visualized their aspirations being fulfilled in the new democratic secular republic. SCs/STs were provided with the reservation system in educational institutions, government employment and state and central legislatures. Untouchability was abolished. There were provisions for the improvement of backward classes laid down in the Constitution. The minorities were guaranteed all protection from the onslaught of the majority. The right to run educational institutions of their choice with a view to help minorities preserve and develop their culture was granted. The Constitution also guaranteed to all citizens equality before and equal protection of law. But in spite of a Constitution described by some observers as an instrument for socio-economic transformation, right from the beginning, there started emerging a vast gap between the stated objectives and actual performance of the government both in formation of policies and their implementation, more so in the latter. Various reasons and explainations for that has been provided by many observers and in critiques from different perspectives and ideological preferences. Within these, one generally agreed reason for non-fulfillment of many constitutional goals has been the initial continuation of and later further decay in the Indian administrative structure including the law and order machinery.

Without entering into the debate on general nature and role of civil and police administration during colonial and post-independence periods, one can at least agree with the observation that to begin with, although ruler-oriented, pro-rules and not pro-people these services were more or less competent, motivated and above all neutral. But during last fifty years, over a course of time, neutrality and independence have given way to jobbery and politicking for receiving undue favours. As a result both the IAS and IPS have suffered a measurable decline in terms of professionalism and integrity. In recent years, these standards have almost reached their nadir. The Gujarat carnage (2002) once again proved that the system and the administrative the law and order machinery in India, cannot be trusted to act with fairness and objectivity. Rather than follow dictates of the Constitution most of them got swayed by their communal prejudices and willingly allowed themselves to be governed by the local politicians forgetting that they were duty-bound to save the lives of innocent citizens. This observation in fact is more applicable to the police force.

The excessive use of force, when strictly not warranted, and a failure to maintain a posture of neutrality between communities, are according to a former senior police officer, R.K. Raghavan, two distressing features of the Gujarat scene, and in fact not for the first time. Various commissions of enquiry appointed after communal riots have in general pointed out that the police were partisan in favour of the majority Hindu community, or they had failed to anticipate trouble or had acted indecisively at the beginning of trouble to bring the situation under control.

It is also true that most incidents of communal tension, particularly riots, are usually planned in advance. This planning is done by some political party or even by some anti-social elements to serve their own interests or those of their political patrons. When a riot is pre-planned, an appropriate atmosphere needs to be created and this is often done with a view to raise communal temperature by spreading some atrocious rumour. This greatly helps in spreading communal violence and also in justifying it. In other words, the violence acquires legitimacy in the eyes of people of community which is aggressing against the other. The role of the administration and the police in such cases becomes much more complex and even difficult. The police officials cannot normally ignore the instructions from their ruling political bosses. It is not always true that the police has a free hand to deal with a situation. It has to face several constraints as the political bosses themselves do not have a clean hand. In the case of the Gujarat carnage, for example, there were complaints that a few senior police officers who acted firmly to protect Muslims were transferred out on unspecified grounds, thereby transmitting the message that the state government was not in favour of safeguarding the minority community.

The role of police, while dealing with minorities, particularly during communal riots, thus remains controversial. There are views suggesting that the police personnel themselves have become much communalized over the years. At the same time it is also pointed out that policemen behave harshly with all weaker sections of society, mostly involving poor of the upper castes and of course dalits. It is also partly because of the whole corrupt political atmosphere in the country. As pointed out above, it is said that not only the police and paramilitary forces have failed in quelling communal riots and disturbances, but the very governments which pretend to be secular and democratic have politicized these forces due to their own communal and non-secular outlook. Similarly there have been debates about the methods of recruitment and training of police personnel, the powers vested in them, their service conditions and accountability. Some observers, for instance, suggest that police officials, particularly at lower level, are terribly overworked, more so during communal disturbances. They are often required to perform round the clock duty on such occasions. Also they perceive danger to their life. The tension of their working conditions make them highly inflammable and they tend to overreact. They take revenge against innocent persons. They are also deeply affected by communal propaganda like any other ordinary citizen.

Whatever may be the explanations, there now is a general feeling that the Indian Police personnel are not as objective as they should be in protecting minorities. This, as said in the beginning , is not conducive for the stability and development of the nation. Police, for the common man, personifies State power, he or she, gets alienated from the State itself due to police behaviour. To realize the developmental objectives of the State, apart from other things, there also has to be a sea-change in perceptions of the public in general and vulnerable sections and minorities in public vis-à-vis the police.

It is against this background, the papers in the volume, are just not critiques of police behaviour and attitude but attempt to analyse various aspects leading to such situation. While highlighting the gravity of situation the purpose here is to sensitize the police, the civil society, and administration and persuation for necessary but long over due reforms.

Asghar Ali Engineer's paper 'Making and Unmaking of Muslim Stereotypes', written on the basis of his vast experience of conducting enquiries into incidents of communal riots and conducting training programmes for police personnel brings out the psycho-social attitude of the personnel as part of the large society in perpetuating carrying certain stereotypes about the Muslims, particularly their being responsible for partition of the country and deserving to be punished for that. Engineer finds out text books, popular literature and a section of press, especially the language press contributing to this stereotyping rather than looking into the fact that not more than 5 per cent Muslims had supported the creation of Pakistan and a larger section decided to stay in India even after partition, believing this to be their homeland. Engineer also asks the question that how can the present generation of Indian Muslims who were not around at the time of the partition and had nothing to do with the creation of Pakistan can be held responsible for that? Creation of this stereotype, however, helps some politicians to create vote banks for them. Engineer, finds police personnel also influenced by such propaganda. The way out, according to him lies in changing the recruitment system and reforming the training system significantly. There is need for reflection of plurality of society in the police force also.

My paper on 'Minorities and Police in India' provides an overview of the situation and analyses the nature of functioning of police when protecting minorities and dealing with them as groups, particularly in situations of communal tensions in the context of state's obligations towards minorities as per accepted international norms and India's Constitution and politico-legal commitments. It tries to locate various reasons for the blatantly partisan role of police vis-à-vis the minorities which has been well documented by various commissions of inquiries and otherwise. The reasons brought out include the continuation of the colonial structure of the police force, the regular political interference in the day to day working of police, social composition and orientation of the force as a mirror of general societal attitude towards Muslim minority in particular and lack of adequate necessary training and proper working conditions. While the police behave harshly with all weaker sections of the society, they are particularly so against minorities for historical and social reasons. While need for reforms and necessary recommendations are available from various sources there obviously is lack of political and administrative will, so the rut continues.

K.S. Dhillon's paper 'Democracy, Pluralism and Police in India' traces the development and transformation of police and its nature from colonial period to independent India. As far as the police, and the civil services in general, are concerned, Dhillon points out that independence was not an abrupt break with the past. While in terms of orientation and class origin the police force remained the same, there set in motion a process of change in their relationship with the new class of politicians. This new relationship rather than improving the nature and functioning of the police further deteriorated it. The much needed reforms did not engage the attention of either the political class or the bureaucracy. The result according to Dhillon is that even after having done reasonably well in many cases, in spite of limitations, the Indian police were not able to live down their historical legacies. Delineating the long course of historical developments from colonial period to the present in the context of socio-political changes, Dhillon analyses the recommendations of the National

Police Commission for changes and finds even those wanting in the present context. He is also of the opinion that judicial activism has limited role in changing the scenario. The need according to him is for radical reforms which can be stimulated only by public awareness of their rights and powers in an enlightened but assertive manner.

R.K. Raghavan in his essay 'Maintaining Social Order' delineates the system of police functioning in handling situations of social disorder, including inter-religious riots. He analyses this in pre and post-independence periods. In both these periods the police had been subjected to myriad influences but of different types. Raghavan suggests that in the pre-independence period while the initial police response was defensive and tardy, a degree of professionalism was acquired in course of time. In independent India the decay of the police has been extensive, and the force has been criticized widely for functioning as the handmaiden of the political party in power. This impression has unfortunately become stronger over the years. According to Raghavan while police has been facing new types of problems and pressures, in the absence of proper training, orientation, sufficient manpower and autonomy, their responses have remained inadequate. Non-implementation of the National Police Commission recommendations, Raghavan points out, is one major reason for police subordination to the political executive instead of the law of the land. As long as politicians look upon the police as a tool to settle political scores with adversaries, nothing will alter.

Prakash Louis's paper on 'Place and Role of Police in a Plural Society' looks into the emerging questions like, is the police protective, detective or repressive? He examines these questions in the light of the Constitution of India envisaging a socialist, secular and democratic form of government. Louis while agrees that like any other police in the world, Indian police is also part of the existing social order, suggests that here due to the existing socio-political, economic and cultural system the police force is treated with callous apathy and animated hostility. He makes a class analysis of the socio-political power-structure prevailing in Indian society, which the police is part and parcel of-Looking into the police role in communal situations, particularly in Gujarat he expresses concern about the direction of the politicization of police that is taking place. While at the senior level there are both types of officers, at lower level of officers and constabulary, communalization is all pervasive. Considering this to be a threat to the very norms of democracy in a plural society Louis poses the question 'Is the Indian society and polity willing to engage in the much needed task of police reforms?'

P.D. Malaviya's paper 'Police and the Minorities in India' tracing the causes for police bias against religious minorities, particularly since the 1970s, provides some useful suggestions for the change. According to him the causes of change in police attitude and behaviour today include, policemen's exposure to communal virus prevailing in the society, corruption and indiscipline in the force, domination of the ruling political elite over the police force, among other things. Malaviya also finds some problems with the recommendations of the National Police Commission in the matter, particularly with regard to police being subjected to overall guidance from the government in preventive tasks. This according to him is so because in the present scenario there is no certainty that there will always be a secular government in all the states or that communal riots will not be engineered to settle power-struggle within a secularist party when it is in power. Malaviya, therefore feels that the only solution lies in bringing the weight of public opinion to bear against the misuse of the police by the ruling elite. He also suggests that the police should work in an open manner, and police priorities be aligned with public concerns.

A.R. Vijapur and Md. Mohibul Haque, in their paper titled 'Endangered Minorities in India: Understanding the Role of Police' focus on how the rights of minorities stand unprotected because of the most visible hands of the state, i.e. police turning against them. They analyse the police attitude towards minorities in the wider context of the general picture of police which is one of fear and disgust as also the enormous legal powers they enjoy. This detestable attitude of police towards the general public, according to the authors assumes a larger and more vicious magnitude when police minority relations are analysed. The situation has further deteriorated because of the dirty alliance between an institution for maintaining law and order and an ideology for creating communal hatred. The authors fear that the Indian State will pass into a phase of total anarchy if the communalization of its most visible hand continues like this.

K.S. Subramanian's paper 'Police and the Minorities: A Study of the Role of the Police during Communal Violence in India' after reviewing the phenomena of communal violence during the last fifty years analyses the role of the police in some major instances in the recent period. This he studies in the background of the emergence of a aggressive form of Hindu nationalism from the mid-1980s to the 1990s and thereafter. Subramanian, discusses the Gujarat carnage in some detail and brings out, how police remained ineffective because of the nature of politics prevailing in that state during the last decade. He also suggests that to understand police participation and apathy, the historical background of the inherited administrative machinery in South Asia, which is basically regulatory rather than developmental also needs to be appreciated. Subramanian, therefore concludes that unless far-reaching reforms are carried out, the phenomena of socio-political violence witnessed recently in Gujarat and elsewhere is likely to continue. Like some other writers, he also feels that at present political will to carry out these reforms is lacking mainly because communal mobilization for political gain has become an important factor for professional politicians.

Arshi Khan in his paper 'Police Prejudice against the Muslims' looking in the context that the role and attitude of the police are crucial in the case of the protection of minorities and their rights suggests that in India affirmation of the minimum rights to life and security stand negated by the wide powers vested in police and their prejudiced attitude. According to him the majoritarian attitude of the Congress and the question of communal settlement raised by the Muslim League which dealt a death-blow to the process of Hindu-Muslim unity during the national movement had shaped the communal psychology of the police personnel. This has been further accentuated due to rise of communalism, violence, and exclusion of minorities particularly the Muslims.

In his paper 'Police Partisanship during Communal Riots: Need for its Secularization and Pluralization' Iqbal Ansari while bringing out the well documented partisan role of police during communal riots suggests some of the reforms measures that are required to be implemented for good governance in making the police function again as an instrument of the rule of law. His recommendations include setting up of statutory State Security Commissions in the states for making the police autonomous and accountable, introduction of special courses, as part of training, for eradication of communal prejudices, amendment of the police manual and riot control schemes, adequate representation of minorities in state and central police forces, etc. All these he suggests in the context that in a democratic system the police cannot perform its basic duty, if it is organized as a ruler appointed body carrying out policies formulated on the basis of political calculations.

Chaman Lal, in his paper titled 'Need for People Friendly Police' discusses the role of police in a democratic republic. In that context he finds that the present structural basis of police based on the 1861 Police Act is not conducive to that as the sole purpose of this Act was to provide for a police which could prevent and investigate crime, maintain order and protect the overall colonial interests. The concept of a people friendly police was alien to this Act and the citizen as an entity did not figure in it. He points out that even after independence, police had been thinking largely about its combat capabilities only. Because of that, the police tackles problems of communalism, terrorism, insurgency, left-wing extremism, etc., only by treating their symptoms without analysing the root causes. He points out that whenever temporary success is achieved through expediency, a heavy price has to be paid in the long run. Chaman Lal also brings out some of the problems the police faces, particularly with extra emphasis being laid on human rights some times. He accordingly brings out urgency for police reforms and a change in police-civil society relationship.

H.S. Phoolka's paper 'The Infamous Carnage of November 1984' and that of Vrinda Grover 'Institutional Impunity' are case studies of the 1984 anti-sikh riots in Delhi and the role of the Police in those. Both Phoolka and Grover had made extensive surveys among riot-hit areas and people. Therefore the papers are based on ground realities. According to Phoolka violence against Sikhs in Delhi was not a communal riot. It was a violence in which one community was targeted. During this violence, the attitude of the police was so atrocious that it cannot merely be called a bias or prejudice. Not only ordinary Sikhs, even the then President of India, being a Sikh was not spared. The police's conduct during the carnage and thereafter bear out the assessment that it was working to a plan. Phoolka, to substantiate his point, presents statistics of those killed and arrested from among the victims rather from among the accused. He also points out the nature of police action at specific places in the city.

Vrinda Grover's paper is basically the affidavit she filed before Justice Nanavati Commission of Enquiry that was appointed to look afresh into the riots and ascertain the identity of the perpetrators and the responsbilities of those required to control. Grover in her affidavit based on the study of various documents submitted before the first commission of enquiry (Justice Ranganath Misra Commission) and in various courts of law and judgements brings out how the police investigation in riot cases was faulty and biased. She cites cases and observations of judges to highlight how during the carnage, law and machinery was completely paralysed because of inaction/connivance of the police. In addition the police inaction and complicity during the violence and killings as evidenced by their non-recording or delayed recording of FIRs and statements weakened the case of prosecution and enabled the accused to secure an acquittal. By bringing out the police attitude and behaviour Grover corroborates the findings of various enquiry reports pointing out the anti-minority bias of police that determines their actions, conduct, decisions and orders. Along with some other writers in this volume she also opines that the political will to overhaul the present structure of functioning and accountability of the police is obviously lacking as the current arrangement suits the vested interests of those in power.

Ajay Mehra in his paper tracing the history of Police Reforms in India from 1950s brings out that while the need for police reforms was not missed by leaders, in due course the political class found the the colonial culture of police useful for them. Therefore the useful reports prepared by commissions were consigned to cold storage. Another reason for lack of reforms, Mehra points out is the fact of law and order being a state subject and reluctance of the Union government to interfere in that for obvious reasons. Mehra analyses the National Police Commission (Chaired by Dharma Vira) Report in particular and finds it to be comprehensive and relevant even today. He therefore recommends a fresh debate on the NPC report and urgent initiation of police reforms in the interest of consolidation of democracy and fulfilment of people's aspiration.

CHAPTER 1

Making and Unmaking of Muslim Stereotypes

ASGHAR ALI ENGINEER

Recently a few trainee police officers in UK were suspended for their racial remarks against Asians. The BBC had made a secret film on these trainee officers and they were caught passing racist remarks against Asians. It came as a shock to the authorities and immediate action was taken against the concerned officers. According to newspaper reports four British police officers had been suspended following allegations of racism prompted by the BBC documentary.

This was the biggest survey of the forces ever undertaken. Nearly 13,000 officers were scanned for sexual and racist attitude among the police force. The study led by Professor Gus John, a key adviser to Home Secretary David Blunkett on race issues found evidence that at virtually every stage of the prosecution process Asian and black people appeared to suffer discrimination.

Britain is becoming a pluralistic society and the authorities are worried that the police may not have the right attitudes to handle law and order in the new pluralistic set up.

It is in sharp contrast to the attitude of Indian authorities towards those policemen who publicly display their anti-minority bias. No action has ever been taken against any erroneous police officer. Every communal riot has its own story of police atrocities towards minorities.

It is quite clear from what is stated above that the Indian police, in general, with some honourable exceptions at higher echelons, is strongly biased against minorities. So is the UK and USA police. The Situation in India perhaps is somewhat more serious.

I have been an observer of the communal situation since the Jabalpur riots of 1961 and there is no major riot that I have not covered personally. I have been to all those places—Ahmedabad in 1969, Bhiwandi in 1970, Bihar Sharif in 1981, Meerut and Baroda in 1982, Nelli in 1983, Bhiwandi–Mumbai in 1984, Ahmedabad in 1985, Meerut in 1987 and Bhagalpur in 1989. Of course, I am a denizen of Mumbai and I was in Mumbai in 1992–3 and again in Ahmedabad in 2002 when riots of unprecedented dimensions raged in these cities. I have visited these places personally, and not only talked to victims but also to the police in all these places. In my travels to the riot-torn places I have found both types of police personnel—secular policemen who were really worried, because they were helpless and they couldn't do anything, and also policemen who were communalists to the core.

I can offer many instances from these riots. I went to Nelli in 1983 where 4,000 people were slaughtered—Muslims of the so-called Bangladeshi origin. When I talked to some senior policemen and asked them what caused these riots, they replied, 'You know, these Muslims raped Hindu women, cut off their breasts and carried them on their shoulders'. This was a rumour set afloat by vested interests to provoke rioting. To my shock I found that police officers too were indulging in such rumour mongering. Having means at their command, they could investigate and find out the truth. But instead they chose to lend credence to these rumours. In Mumbai, I talked to many constables, and whichever constable I talked to invariably had a copy of *Saamna* (the official organ of Shiv Sena) in his hand. Now, if they read *Saamna*, we can understand the kind of influence working on their minds. In fact, one constable told me, with a considerable amount of pride, 'Just take off my *vardi* (uniform) and you'll find a Shiv Sainik beneath'. They even said that their basic loyalty was not to the rule of law but to Shiv Sena. It is no surprise that Srikrishna Commission has named 32 police officers, right from the IPS down to the level of constables, as guilty of communal conduct. The learned judge has passed severe strictures against them.

In Jabalpur, in 1961, the armed constabulary got into Muslim houses, molested Muslim women, snatched their necklaces along with all the valuables they could lay their hands on and generally looted their houses. During the riots, a local paper carried a headline that in a particular mosque there is a transmitter and they are receiving instructions from Pakistan on that instrument. Accompanied by veteran social activists like Subhadra Joshi, B.D. Joshi, S.B. Kolpe and others and also by police officials, I rushed to the mosque. We did not find even a transistor, not to speak of a transmitter. When I asked a journalist belonging to the paper why such trash had been published, he replied, *Saab, aap log bahar se aatey hain . . . chale jayenge . . . hamey to shehar main rehna hai aur hamari roti bhi kamani hai.* The message was very clear—'Whatever the truth, we have to write what our owners want us to write in this climate of surcharged communal feelings'.

Another story that a Hindu girl, Usha Bhargav was raped by a Muslim youth turned out to be equally false. All that happened was that Usha Bhargav and a Muslim youth loved each other and wanted to marry. This was simply unacceptable to her community and the canard was created and spread duly assisted by the local media. Unfortunately, Usha Bhargav became the first victim of the canard. Being a sensitive young woman, she could not take the supposed rape charge and committed suicide. Taking cue from this unfortunate incident the violence—probably the first major riot in independent India—spread throughout Jabalpur and beyond it.

I would not like to tar the image of the entire police force with the same brush. I have found many police officers very honest, quite impartial and secular in the discharge of their duties. I must put on record the excellent work done by Satish who was the Commissioner of Police in Mumbai after the communal riots. After his duty hours, he would go to *mohalla* after *mohalla* inhabited by Muslims and spend hours there listening to what the Muslims had to say—their problems, their experiences, their perception of the role of police in communal riots, etc. There is Powar who was additional commissioner of police when violence took place in 1992–3. He saved the lives of several Muslims in Devnar area. Many Muslims told me that but for Powar, the casualty number of Muslims would have been much higher. Similarly, in Pydhuri area, many Muslims told me about the upright conduct of Zende who was the assistant commissioner of police in that area. There was Sanjay Pandey in Dharavi who handled the endemic communal situation in that area in an honest and upright manner.

In one of the workshops that I conducted Sanjay Pandey was present. During the tea break, he took me aside and told me 'Engineer Saab, why are you so soft and guarded in your assessment of police role in communal riots? Why don't you bring out the police role in 1992–3 riots in a forthright manner?' Sanjay Pandey was such an honest and bold person. It need not surprise us that he was penalized for his boldness. He was transferred to an unimportant department. He was demoted and hounded out. Disgusted, he resigned and left the police force. There have been others like O.P. Bali, Suresh Khopado, Vibhuti Narain Rai, Vikas Narain Rai, S.M. Mushrif, V.N. Deshmukh and others, who had performed examplary service.

At lower levels in the police force, the situation is pretty dismal. I have conducted several workshops with 'ordinary' policemen. These people carry certain stereotypes about the Muslims. In one workshop, I asked a policeman, 'If I utter the word 'Muslim', what is the first image that gets registered in your mind?' He replied honestly, 'That of a criminal.' I persisted, 'But why should a Muslim be associated with crime?' 'All Muslims are criminals. In one way or the other, they are associated with Dawood Ibrahim. He is their hero.' Another constable replied, 'When you say the word 'Muslim', it brings to my mind the image of a cruel, heartless person.' 'But why?' 'Look here, Sir. They eat all kinds of meat—mutton, chicken, fish, even beef. They don't spare any animal, not even the poor, humble cow.' I asked this constable, 'But even Hindus take meat. There are certain castes and groups within the Hindu fold which take even beef. Then why should the Muslims be called cruel simply because they eat meat?' The constable felt that his argument had got a little weak. But he came out with a rebound, 'Their religion is cruel. Anyone who follows that religion becomes cruel.' So this is the ground reality. It is a social malady and unless we address it squarely, we shall not succeed in secularizing the police force.

We have to confront this stereotypical image of the Muslim community and try to change it—especially in the minds and psyche of the police force. This can basically be done at three levels. One is the family atmosphere, the second is the school textbook, and the third is the media. All these contribute to a distorted image of the Muslims that we see embedded in the psyche of the police force. The fulminations of the communal politicians, who incite raw, atavistic feelings among the people, only add to this phenomenon.

We also see gross discrimination when it comes to penalizing people for inciting communal feelings. Let me give you an example. It is again from the Marathi daily *Saamna* run by Shiv Sena. This paper has been regularly publishing inflammatory material often vilifying the Muslim community. But the police force has not dared to check it, or file a case against it. There is an Urdu paper published from Mumbai which once carried an inflammatory article on communal violence that took place in Meerut in 1987. The editor of the paper was immediately arrested, and rightly so. But why is no action taken against *Saamna*? Why this discrimination? If law is to be applied, it should be done with impartiality and objectivity.

I have been repeatedly arguing that vernacular language papers betray pronounced communal proclivities and this works on the psyche of the readers, including the police force. In 1982, I went to Meerut to report on the communal riots that had taken place there. During my visit, I also went to the infamous Feroze Building where the PAC had opened fire rather indiscriminately killing a large number of people. Almost at the same time, veteran leader Subhadra Joshi too visited the spot. Later, she held a meeting for peace and communal harmony. But the next day, one local Hindi paper reported: *Subhadra Joshi ki meeting mein sampradayikta ka nanga naach* (naked display of communalism at Subhadra Joshi's meeting). This was a total distortion of the purpose of the meeting and what had transpired there. Now, when an ordinary policeman reads such news reports day after day, how is he going to be affected? Obviously, he will have a very distorted perception of the Muslim community which will affect the discharge of his duties in a volatile communal situation.

Yet another incident took place in another police training session where I was lecturing a group of women constables. During the question-answer session, a woman constable stood up and asked me, 'Sir, don't you think that all Muslims are loyal to Pakistan?' Now, this question of Muslims identifying themselves with Pakistan is another stereotype that rankles in the hearts of the Hindus, except those who are strongly committed to secularism. Any discussion on this issue leads to the bigger question—whether it was right or wrong to divide the country. Muslims are paying the price for the blunder of Pakistan because our textbooks are presenting facts regarding the partition in an insidiously communal way. They are not giving the whole truth.

Our textbooks and popular literature on partition presents the issue in such a way that it makes every Muslim responsible for the genesis of Pakistan. The historical fact is that not more than 5 per cent Muslims had supported the creation of Pakistan while 95 per cent had either nothing to do with Pakistan or they were politically and emotionally opposed to it. These facts are not known to ordinary people. That is why during the communal riots, when police arrests Muslims, they also taunt them by asking them to go to Pakistan.

Such perceptions, and utterances on the part of the police are indicative of the kind of environment that still persists in our country.

Moreover, the present generation of Indian Muslims, who were not around at the time of the partition and could not have anything to do with the creation of Pakistan, cannot be held responsible for whatever happened at that time. Let us not get caught in a time warp.

Now, let us delve a little deeper in the social background of the demand for Pakistan. The 5 per cent of Muslims who had a sneaking desire for the creation of a separate Muslim nation came from the elite class. They saw their future as being bleak in India and they sensed opportunities for quick growth in a newly carved nation. Eminent sociologist Professor Hamza Alvi, who is presently based in Pakistan, has repeatedly argued that it were the salaried classes among the Muslims who were responsible for the creation of Pakistan. In modern-day India, the Muslim representation in the civil services does not go beyond 2–3 per cent. But at the time of the partition, the Muslim representation in the police, the army, the educational services and in other areas was much higher. All these people rushed to Pakistan. They thought that in independent India, their representation in the services would go down. That was the fear and for that they supported the Pakistan movement. There were no capitalists among the Muslims. So it was not a capitalist conspiracy. There were, of course, the feudals and they too joined the Muslim League. But what had the Muslim masses to do with Pakistan? For a tonga-wallah, a mechanic, a peasant—Pakistan did not matter at all.

Let me narrate a very interesting experience that I had in Karachi. While waiting for a friend to pick me up, I saw a sweeper sweeping the street in front of me. Out of sheer curiosity, I asked the person his name. He happened to be a Dalit Hindu. I asked him why he did not migrate to India at the time of Partition. His reply was revealing. He said, 'Sir I'm a sweeper and my job is to sweep streets. It does not matter whether the street is in Pakistan or in India.' That precisely must have been the logic of ordinary Muslims at that time. That was the reason why an overwhelming majority of Muslims preferred to stay back. Only the zamindars, the bureaucracy, the police and the army officers and their dependents migrated. When at the many workshops where I speak I reveal these facts to the trainees, they tell me that they did not know these. From this point begins the process of rethinking and change. This intellectual impact is very important.

But our education system, our media, our political establishment are not doing it. On the other hand, they are accentuating the cleavage. So in this scenario, how can we expect our police force to rise above prejudices and to be even-handed in a communally sensitive situation?

We often hear of policemen raping Muslim women. Such acts are justified by saying: 'During the Muslim rule, the Hindu women were molested. What's wrong in doing the same to them now when the power is in our hands?' Such notions are injected into them through our textbooks. Often, even educated Hindus say: 'The Muslim rulers demolished our temples. They harmed our religion and culture.' Such ideas, if left unconstested proliferate and infect a lot many people, even educated and intelligent ones.

We have developed a history module for our workshops. We take up topics like medieval history and communalism; British rule and communalism; genesis of Pakistan and Communalism; post-independence India and the re-emergence of communalism and the like. We explain everything to them: how to understand medieval history, the truth behind the temple-mosque controversy, and the behaviour of the rulers towards the ruled in medieval ages, etc. This comes as enlightenment to people. These are simple things but these have never been told to them. All they have been told about are real or supposed ill doings of Mehmood Ghaznavi and Aurangzeb. The entire history of medieval India veers round these villains. Then some of our political parties or leaders create and nurture Hindu vote banks by making fantastic claims that 3,000 temples were converted into mosques. Such ideas are drilled into the minds of common people day-in and day-out. How can our police personnel remain immune to such propaganda?

I can offer some suggestions to rectify the situation. One, training courses must be conducted at the stage of recruitment itself. This will remove from the mind of the new entrants distorted perspectives and false stereotyping. In other words, at the time of recruitment, we must ensure that the person has the right attitude. But who will do such screening? A large number of recruiting staff may themselves be affected by the communal virus. In spite of these snags, we must put in place a system of recruitment where only those persons are allowed to join the police force who are secular in outlook or at least do not have crude communal prejudices. We can definitely devise means for ensuring this.

Two, we must see to it that our police force is truly reflective of the diversity of our society. If our police force is diverse, if social diversity is reflected in recruitment, it will lead to closer interaction and ultimately melting away of insidious stereotypes that member of different communities may have about each other. Stereotypes get engendered in isolation. If I remain in isolation from the Hindus, then anybody who tells me anything about the Hindus, I will believe it. But if I am interacting with the Hindus, then such stereotypes will not hold true for me. The Hindus and the Muslims, who have been interacting, develop a healthy attitude towards each other. Without social interaction, the Muslims will continue to describe the Hindus as *kafirs* (which, incidentally, is not a Koranic injunction) while the Hindus will continue to see the Muslims as violent and aggressive.

Unfortunately, at present, the police force has a minuscule number of Muslims. The Muslim representation in Maharashtra Police is less than 2 per cent. It is not, therefore, surprising that the general attitude of the state police towards the Muslims is prejudiced. Diversity in representation would go some way in mitigating this problem.

Three, our textbooks are doing great damage to the composite fabric of our culture and must be revised. Our culture is a composite one and all communities—including Muslims—have contributed to it. I cannot think of any community which has not had a role in the flowering of Indian culture and civilization.

This composite culture gets reflected in our day-to-day life. I once had a Muslim friend who hailed from a rural area. Every week he used to narrate to me portions of the *Ramayana*. He used to take part in *Ramleela* in his village. Thus my entire knowledge of the *Ramayana* has come from a person who was, by faith, a Muslim. He would tell me about Lord Rama's idealism, about Hanuman's devotion, about Sita's loyalty and so on. We had Bhakti saints and Sufi mendicants who attacked religious orthodoxy and talked of the unity of mankind. This is the composite culture that I am talking about. This composite culture should be made a part of the police training. If only these communal stereotypes and ingrained prejudices are drained out and a healthy attitude towards the minorities inculcated, the police force can serve the society in a far more efficient and productive manner.

What is needed is to sensitize the police to communal and racist situations in a multi-racial and multi-religious society. India is bewilderingly diverse and a police officer should be thoroughly aware of this social situation. His thinking should be purged of all majoritarian ethos or majoritarian arrogance. A qualitative democracy should ensure equal rights for all, whether belonging to majority or minority.

To thus educate the police a thorough training programme is needed. But there is no such effort and the training module for the police does not include any such material.

It would be in the interest of our multi-religious and multi-cultural society to train policemen to appreciate diversity and respect it. Such training would ensure much better law and order in the society. We do have a multi-religious and multi-caste society but we have still to develop a multi-religious cultural ethos.

CHAPTER 2

Minorities and Police in India

AMARJIT S. NARANG

The overwhelming majority of societies today are multi-religious, multi-ethnic and multi-lingual in character. Most of these, having accepted various UN declarations particularly relating to human rights, have agreed to the goal of establishing and promoting a just social order in which every person could freely enjoy all basic human rights irrespective of numerical strength, caste, creed, race, sex, place of birth, colour, language, political opinion or status. There is affirmation to the ideal that all human beings are born free and equal in dignity. All persons are equal before the law and are entitled, without discrimination, to equal protection of law. The states have accepted to act promptly to protect the right to freedom of thought, conscience, religion and belief in all its aspects. Yet reports of ethnic discrimination and religious intolerance come from many states. Though in all liberal democracies one of the major mechanisms for accommodating cultural differences is the protection of the civil and political rights of individuals, a gap in many states persists between the legal precepts and actual practices. Many have proven unable to create or sustain any strong sense of solidarity across ethno-national lines. The global experience, however, suggests that if minorities are not protected and their rights not safeguarded, the societies and states face conflictual situations and social tensions. To avoid these, as also to respect the principles and conventions on human rights, it is essential that in a plural society there must be adequate measures for the protection of the ethno-religious minorities. The 1981 United Nations Declaration on the Elimination of All Forms of Intolerance and of Discrimination Based on Religion or Belief articulated the right to freedom of religion and gave specific recognition to the rights and freedom from discrimination based on religion contained in the major human rights instruments. It stated, 'Discrimination between human beings on the ground of religion or belief constitutes an affront to human dignity and disapproval of the principles of the charter of the United Nations'. The States are also expected to protect such freedoms by placing them in the constitutions and supreme laws and declaring them immune from invasion by public authorities. By setting out such principles, by placing all public authorities under a solemn obligation to respect and observe them, and by indicating how the rules to implement them will be made, applied and adjudicated, they establish standards for legislators, administrators, police and judges.

MINORITY PROTECTION IN INDIA

India is a liberal, democratic, plural society with a number of minority communities inhabiting it. It is the origin of several major world religions and others have established themselves on its soil over the centuries. There has been considerable interaction between their different worldviews, rituals and customs. There are eight main religious communities in India: Hindus (82.7 per cent of the population), Muslims (11.8 per cent) Christians (2.6 per cent), Sikhs (2 per cent), Buddhists (0.7 per cent), Jains (0.5 per cent), Zoroastrians (0.3 per cent) and Jews (0.1) per cent. The indigenous peoples (adivasis), whose beliefs, rituals and resources are uniquely associated with their ancestors and the forest, constitute 7.8 per cent of the population (60 million). While many indigenous communities have a close affinity with Hinduism, sizeable groups have converted to Christianity and some to Islam.

India is a common law country and her Constitution contains detailed provisions on the protection of individual rights. The courts have power to declare invalid any laws passed by the Parliament or State Assemblies if they contravene the Constitution. Articles 25 to 30 in Part III of the Constitution extend these guarantees to all categories of minorities—religious, cultural and linguistic. Article 25 relates to the freedom of conscience and religion. All persons are equally entitled to profess, practice and propagate religion subject to public order, morality, health and other provisions of that part. The individual as well as a religious community is free to avail itself of this right and it can have a collective manifestation. The Indian state is secular in the sense that it is meant to treat all religions equally and keep its distance from every one of them. The former President of India, Dr. Radhakrishnan, noted that in India 'we hold that no religion should be given preferential status'.

Article 51 A of the Constitution imposes a positive duty on citizens 'to promote harmony and the spirit of common brotherhood amongst all people of India transcending religious, linguistic and regional or sectional diversities; to renounce practices derogatory to the dignity of women . . .' Article 25 of the Constitution guarantees not only freedom of conscience, free profession and practice of religion, but also the right to propagate religion. Article 25(2) (b) provides that the state can make law for social welfare and reform or the opening of Hindu religious institutions of a public character to all classes and sections of Hindus. The freedom to manage religious institutions and their property is constitutionally guaranteed (Article 26). Aid may be provided by the state as long as it is non-discriminatory while individuals are guaranteed freedom as to payment of taxes for the promotion of any particular religion (Article 27).

Educational institutions recognized by the state or receiving state funding cannot impose religious teachings without the individual's consent or the parent's or guardian's if the student is a minor. The customary and codified personal laws of different communities remain protected. The statutes also provide for the liberty of children to develop their own religious convictions. Article 29 and 30 of the Constitution protect the cultural and educational rights of minorities. Any section of the citizenry with a distinct language, script or culture of its own has the right to conserve it. No one can be denied admission into any educational institution, maintained by the state or receiving state aid, on the grounds only of religion, race, caste or language. Article 30 guarantees to minorities, both linguistic and religious, the right to establish and administer educational institutions. The state cannot discriminate against such institutions either in granting recognition or in providing aid.

MINORITIES AND THE POLICE

In spite of above provisions in India, there is a widespread feeling today that the rights of minorities stand unprotected. Despite the safeguards provided in the Constitution and the laws in force, there exists a feeling of inequality and discrimination among the minorities. There is a general feeling that the police, which is meant to protect them, actually plays a blatantly partisan role. In recent times, the media has extensively brought to light the savage carnage in many parts of Gujarat that followed the horrific torching of a railway compartment in Godhra on 27 February 2002. A number of impartial reports make it clear that the police here aided and abetted the rioters against the minority community. Harsh Mander, an IAS officer in Gujarat and who resigned in sheer disgust, wrote, 'The unconscionable failure and active connivance of the state police and administrative machinery is also now widely acknowledged. The police is known to have misguided people and provided shields to crowds bent upon pillage, arson, rape and murder and were deaf to the pleas of these disparate Muslim victims, many of them women and children' (Mander: 2002).

The incidents in Gujarat were not unique. This has been happening all over the country in one form or the other. Since 1960, in almost all communal riots that have occurred, the same picture has been painted in the same colours—a picture of a helpless and often deliberately inactive police force that allowed vulnerable members of all communities to be looted and killed in its presence. A senior police officer, V.N. Rai, says that on every occasion that the police have failed in their primary duty, whether in 1984, when thousands of Sikhs were massacred all over the country, or in 1992 when the mosque in Ayodhya was demolished in full view of tens of thousands of policemen, commissions which were set up to enquire into these incidents have always indicted the police for their partisan behaviour, their deliberate inaction in providing protection to the lives and properties of the minorities and their criminal involvement in violent and murderous attacks and looting of property.

Justice Madan Commission Report on Bhiwandi riots (1970) observed, 'Discrimination was also practiced in making arrests and while Muslim rioters were arrested in large numbers, the police turned a blind eye to what the Hindu rioters were doing. Some innocent Muslims, who went to take shelter at Bhiwandi Town Police Station were arrested instead of being given shelter and protection.' About Jalgaon riot of 1970, the commission makes the following observations: 'The real reason for the inadequacy of the measures taken by authorities was the communal bent of mind of some officers and the incompetence of others. . . . No attempts were made to check the rioting and arson at Joshi Peth, though fifty-four Muslim houses were set on fire there and the flames could be seen even from a distance of two miles'.

Justice Jaganmohan Reddy Commission Report on the Ahmedabad riots of 1969 is quite revealing. The report observed 'This commission of inquiry has cited more than half a dozen instances where Muslim religious places adjoining police lines or police stations were attacked or damaged. The argument advanced by the police officers that because they were busy quelling riots elsewhere, these police stations were shorn of adequate strength and hence these attacks on religious places could not be prevented, did not impress the commission. It has made this observation because not a single case of damage to a Hindu place of worship near a police station was reported to the commission.

Justice Joseph Vithayathil Commission Report on the Tellicherry riots, 1971 points out:

> The evidence of the deputy SP says that while on patrol duty he had to curb many among his rank and file who could not restrain themselves when they met Muslims on the road. Similar evidence was given by the sub-collector and other witnesses who have testified saying that while chasing away some Muslims, many policemen yelled at them to go to Pakistan. At Mattambaram one or two of them got into the mosque and besides beating Usman Kutty Haji, a very respectable person, broke the tube-light and chandeliers in the mosque. There is nothing to show that there was any justification for this action. . .

Justice B.N. Srikrishna made the following observations in his report on Bombay riots 1992–3, 'The Commission is of the view that there is evidence of police bias against Muslims which has manifested itself in other ways like the harsh treatment given to them, failure to register even cognizable offences'. That there was a general bias against the Muslims in the minds of the average policemen, was evident in the way they dealt with the Muslims, and even accepted by V.N. Deshmukh an officer of the rank of additional commissioner. This general police bias against Muslims crystallized itself in action during January 1993.

The response of the police to appeals from desperate victims, particularly Muslims, was cynical and utterly indifferent. On occasions the response was that they were unable to leave appointed post; on others, the attitude was that one Muslim killed, was one Muslim less.

Police officers and men, particularly at the junior level, appeared to have an inbuilt bias against the Muslim which was evident in their treatment of the Muslim suspects and victims of riots. The treatment given was harsh and brutal and, on occasions, bordering on inhuman, hardly doing credit to the force. The bias of policemen was seen in the active connivance of police constables with the rioting Hindu mobs on occasions, also with their adopting the role of passive onlookers on such occasions, and finally, in their lack of enthusiasm in registering offences against Hindus even when the accused were clearly identified.

Even the registered riot-related offences were most unsatisfactorily investigated. The investigations displayed lack of enthusiasm, lackadaisical approach and utter cynicism. Despite clear clues the miscreants were not pursued, arrested and interrogated, particularly when the accused happened to be Hindus having connections to Shiv Sena or were Shiv Sainiks. This general apathy appears to be the outcome of the built-in prejudice in the mind of an average policeman that every Muslim is prone to crime.

While there are a number of useful studies on Hindu-Muslim violence in India, the report of Vibhuti Narain Rai is important as it was authored by a serving senior police officer of Uttar Pradesh, which has a record of persistent Hindu-Muslim violence. The author studied the role of the police in the Hindu-Muslim violence during the pre-independence and post-independence periods in Kanpur (1931), Ranchi (1967), Ahmedabad (1969), Bhiwandi and Jalgaon (1970), Banaras (1977), Jamshedpur (1979), Meerut (1990), Bhagalpur (1989), Ayodhya (1992) and Mumbai (1992–3). His main findings with respect to the role of the police in these cases were as follows:

(i) The police behave partially during most riots. In all the riots discussed in the study, the police did not act as a neutral law enforcement agency but more as a 'Hindu' force.

(ii) Perceptible discrimination was visible in the use of force, preventive arrests, enforcement of curfew, treatment of detained persons at police stations, reporting of facts and investigation and detection and prosecution of cases registered during riots. Muslims suffered in all the above mentioned areas.

(iii) The perception by Hindus and Muslims of the police during communal strife is diametrically opposed. Hindus view policemen as their friends and protectors during communal riots. Muslims, by and large, consider policemen as their enemies in similar situations.

(iv) An average policeman does not shed his prejudices and predetermined beliefs at the time of his entry into the force, and this is reflected in his bias against Muslims during communal violence.

(v) The expectations of the Indian society from average policemen are communal. The policeman is believed to be a protector of the interests of his community.

(vi) The inimical relationship between the police and the Muslims make them over-react in a confrontation like situation. (cited by Subramanian 2002)

Thus, there is clear evidence from various reports and studies that the role of police in majority-minority relations, particularly during communal riots, has been far from desirable. It is a sad fact that a large number of police officers have not just failed to control riot situations but have actually given the culprits their active support. This naturally raises important questions about the nature and working of police as an institution of the Indian state.

THE CAUSES

The first point to understand here is that the Indian police system is a creation of the British Raj which employed the police as an instrument of oppression to perpetuate their rule. The police in India still functions under the Police Act of 1861 which was mainly designed to control a subject people. In effect the Act made provision only for two purposes, i.e. the establishment and administration, under strict magisterial control, of a single unified police force in every province and using it to keep the people of the country effectively suppressed. In the words of Dharma Vira who headed the National Police Commission 'the police in India is not organized for impartial law enforcement, it is rather a policy enforcement subordinate body'.

David Arnold has observed that the evolution of the Indian police during the nineteenth century was conditioned by the political needs of the British colonial regime. The distinction between political and crime control functions of the police did not in fact exist. The British Indian police, modelled on the colonial Irish police, was a centralized paramilitary force. Its chief officer was called an inspector general of police, an apt designation for the head of a colonial paramilitary police. The officer was directly responsible to the chief secretary of the government. Its availability as an armed force under civilian control and its centralized paramilitary character made it useful to the government of a restless and violent country. By the late 1850s, the basic structure of the Indian police as a partly military and partly civilian organization had become established. After the mutiny of 1857 and the transfer of governance of India to the British Crown, the Code of Civil Procedure, 1859, the Code of Criminal Procedure, 1861 and Indian Penal Code, 1860 were enacted. The Police Commission of 1860 led to the formulation of the Police Act of 1861. The recommendations of the Police Commission of 1902 were intended mainly to strengthen the police more fully to take over the responsibility of the army to maintain internal control and to counter the emerging strength of the nationalist opposition to British rule. Special attention was paid to the armed police and the CID, which became the growth areas claiming a larger share of the budget (cited by Subramanian). The re-organized police of British India could not come up anywhere near the levels of efficiency or public acceptance which the British police had attained within just two decades of their reorganization in 1829. The Indian police were not perhaps expected to emulate their British counterparts for elementary reasons that whereas the former served the imperial interests of a colonial government, the latter catered to a nation of freedom-loving people, long used to enjoying some basic civil and individual rights. Moreover, while the Indian police was an imposition from above which the large mass of the people considered as hostile and offensive, the British police had developed from below in a natural process of evolution (Dhillon, 1995: 115).

In the aftermath of the grim and bloody situation of partition, the leaders of the Indian Independence struggle had resolved to retain a powerful bureaucratic and police structure inherited from the colonial legacy of governance. Their expectation was that it would act as a sturdy bulwark, a steel frame, to strengthen the unification of a vast, diverse, volatile land. While the objective of the Constitution adopted for free India was the creation of a society where all citizens, irrespective of religion, caste, class and gender would enjoy the equal protection of the state, the colonial administrative, judicial and law enforcement structure, was retained. The dawn of independence in 1947 saw no basic change in its police structure. In fact independence in the subcontinent was not an abrupt break with the past. It did not constitute a clearly defined watershed as far as its general administration was concerned. The basic unit of administration, i.e. the district continued to be administered by a collector-cum-district magistrate who remained almost indistinguishable from their pre-independence forerunners in their styles of functioning and modes of accountability. The need for reforms in the Indian police did not engage the attention of either the political class or the bureaucracy for several decades after independence, though dissatisfaction was frequently voiced with police performance, specially their attitudes to the common man and the frequent use of force in law and order situations (Dhillon, 1995: 254). What has happened subsequently is the 'massive growth of centralized police power'.

Post-independent India has witnessed no attempt to separate the political and crime control functions of the police. This is allied to the failure to separate the law and order functions from the investigative functions at the field level. A visible neglect of investigative functions at the cost of the law and order functions has grown. Further, there has been a steady increase in the numbers of armed police at all levels, especially at the central level. The increasing importance of the intelligence police is to be added to this, again especially at the central level. This police and administrative structure headed by the IAS and the IPS has pre-existed and survived the Indian Constitution and is the cause of many a malaise in India today. However, this administrative structure has played a crucial role in maintaining the post-colonial status quo in India.

The above mentioned unreformed police has further allowed itself to be overwhelmed by the extraneous influences, particularly the political interference. Political interference takes place in different forms: The Police Act of 1861 does give the political executive the power of 'superintendence' over police working. Obviously, this was intended to ensure that the police conducted themselves according to the laws of the country. In the colonial era, the foreign government interpreted this power in such a way as to shift police loyalty from the rule of law to the rulers themselves. This approach was found convenient later by the so-called people's representatives to get their dirty job done by the police with little or no accountability and in complete disregard of the demands of justice. Superintendence, in the name of democracy has become a license for politicians to interfere in investigations of crimes over which even courts have very little powers, in posting and transfer of policemen and in pressurizing the police to act in partisan ways (Madhava Menon, 1997).

Influential politicians interfere in the day-to-day working of the police at different levels of administration. Transfers and postings are used conveniently to break the back of honest officers and to reward the pliable and corrupt ones who use their powers to selectively advance the interests of politicians or parties.

The police are invariably helpless when an MLA or MP throws

his weight about. At times politicians themselves commit crimes and try to escape the clutches of law by the strength of their political clout. If an honest policeman is made ineffective or taken to task for performing his duty, the police cannot be expected to act fearlessly and honestly.

Harsh Mander points out that until the 1980s there was an unwritten agreement in our polity that even if politicians inflamed communal passions, the police and civil administration would be expected to act professionally and impartially to control the riots in the shortest possible time, and to protect innocent lives. There were several failures in performance, and minorities were targeted in many infamous riots, but the rules of the game were still acknowledged and in the majority of instances adhered to, which is why the higher civil and police services were regarded to be the steel frame, vital to the preservation of the unity and plurality of the country. The 1980s saw the breaking of this unwritten code which led to corrosion and near collapse of the steel frame. It became frequent practice for the higher civil and police authorities to be instructed to actively connive in the systematic killing of the minority community, by delaying, sometimes by several days, the use of force to control riots. Local state authorities complied and rioters were left unrestrained by the state power for their orgy of mass murder, arson and plunder. Civil and police authorities today openly await the orders of their political supervisors before they apply force, so much so that it has become popular perception that indeed they cannot act without the permission of their administrative and political supervisors and ultimately the chief minister (Mander, 2002). The decision to arrest and release people are made entirely on political considerations. People have increasingly come to the conclusion that the police force has been reduced to an instrument of tyranny in the hands of the rulers and more so for the minorities and the underprivileged.

Apart from the political interference, social composition and orientation has made policeman and administrators commonly prejudiced. In this context, some studies have shown that there is a close linkage between anti-Muslim violence in India and the way Pakistan, as a perfidious Muslim neighbour, is perceived by sections of the Indian public and politicians. It has been argued that in a communal movement, the government is thematised, but in an ethnic movement, the ethnic other is thematised as an enemy of the nation state. In the latter case, there is a clear majority and a clear minority.

The minority is portrayed as anti-national. After the partition of India in 1947, the idea of the nation state was etched clearly in the Indian consciousness. Pakistan as an enemy state figures prominently in India in moments of ethnic strife. The tendency in ethnic movements has been to vilify the minorities as traitors to the nation, who act at the behest of hostile countries. For example, some leaders of the recent anti-Muslim violence in Gujarat went to the extent of calling for the dismemberment of Pakistan (Subramanian, 2002). The perception of Pakistan as a hostile Muslim neighbouring state in the Hindu mind has led to the development of a negative stereotype of Indian Muslims. According to V.N. Rai, an average policeman does not shed his prejudice and predetermined beliefs at the time of his entry into the force, and this is reflected in his bias against Muslims during communal violence.

In 1982, N.C. Saxena, the then Joint Secretary of the National Commission for Minorities reported after inquiring into Meerut riots, 'The district administration perceived threat to public peace only from Muslims . . . the order from the senior officers in the district to the police could be summarized in one phrase: Muslims must be taught a lesson; the Provincial Armed Constabulary and the police faithfully implemented this policy'. Carrying out a study on the attitudes and perceptions of the magistrates and senior police officers about various communities, Saxena made the following conclusions:

(b) Muslims are excitable and irrational people who are guided by their religious instincts. Hindus, on the other hand, are law abiding and cooperate with the police in controlling communal violence.

(c) Riots are started by the Muslims and they invariably take the first opportunity to strike at the other community and the police.

(d) In all other previous riots in the country before the current riot, Muslims took the upper hand which resulted in huge loss to the Hindu community. Therefore, there is moral justification if in the current riot, casualties on the Muslim side are heavier.

(e) State governments attach a great deal of importance in ensuring quick control of rioting. Since Muslims are aggressive, it is necessary that they are taught a lesson through arrests, firing and third degree methods.

The study further reports that 'the P AC treats Muslims as monsters, criminals and suspects. It has led to loss of faith among Muslims in the fairness of administration. They have started patronizing anti-social elements for their defence and in the recent riots, attacks on police from the Muslim side have also increased. Police-Muslim confrontation, if not checked, may lead to terrorism just as in some countries like Philippines and Thailand, Muslim terrorism has assumed an alarming proportion.'

In his dissertation on *Perception of Police Neutrality During Hindu-Muslim Riots in India,* V.N. Rai reports the following findings based on field study:

(a) The police behave partially during most riots. In all the riots discussed in this study, they did not act as a neutral law enforcement agency but more as a 'Hindu' force.
(b) Perceptible discrimination was visible in the use of force, preventive arrests, enforcement of curfew, treatment of detained persons at police stations, reporting of facts and investigation, detection and prosecution of cases registered during riots. Muslims suffered in all of the above mentioned areas.
(c) An average policeman does not shed his prejudices and pre-determined beliefs at the time of his entry into the force, and this is reflected in his bias against Muslims during communal violence.
(d) The inimical relationship between police and Muslims make them over-react in a confrontation-like situation.

Of course, it will be fundamentally wrong to label all the police officials as biased against the minority. Particularly among the senior officers there are those who fight for their convictions and even suffer. The picture, however, radically changes when it comes to lower level officers. They are much more communalized. It should also be stated that they behave harshly with all weaker sections of the society (Engineer). Apart from their social mindset, lack of training and proper working conditions are also responsible for such an attitude. They are terribly overworked during communal disturbances. They are often required to perform round-the-clock duty on such occasions. They hardly have time to go home. Also, they perceive danger to their life. It is not easy to work in such conditions. Such tensions make them highly inflammable, and they tend to overreact to any situation. They take revenge on innocent persons. Also, they are deeply affected by communal propaganda which, for historical and social reasons, remains biased against Muslims. The numerical social composition of the police and paramilitary forces and other wings of law-enforcement machinery with gross under-representation of minorities, especially Muslims, at all levels and ranks again helps in intensifying and entrenching the biased perceptions and communal behaviour against minorities. At present, in the given situation, there seems to be no way that the majority of the police force can be insulated from the onslaught of intense communal propaganda. It is true that our men and women in khaki work under conditions of great stress, with long hours, inadequate facilities and uninspiring training. Even so, whenever commanded by leaders of character, who are non-partisan, professional, fearless and lead from the front, the same forces are known to perform peace admirably (Mander, 2002). But this is possible only with the encouragement and consolidation of secular values in the society on the one hand and radical police reforms in justice and law enforcement system, particularly paying attention to the need of proper training and change of orientation.

NEED FOR REFORMS

Police reforms in India are critical now, more than ever before. Apart from other aspects of police functioning, there is an urgent need to formulate a system to develop a neutral, secular, non-communal police force which will act as per the law of the land without fear or favour and free from extraneous interference. Commission after commission and one agency after the other have continually been stressing the need for this (Pillai, 2002).

Some 25 years ago the Shah Commission, which went into the excesses of the Emergency, said: 'The Government must seriously consider the feasibility and the desirability of insulating the police from the politics of the country and employing it scrupulously on duties for which alone it is by law intended. The policemen must also be made to realize that politicking by them is outside the sphere of their domain and the Government would take a very serious view of it.'

The National Human Rights Commission (NHRC) has underlined the need to proceed without delay to implement reforms that have been repeatedly recommended in order to preserve the integrity of the investigating process and to insulate it from extraneous influence.

The recommendations of the National Police Commission (1981) have long been forwarded to the State but the crucial recommendations regarding the constitution of the security commission, selection of the director general of police, protecting the police from the political process have not been implemented.

There is an obvious 'lack of political and administrative will' to implement the above recommendations as pointed out by the NHRC. The Commission has urged the government 'to revive quality of policing in this country and to save it from catastrophic "extraneous influences" that are ruining the investigation work of the police – taking the situation in Gujarat as a warning and catalyst to act with determination to implement various reforms recommended.'

The Supreme Court in the case of *Vineet Narayan* vs *Union of India and others* (1998 (a) SCC 273) has pointed out the need for establishing a mechanism for selecting the DGP and police officers of and above the rank of superintendent of police. But no action was taken despite the observation of the Supreme Court in 1997 and the letter from the Union Home Minister—the late Indrajit Gupta (Pillai, 2002).

Unfortunately, the crying need for police reform has remained ignored. But society cannot allow the police any more to drift with less and less accountability. The government must give top priority to police reform in the interest of the nation without extraneous consideration. On the one hand police training and orientation should become conducive to values like the spirit of tolerance, respect for the view of others, even-handed treatment of all sections of society, concern for human rights, and cultural sensitivities of minority communities. On the other hand, steps to improve the morale of the police should also include proper career planning, better emoluments, improved housing, welfare measures and social amenities for lower level officers and constables.

REFERENCES

Ansari, Iqbal, 'Partisan Police', *The Times of India*, 16 April 2002.

———, *Report on Communal Riots: Prevention and Control,* New Delhi: Minorities Council of India, 1999.

Dhillon, K.S., *Defenders of the Establishment*, Shimla: Indian Institute of Advanced Study, 1995.

Engineer, Asghar Ali , 'Role of Police in Gujarat Carnage', *Secular Perspective* vol. V, no. 12, June 2002.

Mander, Harsh, 'Protectors turn Predators', *Communalism Combat*, September 2002.

Menon, M.R. Madhava, 'Police, People and Politicians' *The Hindu*, 13 November 1997.

Nayar, Kuldeep , 'Governance and the Police', *The Hindu*, 29 October 1997.

Pillai, V. Kannu, 'Reforms Now', *Communalism Combat*, September 2002.

Rai, Vibhuti Narain, 'Letter to IPS officer in Gujarat', *The Milli Gazette*, 1–15 June 2002.

———, 'Law and Order: Who Cares?' *Communalism Combat*, September 2002.

Surahmanyam, K., 'Policing the Police', *The Times of India*, 19 September 1999.

Subramanian, K.S., *Police and the Minorities: A Study of Police Role in Communal Violence in India*, mimio, 2002.

CHAPTER 3

Democracy, Pluralism and Police in India

KIRPAL SINGH DHILLON

India inherited at the time of independence a civil service which, though of colonial origin, had by the 1930s, acquired a largely objective, paternalistic, and benevolent slant in the performance of its functions. As between the paramount power and the Indian masses, the services generally exercised their administrative discretion in an efficient but neutral manner. Through training and upbringing in the service, the superior cadres consistently imbibed the qualities of fair play, justice, probity and transparency in their official dealings. High salaries, and unlimited opportunities of promotion to the highest office in the government, attracted the best available talent to the civil services. The elite character of the Indian civil service was deliberately kept undiluted by conscious effort and constant review. Thus, the new government of independent India not only stepped into the shoes of the erstwhile colonial power without much difficulty and transfer of power was accomplished smoothly and painlessly, the post colonial state was also able to handle the genocidal post-partition riots and the rehabilitation of a massive refugee population with a fair degree of success. India was able to deal with the immediate post-partition problems and their long-term fallout quite effectively as it inherited a fully functioning central secretariat at Delhi and also because Indian political leaders had over two years of experience in governance from 1937 to 1939, when they had held ministerial positions in the provincial governments constituted under the scheme of the 1935 Government of India Act.

Independence in the subcontinent was not an abrupt break with the past. It did not constitute a clearly defined watershed as far as general administration was concerned. For instance, though the institution of the viceroy and governor-general was replaced by an Indian President with the coming into force of the new Constitution in January 1950 and the control of the new governments in Delhi and the state capitals came to be vested in the councils of ministers, headed by the prime minister and state chief ministers respectively, the mechanics of the system showed little signs of change. The basic unit of administration, i.e. the district continued to be administered by a collector-cum-district magistrate with the assistance of some half a dozen district level officers, under the distant supervision of the divisional commissioners and the state governments. For about two decades in the immediate post-independence period, the district officers were almost indistinguishable from their pre-independence forerunners in their styles of functioning and modes of accountability. The tone and tenor of their behaviour and conduct was still determined by their ICS mentors and the erstwhile service traditions. As the methods of recruitment of higher civil services did not change, the quality and class origin of the recruits remained the same. However, with the new generation of politicians becoming more assertive, a process of change in the relationship between politicians and civil servants was duly set in motion. Unfortunately, such a process, in the long run, led to an inevitable erosion of the values and ethos of the Civil Service. Later with a massive expansion in governmental responsibility for management of diverse economic activities and a burgeoning public sector, the intake into the superior and other civil services multiplied manifold, thus further diluting the basic fibre of a service, which prided itself on its exclusivity and elite character. The civil service, which had helped the British colonial power administer this vast land for over hundred year and, in the words of Philip Mason, the eminent historian of Indian district administration, quietly altered their role from 'Founders' to 'Guardians', had lost much of its élan and become flabby, diffident and weakened. Inflationary pressures reduced the real value of their already reduced salaries and their curtailed status no longer attracted the best candidates in an expanding job market. Even the standards of probity nosedived and venality, unthought of earlier, became widespread. Administration in all spheres became lax, inefficient, ineffective and lost its traditional reputation for objectivity and fair play. Reservations and quotas for the depressed and backward castes to help them enter the superior civil services and the police further diluted the strength and character of the civil service. Thus, even though no formal alteration was made in the laws and procedures, laying down the work and conduct of the bureaucracy, a marked change in their outlook, attitudes, values and approaches had occurred by the mid 1970's. With each passing decade, the deterioration in their moral fibre also became more and more prominent and their sense of propriety more fragile. By early 1997, the civil services had become almost fully politicized, demoralized and had lost their operational confidence and efficiency and were disinclined to regain or exercise their traditional initiative and dynamism. They had also abdicated, more or less totally, their functional autonomy and commitment to objectivity, neutrality and the rule of law. It will perhaps not be incorrect to characterize the civil services fifty years after independence as but a pale shadow of their pre-independence cousins, in all of South Asia, including India, Pakistan and Bangladesh.

The superior police service, redesignated after 1947 as the Indian Police Service (IPS) to distinguish it from Indian (branch of the Imperial) Police (IP) of the British era was constituted, along with the Indian Administrative Service (IAS), successor to the Indian Civil Service (ICS), as an All-India Service to fill up leadership positions in the Indian police, both in the states and at the national level. The mode of recruitment to the IPS and their training programmes for a couple of decades after independence were not much different from those followed for the officers belonging to the erstwhile IP. Thus, the culture, character and functional styles of the initial entrants to the new service did not materially change. The scheme of examinations for entry into the All-India and Central Services was such that although the prescribed minimum educational qualification for all was graduation, a candidate could secure appointment to the IPS by successfully competing only in five (3 compulsory and 2 optional) subjects, while all other services required the candidates to clear six papers (later upgraded to eight for the IAS). This bred a sense of inferiority in the IPS officers, which together with their lower pay-scales and much less variety and fewer senior jobs available to them compared to their colleagues in the IAS would in a few years change the complexion of the service by corroding its attractiveness as a top career choice for ambitious young persons. It would also lead to a sense of frustration and loss of zeal in the absence of regular periodical promotions to higher positions. Although some corrective measures were taken later, the IPS remained the last option for bright young persons seeking a career in the higher civil services. The IPS officers were also considered and generally treated as peripheral to the centrality of district and divisional administration whereas the IAS district magistrates and divisional commissioners were accorded almost exclusive importance. It was not until the late 1980s, when the sharp deterioration in the security environment, spread of terrorism and massive public disorder together with a heightened threat perception of the life and free movement of the ruling political classes, drew the police services closer to the seats of power and the role of police officers were recognized as vital and important to the administration. In a way, this turn of events restored to the IPS a status somewhat identical to the pre-independence service in its equation with the IAS and other services, which had been lost in the initial enthusiastic pre-occupation of governments with developmental activities. However, this would also lead, in another few years, to a runaway proliferation of senior posts which besides making the service top-heavy, would lead to factionalism, indiscipline, careerism and venality. The trend of creating a disproportionate number of senior jobs was initially set by the IAS, to be followed with equal indifference to the requirements of efficiency and compactness in the central services and the IPS. By the end of the 1980s, central and state secretariats had become grossly overpopulated.

The flaws which crept into the IPS due to its sidelining in the beginning and faulty cadre management later along with proliferation of senior posts and a history of a long time unfriendly relations, even hostility, between the police and the public, soon led to a sharp erosion in the capacity of the IPS to provide effective leadership to the Indian police. The standards of efficiency, honesty, integrity and diligence declined with each passing year and the subordinate ranks never popular with the citizens, became even more unwanted, despised and scorned by large sections of society. IPS recruits joined the Service with considerable zeal, dedication and a high degree of idealism, but turned into unenthusiastic cynics within a few years of confrontation with ground realities. It was generally believed that most recruits had to unlearn several lessons in police work and methods of investigation taught to them in the training institutions, if they were to succeed in real life police situations. In fact, many of the training schools for constables and sub-inspectors enjoyed highly unsavoury reputations as breeding grounds for undesirable police subordinates. A progressive deterioration in the quality of supervision by senior officers did not help eliminate such malpractices. At a later date even the recruitment procedures for subordinate police ranks would be manipulated to promote nepotism, favouritism, political intervention and even corrupt practices. In the state of Haryana, the High Court set aside the recruitment of hundreds of constables on grounds of irregularities. This was not the only case of its kind. In many states, recruitment to constables and upper subordinates was held up for several years as the administration were unable to evolve a foolproof method of intake, which would not be open to misuse. The Punjab Police Department was at one time carrying a shortfall of more than three thousand constables, i.e. one tenth of its total strength (1984) due to fears that a fair recruitment could not be ensured. In any case, since the Punjab police was predominantly Sikh, the central government did not want to add more Sikhs to the force in the wake of rising Sikh militancy. In Bihar and UP, hundreds of posts of sub-inspectors were created in 1995 and mostly filled up with relatives, kinsmen and favourites of powerful politicians and other influential persons. It can, perhaps, be safely assumed that a programme of fair selection to the powerful position of police subordinates was neither practiced nor favoured by any political party, which happened to be in office in any part of the country. Obviously, a police force composed largely of such members cannot be expected to be either fair or honest in their dealings with the public or in the discharge of their duties.

The need for reforms in the Indian Police did not engage the attention of either the political class or the bureaucracy for several decades after Independence though dissatisfaction was frequently voiced with police performance, specially regarding their attitudes to the common man and the frequent use of force in law and order situations. The generation of police officers who held positions of authority in the immediate post-independence period were quite happy with conducting the affairs of the departments under their control in accordance with the practices and traditions they had learnt from their British mentors. They still swore by the virtues of the Indian Police Act of 1861 which, according to them, had contributed to a large extent in providing conditions of stability, peace and order in the subcontinent for a century and could continue to regulate the raising, disciplining and functioning of the Indian Police in future too. It was in this belief that the centenary of this Act was observed with great fanfare in 1961. Not many voices were being raised by social scientists and the new generation of police leaders as to how the efficacy and relevance of a legislation enacted by a colonial administration would suit their needs in a changed historical context. Questions were also asked and doubts expressed about whether a police force organized under the hundred year old Act, would be a proper medium to serve the police of a free and democratic India with a Constitution laying a great deal of stress on basic human rights and fundamental freedoms of its citizens. Indian police, frequently and expectedly, came into conflict with the leaders of public opinion as to the method and strategies they adopted in the discharge of their duties. Over a period of time, such conflicts would tend to distance the policemen further from the common law-abiding Indian citizen and oblige the Police to rely more and more on the manipulative touts and other ruffians living on the fringes of law, for even their day-to-day functioning as well as collection of evidence while investigating offences. They had to routinely depend on professional witnesses to support the prosecution evidence in courts of law. A later generation of enlightened public leaders would understand and appreciate the dilemma of a police force raised by a colonial enactment but expected, in a totally changed environment, to function in a system of democratic self-government. But they would do nothing to alter the situation except to indulge in platitudes at Police parades and seminars, partly because they were far too busy in politicking, but mainly because they had come to realize that a colonialist police would serve their special interests much more effectively and without protest than a force more in tune with the democratic aspirations of a free people. Police leaders on the other hand, who were painfully aware of the basic asymmetry between the legal provisions regulating the police functioning and organization and the public expectations from the force, gave vent to their feelings in many a seminar and conference but could not make their views prevail in an administrative set-up dominated by advocates of the status quo. In the event, the Indian police continued to be governed by a piece of legislation enacted in 1861 in a totally different context in the closing years of the twentieth century. Even the extended labours of a National Police Commission, presided over by an eminent civilian (a former cabinet secretary and governor of several states) and consisting of a top social scientist, a well-known judge and two of India's outstanding police leaders, failed to make a dent in the attitudes of the anti-reform lobbies in the civil service and the no-changers among the politicians.

Hamstrung as the Indian Police have been on account of legal infirmities inherent in the manner of its reorganization in 1861 and the long historical legacy of public hostility and apathy, they have not failed to display an extraordinary degree of capability to handle numerous challenges to social harmony, public order and national integrity. They have weathered many a storm and faced several explosive situations during the five decades India has been free. Not that they have covered themselves with glory but a considerable measure of credit cannot be denied to them for securing to the majority of Indian citizens a peaceful environment and an orderly way of life. To start with, the horrendous spate of sectarian killings, arson, plunder and cross-migration of millions of people from India to the newly created dominion of Pakistan and from there to India, following Partition, stretched their resources to the maximum. Suddenly the entire social fabric showed signs of a rupture with an unending stream of refugees flowing into the truncated state of east Punjab, Delhi and parts of UP. The Indian Police, depleted as they were of the superior cadres with British officers having left and Muslims opting for Pakistan, were called upon to undertake abnormally complex tasks. As is common when such large-scale displacement of populations take place, the crime graph rose sharply. The police in the affected areas had to substantially revise their crime records, history sheets and surveillance lists. All this required considerable effort, initiative and hard work on the part of the district police officials and those at supervisory levels.

Not the least of their successes lay in the near peaceful conduct of fourteen gigantic general elections to the Indian parliament and also more frequent ones to the state legislative assemblies. These elections, of late, have been quite complex requiring a massive deployment of Police and paramilitary forces not only for manning the polling stations and ballot boxes but also to strengthen preventive arrangements to curb all violent outbursts of anger in the post-election phase. Besides most candidates had to be provided personal security in view of the threat to their lives and persons. With several parts of the country in the grip of terrorism, militancy, violence and secessionist agitations, it is not easy to tackle the problems arising out of such situations. Add to this the bizarre nature of the Indian electorate, largely illiterate and ill-informed, and the large number of partyless candidates in almost every constituency. The sheer size of the electorate is mind-boggling and the sweep and spread of the exercise is stupendous. Without the active involvement of large bodies of policemen, the process of a free and fair election would be unthinkable in this land of subcontinental dimensions. It is not often realized that democracy in developing societies with low literacy percentages is a fragile enterprise which needs extensive safeguards enforced by a strong internal security apparatus. Indian Police, despite its many weaknesses, have more or less been successfully employed to fulfil their mandate in this process of reconstitution of democratic institutions time and again. The smooth working of our legislatures, the security of parliamentary and legislative houses, the personal safety of legislators and members of parliament as also the undisturbed conduct of scores of other functions pertaining to parliamentary democracy would become impossible without the participation of police and security agencies in the process, in a major way.

However, the Indian Police were not able to live down their historical legacies—an unfriendly even hostile citizenry, a habit of servility to the State structure and the entrenched elite classes, an oppressive attitude towards the common poor citizen and deprived sections of society. Also a general lack of concern with public welfare, in spite of a growing awareness among some, a least, in the new generation of IPS officers about the crucial connection between police performance and public support. Intensive introspection within the department, and prolonged debates without it, to pinpoint the causes of police failure on this score and suggest remedial measures, did not produce any noticeable or worthwhile improvement in the overall performance, in the absence of an informed and sincere response from the political authority. Nor were the administrators belonging to the IAS overly interested in Police reform, which would take away from them the powerful positions of the district magistrate and home secretary, as any step in the direction of its modernization would evidently confer on the police greater degree of functional autonomy, which is how all police agencies in advanced societies function. The initial enthusiasm in police organizations as well as in some state governments regarding reforms, led to the setting up of Police Commissions in state after state and subsequently at the national level. Almost all of these commissions and committees produced voluminous reports and broad-based recommendations aimed often at drastically changing the character and functioning of the police in Indian states. Understandably, none of these bodies succeeded in their efforts and their recommendations were generally allowed to gather dust in the record rooms of the states. Most governments and bureaucrats, even police officers, would lose interest in these inconclusive and futile exercises and the persistent erosion in police effectiveness and efficiency would be sought to be overcome by a disproportionate increase in the strength of what is called the state armed police and by creating, at the national level and under the control of the union home ministry, a number of paramilitary forces (PMF). This would make the situation even more confused and messy, as larger the component of armed police in a country's social defence system, the greater will be its irrelevance to the common citizen whose primary need of security of person and property can be best met by a neighbourhood policeman posted at the local police station and familiar with the locality, its people and their problems, as was pointed out so forcefully by Lord Scarman in his enquiry report on the Brixton riots in England sometime ago. However, the governments both at New Delhi and the state capitals were happy to have at their disposal well-armed and well-organized forces to play with and to be put, not always, to the best use. An abnormal increase in manpower also implied considerable wastage in its deployment thus proving to be a highly uneconomical arrangement. It is axiomatic that a vast expansion of the armed forces would sooner or later heighten both the extent and intensity of the violation of human rights and fundamental freedoms of the people, as armed contingents in developing societies have a marked tendency, and long history, of preying upon the public they are employed to serve. Sociologists would possibly have formulated hypotheses to explain the phenomenon but ground realities in Jammu & Kashmir, Punjab, the North-East and some other parts of India would make the point quite forcefully. As time went by the police and its allied forces would increasingly become more and more unpopular with the common Indian as the country proceeded to consolidate its freedom decade after decade.

Independence, to a partitioned subcontinent in 1947, brought in its wake an unprecedented outbreak of savage violence and plunder on both sides of the new frontier and generated probably history's most massive migration of whole populations suddenly designated as religious minorities in the new nations of India and Pakistan. However, after the traumatic events following Partition had finally petered out, the age-old sectarian cleavage between the majority Hindus and the Muslims, still a sizeable minority in the new India, seemed to have lost its severity for a couple of decades. But the respite proved to be short-lived and serious Hindu–Muslim riots broke out in several states in the early 1960s. It is not as if the period between 1947 and 1964 when widespread riots took place in many parts of the country, was entirely free of such incidents. Whereas the total number of reported incidents over the period 1950 to 1963 was 1,141, giving an average of 81.5 per year, in 1964 alone the number was 1070. The year 1964, besides being a particularly bad year for sectarian violence, also clearly signified the commencement of the process of a major worsening of the communal climate in India. For the seven year between 1964 and 1970, the average number of incidents per year was 424.42 as against 81.5 for the preceding fourteen years. Not only had the number of incidents risen sharply, the area affected by sectarian violence had also steadily expanded. In 1961, only 61 districts in the country had experienced communal violence. By the end of the decade, their number had gone up to 216, forming about 70 per cent of the basic administrative units. In 1986, the union home minister identified 88 districts as hypersensitive and a further 98 as sensitive from the communal angle. Evidently, sectarian conflicts have emerged progressively as a major problem in most parts of India and increasing administrative and political resources have to be employed for their containment. It is one of the several areas where the police have been less than successful in evolving an effective response. While major incidents are generally confined to urban areas, India's villages are also getting increasingly affected by the virus. Rural violence is more dangerous because the police has only a marginal presence in those areas. Although fewer incidents of sectarian riots were reported in the decade 1971 to 1980 (2,572 as against 7,664 for the preceding decade) the severity of violence was much greater as the death toll per incident was higher at 0.46 against 0.40 during the 1960s. The difference on account of injuries was even greater, being 5.94 per incident as against 1.52 in the 1961–70 period. The number of policemen killed had risen from only 1 in 1961–70 to 13 in 1971–80 and the number of policemen injured had gone up by 78 per cent. Obviously the scale and magnitude of violence in each successive decade was becoming more systematic, well-directed and calculated. There was increasing use of firearms, explosive devices, remote-controlled bombs and other sophisticated and more deadly weaponry both for offence and defence. Hindu–Muslim discord peaked in the destruction of the centuries old Baburi Masjid at Ayodhya in UP in December 1992 by a stridently communal organization, openly supported by a Hindu dominated political party. A series of bomb blasts in Bombay, widely believed to be a retaliatory act by Muslim hardliners in January–February 1993 caused a large number of deaths and damage to property. However, after those deadly occurrences, an uneasy peace seems to have returned in most parts of the country, with encouraging indications that the majority among the Muslims have begun to favour a review of their religious assumptions to come to terms with mainstream political realities, though many voices still preach a seperatist line. The Hindu revivalist movements, unfortunately, are assuming even harder postures. Sectarian conflicts among the two major communities in the country, although not wholly a law and order matter, reflecting as they do a certain failure of the political leadership to solve the ethnic issues inherent in the pluralistic nature of India's population, does nevertheless pose a major challenge to the police and administration in the districts. Due to legal infirmities, dual responsibility of the police and magistracy in the non-commissionerate locations, and the long-standing dependence on the use of force in such situations; the handling of riots, in most cases, usually generates a chain of complaints, and demands for judicial inquiries. Most complaints relate to reckless use of force, targeting of minorities, indiscriminate arrests, rude behaviour and long periods of restrictive orders.

Although there were several incidents of terrorism and violence during India's long struggle for freedom, resorting to extremist methods was not favoured as a legitimate means to that end by the mainline political leadership and never gained acceptance. The multiple pluralities in India's vast (and ever-growing) population along ethnic, linguistic, regional, cultural and religious line make it a very difficult country to govern specially so when its neighbours, because of their own in-built insecurities and weaknesses, spare no effort to destabilize their giant neighbour. The many diversities in the Indian people, which lay dormant during the long colonial period, became a major cause for concern after independence when the country adopted one of the most modern, liberal and secular Constitutions of the present times. The concept of an underlying civilizational unity in diversity, propounded by India's first Prime Minister Jawaharlal Nehru in the initial heady years of freedom, failed to keep the regional, linguistic and other movements in check for long. Several factors were responsible for stoking fissiparous forces in different parts of India. Not all of them need to be gone into here as they are really the concern of the political scientist. However, some of the causes which generated discontent in sections of the people and led to piling up of grievances on issues relating to autonomy and political disadvantage could be pinpointed. As the source of power and patronage continued to be centred in the Nehru–Gandhi dynasty and their close friends for almost four out of five decades after independence, discontent grew in peripheral and marginalized areas, classes, castes and sections of the people. By mid-1960s, several parts of the country started becoming increasingly restless and disgruntled with the ruling oligarchy, dominated by north Indian upper caste Hindus. The state of Uttar Pradesh (UP) has produced all of India's prime ministers except three. All of India's prime ministers excet five, belong to the highest caste–Brahmin. South is unhappy with the language policy, north-east with denial of religious and tribal autonomy; north-west got alienated due to linguistic, cultural and religious grievances. Then there is the large Muslim minority (130 million at last count) who feel deprived of the fruits of the new economic, social and industrial policies of the nation. There is also the age-old cleavage due to a perceived sense of religious intolerance and discrimination. The Sikhs, a vigorous, vibrant and well-to-do but small farming community (only 2 per cent of India's population) with a recognized reputation for producing good soldiers, felt let down as the Partition of the sub-continent divested them of their large prosperous estates in west Punjab. The slashing down of their representation in the armed forces (nearly 20 per cent at the time of Independence) in keeping with their low percentage in the total population and other discriminatory steps perceived by them as unfair and unjust embittered them further. The north-east, a complex maze of innumerable tribal groups each with their own distinct language, modes of belief and cultural traditions, resented the intrusive policies of the new government in distant Delhi. The British Indian government had largely left the mostly inaccessible tribal tracts unadministered except occasional punitive forays to put down inter-tribal clashes. Feelings of separate identities originally born out of historical reasons and remoteness from mainstream India, were also encouraged by political ambitions of their chieftains and, of course, further nourished by hostile neighbours. It was there that the first flames of terrorism and insurgency erupted soon after independence and have continued ever since. The rest of the country, however, remained free of terrorist violence till well into the 1960s and it was not a noticeable element in the agenda of any political party except the Communist Party of India (CPI) who had spearheaded an insurgent situation in rural Andhra Pradesh (AP) between landlords and cultivators shortly after independence. Andhra Pradesh incidentally, continued to provide fertile ground for the spread of extremist ideology in the form of what came to be called as Naxalism after 1967, from the village Naxalbari in West Bengal where the Maoist movement first took root. Inspired by the Maoist cult in neighbouring China, particularly after the humiliation inflicted by the Chinese army on Indian defence forces in 1962, a breakaway faction of the Communist Party (Marxist) (CPM), known as CPI (ML) introduced an extremist element in the Indian political discourse which would not be extinguished for several years to come. It came to be accepted in the Indian political scene as 'Naxalism' and deeply influenced many political agitations in West Bengal, Bihar, Punjab, Kerala, Andhra Pradesh, Tamil Nadu, Madhya Pradesh and Maharashtra. However, except in Bihar and in the tribal trijunctional areas of AP, MP and Maharashtra, Naxalism was almost wholly contained.

It needs to be mentioned, at this stage, that large parts of India remained outside the control of the central power in Delhi except during the last ninety years of British rule. The binding force of nationhood, therefore, did not come naturally to all Indians when India became independent in 1947. Peripheral areas, therefore did not fully share the long-established 'Indianness' of the central Indian states. Some of them, on the contrary, nursed a feeling of contempt for the poorer, illiterate and less developed people of those states, who in fact, came to enjoy enormous political power in Delhi due to the arithmetic of numbers in a democratic system.

The many diversities of Indian society frequently divide its people into alienated islands unable to accommodate each other's aspirations and demands. Conditions are created which promote discontent, grievance-formation, cultural exclusivity, social aloofness and other such phenomena, occasionally leading also to hardening of attitudes and feelings of separatism and secessionism. Added to these various elements that exacerbate the problems of diversity and disunity is the widespread poverty and illiteracy among the masses and lack of modernism and enlightenment, even in the comparatively affluent sections.

Obviously, distortions in the proper functioning of democratic and administrative institutions in such a milieu are inevitable. Such a situation soon leads to coterie rule by corrupt politicians, bending of prescribed procedures, marginalizing of civil services and exploitation of the wealth of the nation for their own nefarious ends. In such circumstances, the politics of debate and reason gets relegated to the background, problems are neglected, no effort is made to address them through an informed and analytical approach. Discontent is allowed to grow and fester for years, policies of hard blows and appeasement alternate with each other till those in authority lose all credibility and the discontented group feels compelled to wrest the initiative and take the lead in finding solutions to its problems in whatever manner possible. Time and again the Indian State has been presented with 'no-win' situations because the political authority was unable (or powerless) to act in time and the civil service and security forces dithered. Sometimes the ruling political party itself promotes violence and protest to marginalize a rival (regional) party, as happened in the Punjab in the late 1970s and many other states at other times.

Terrorism as a mode of achieving political goals and expressing discontent, disgruntlement and alienation has sporadically been practised in many parts of India but it took virulent form only in the north-east, the Punjab and Kashmir. The fact that all these areas are located along international borders has helped the terrorist groups immensely in enhancing their striking prowess and survivability by seeking shelter in neighbouring countries. With the country's civil services getting highly politicized and partisan, the police agencies compromising their integrity and objectivity and the political class becoming corrupt, inept and self-seeking, terrorism as a strategy to express discontent and grievances as also to influence policy-formation secured widespread acceptance in the Punjab in the 1980s and in Jammu & Kashmir in the 1990s. Since the government itself proved to be indecisive at several vital junctures in the nation's history, occasionally even acting in a biased and motivated manner to further its party interests and distorting the rule of law, most state institutions failed to safeguard democratic norms. Persistent subversion of the pillars of democracy—an impartial civil service, a strong and independent judiciary, fearless media and an autonomous, honest and a truly accountable police force—has prevented the emergence of a vibrant functioning democracy even more than fifty years after the advent of freedom. Increasingly, as the state itself was assuming a less than secular character in pursuit of electoral gains with the security forces of the Union acting in a partisan manner between the two communities, it was not long before a process of insidious alienation started affecting the Muslims in a land that was fast becoming Hinduized.

The course of events in Punjab during the 1980s is illustrative of the worst type of political manipulation mounted to disturb a peaceful region, and sow the seeds of a deadly terrorist movement in order to destabilize a microscopic but self-respecting community. This was evidently aimed at eroding a political rival's credibility and to clear the path for the monopoly of the Congress party at the expense of the only Sikh outfit, the Akali Dal. In the larger context, the calculated manner in which the situation in Punjab was allowed to reach a flash point justifying the use of the Army and heavy armour to mount an assault on the Golden Temple, the holiest of holy shrines of the Sikh people, was a fully planned and deliberate attempt, perhaps to solve once for all the nationality questions in India. And it did seem to succeed in extinguishing the nascent ethnic movements in most parts of the country for the moment, though it is a moot question if it has fully managed to uproot all such movements.

Indian Police, whatever other drawbacks it may have had during the eighty odd years it served the British Indian government since its reorganization in 1861, was scrupulously fair in its enforcement tasks as between different religious groups. The 1920s, 1930s and 1940s of were marked by increasing sectarian conflicts and rioting between Hindus and Muslims in which the police was called upon to display firmness, promptitude and an impartial outlook in their handling. Muslim officers frequently had to escort Hindu Holi processions accompanied by bands playing loud music in front of mosques where Muslims were at Friday prayers—a common enough cause of rioting. Hindu officers were placed in similar situations in respect of their religious beliefs. In both cases, police officers did not flinch from a strict adherence to the dictates of their respective duties. With the dawn of independence, however, Indian Police got sharply fractured along sectarian lines. The polarization was complete by the end of 1946 as the possibility of Partition became evident. Jack Morton, police chief of Lahore was to observe later, 'I was almost at the end of my tether. We'd had rioting since November 1946, there was practically no rest and no sleep. My Sikh and Hindu police were being singled out by Muslim mobs for violence. The Muslims came along to me saying, "You British and your Muslim police can do what they like to us, but we're not going to have your Hindus and Sikhs. We won't answer for the consequences." So it was a very worrying situation because the police were a thoroughly integrated force'. The situation in east Punjab was no different. There the Muslim police were disarmed a few days before the date fixed for the transfer of power and thus became easy targets of vandalism not only by riotous mobs but also their own erstwhile non-Muslim colleagues. Surprisingly enough an identical black spot, which the Indian Police find very difficult to live down, was the disarming and humiliation of Sikh policemen in India's capital city during the Sikh killings in November 1984, following Indira Gandhi's assassination. Communalization of a fairly objective and integrated pre-independence police proceeded at a swift pace in the Hindi-speaking states of UP, Bihar and Madhya Pradesh, possibly with some surreptitious encouragement at the hands of unscrupulous politicians. Strangely, while the political classes regularly expressed disapproval of growing communal bias among the lower constabulary, no effective correctives were applied. Cosmetic measures like increased intake of Muslims in the police, setting up new and novel outfits to add to the already bloated paramilitary and armed battalions, did not help as they did not address the basic issues. Since society itself was being increasingly affected by the evils of casteism, regionalism and sectarianism, police forces could not remain immune to the poison. This was to prove disastrous in the long run.

The pathetic irony of a colonial era police serving a modern democracy was largely lost upon the ruling coteries of politicians and bureaucrats. Even the police leadership were either unaware of or complacent about the systemic shortcomings and cultural constraints, which continued to colour police performance in independent India and widen the historical chasm between the police and citizens. It was only in the third decade after independence that a more enlightened police and civil service leadership and a non-Congress government in Delhi realized the need for change. It was partly due to a growing sense of uneasiness among the middle level IPS leadership, comprising officers appointed after democracy had taken firm roots in the inhospitable soil of a centuries old feudalist tradition but mainly because of the fast deteriorating security environment. The Government of India now decided to get an indepth examination conducted of the whole gamut of police structure, procedures, regulation, practices, organizational and related matters to update and modernize the Indian Police. Last time such a detailed review was undertaken was in 1902–3 by the Second Indian Police Commission. Now

75 years after that event and 30 years after the attainment of independence, a National Police Commission was appointed in November 1977 with wide terms of reference and comprising some of the best brains from the civil service, police, judiciary and social sciences. Dharma Vira, the chairman was a former member of the ICS who had held high positions in the government including those of cabinet secretary and governor of some very important states. The terms of reference were carefully drafted and comprehensive. The commission was asked to:

1. Re-define the role, duties, powers and responsibilities of the police with special reference to prevention and control of crime and maintenance of public order.
2. Examine the development of the principles underlying the present policing system, including the method of magisterial supervision, evaluate the performance of the system, identify the basic weaknesses and inadequacies, and suggest appropriate changes in the system and the basic laws governing the system.
3. Examine, if any changes are necessary in the existing method of administration, disciplinary control and accountability.
4. Inquire into the system of investigation and prosecution, the reasons for delay and failure; the use of improper methods, and the extent of their prevalence; and suggest how the system may be modified or changed, and made efficient, scientific and consistent with human dignity; and how the related laws may be suitably amended.
5. Examine methods of maintaining crime records and statistics and suggest methods for making them uniform and scientific.
6. Review policing in rural areas, evaluate any new arrangements that have been made, and recommend changes that are necessary.
7. Examine the system of policing required in non-rural and urbanized areas including metropolitan areas, and suggest the pattern that would be most suitable.
8. Examine the steps taken for modernizing law enforcement, evaluate the work of police communications, the computer network, scientific laboratories and agencies for research and development and examine to what extent, as a result of modernization of police forces, streamlining of its functions and its restructuring, it would be possible to economize with regard to manpower in various areas of its activities.

9. Examine the nature and extent of the special responsibilities of the police towards the weaker sections of the community and suggest steps to ensure prompt action on their complaints for safeguarding their rights and interest.
10. Recommend measures and institutional arrangements:
    (i) to prevent misuse of powers by the police and to examine whether police behaviour, outlook, responsiveness and impartiality are maintained at the correct level, and if not, steps such as recruitment and training should be taken to improve them;
    (ii) to prevent misuse of the police by administrative or executive instructions, political or other pressure, or oral orders of any type which are contrary to law;
    (iii) for the quick redressal of grievances of police personnel and to look after their morale and welfare; and
    (iv) for a periodic objective evaluation of police performance in a metropolitan area/district/state in a manner that will carry credibility before the public.
11. Examine the manner and extent to which police can enlist ready and willing cooperation of the public in the discharge of their social defence and law-enforcement duties and suggest measures regarding the institutional arrangements to secure such co-operation and measures for the growth of healthy and friendly public-police relationship.
12. Examine the methods of police training, development and career planning of officers and recommend any changes that are required at any time in their service to modernize their outlook and to make the leadership of the force effective and morally strong.
13. Examine nature of the problems that the police will have to face in the future, and suggest measures necessary for dealing with them, and for keeping them under continuous study and appraisal.
14. Consider and make recommendations and suggestions regarding any other matter which the government may refer to the commission; and
15. Any other matter of relevance or importance having an import on the subject.

The Commission also wanted to report on five other critical areas namely, terrorism, intelligence, state criminal investigation departments, criminal justice system and government railway police but were unable to do so, as according to them, they were pressed for time. The reality was somewhat different. The non-Congress government who had appointed the Commission was voted out in the 1980 General Elections and the new central government of Mrs Gandhi favoured neither reforms nor the Commission membership. So the Commission was advised to speed up their work and pack up. Along with them also went the union home secretary and several other big-wigs favoured by her predecessor in office. The commission was finally wound up after they had submitted eight very useful, comprehensive and self-contained reports, in May 1981. In the three and a half years of their labours, the Commission closely examined a number of critical areas pertaining to police and the criminal justice system, interviewed hundreds of witnesses, scrutinized thousands of memoranda, notes, theme papers, enquiry reports, records, even commissioned study projects to some eminent sociologists (including David Bayley of Princeton), and went about their tasks with characteristic thoroughness and diligence. In the process, they came out with some of the most apt solutions to the problems and dilemmas confronting the Indian police for the last several decades, including the draft of a brand new Police Act. However, their reports were not destined to bring about any worthwhile changes in the functioning of the police in India because neither the politician nor the bureaucrat wanted to surrender their hold on the police, as they had found it, not unlike the colonial governments before independence, a very useful (and servile) instrument of oppression. So any reform which promoted a degree of functional autonomy in the police was quickly shot down in the corridors of power. Police thus continued to discharge their social defence role in the same age-old manner and though the prospect of early police reform continues to recede further and further away, every new generation of IPS officers do not fail to show their concern and anxiety about the physical and moral health of the police and security agencies. Their efforts in this regard, though sincere and enthusiastic, do not make much of a dent in the political and bureaucratic citadel of resistence. The reports of the National Police Commission are referred from time to time in seminars and conferences, even in the government files, but without making any material difference to the formulation of policies about the working of police and social security agencies. Occasionally, the debates turn into a mere slanging match between the IAS and the IPS.

Apart from the long felt need for initiating a process of reforms in the Indian Police, an immediate circumstance necessitating the setting up of a National Police Commission in 1977 was the fast growing unrest and discontent in the state police forces, and at least one central paramilitary force, at lower levels. There is no clear evidence that such unrest and the accompanying agitational postures of constables and head constables were inspired by their officers or actively supported by mainstream political parties, though local level maverick politicians did not fail to fish in troubled waters. Also though the middle level officers kept away from any active involvement and did not evade compliance with government directions to deal firmly with the insubordinate and indisciplined policemen leading the movement, they could not but feel sympathetic to the demands voiced by the agitators. The IPS officers on whom fell the responsibility of both containing the emerging situation and articulating the genuine grievances of the force under their supervision and control before the authorities, found it a delicate and ticklish task. For ranged against them were not only the political establishment but also the civilian bureaucracy who had lost no time in perceiving in this situation a ready argument against the growing trend of police autonomy in recent years. A service (the IPS) which was unable to provide effective leadership to its own departmental subordinates could not claim to be treated on par with the IAS. The IPS understandably lost considerable ground in its on-going battle to gain more respect and support from the political class, as a result of the police unrest of the 1970s. The latter occurrence also had a positive fallout in as much as the lower subordinates in the police, always a marginalized lot and in a state of utter neglect, gained recognition as a crucial component in the department. No longer would the finance ministers in the states summarily throw out the recommendations of Police chiefs for enhancement of their emoluments, allowances, rations, housing grants and leave entitlements. The Indian Police forces had not remained immune to agitational activities in the past too—UP and Bihar police during the 'Quit India' phase of Indian freedom movement, Delhi police in the mid-1960s phase of Police unrest. The extent and degree of agitational activities were not uniform in all the districts of a state and in all the states of the country. It varied considerably depending on the leadership qualities of the district superintendents and their rapport with their men. At the state level too those inspectors-generals who had the vision and insight to constantly monitor the morale of the forces under them and could forcefully put up the legitimate claims of the constabulary before their governments for timely acceptance, had much less problems than their counterparts in other states. The unrest and agitations were finally brought under control, though not before many state police forces won the right to collective bargaining and the setting up of grievance redressal machineries at all levels from districts upwards, so that the subordinates' grievances and demands were constantly under review. The National Police Commission too examined the subject in great depth and made several eminently useful recommendations.

Rapid and large scale industrialization and urbanization overtaking already overgrown cities and towns have given rise to gigantic urban conglomerations bursting at the seams. It is estimated that at least three mega-cities with populations exceeding the ten million mark in the next century will be located in India. The resultant strains on civic amenities, quality of life and efficacy of police in containing crime, criminal and antisocial elements are likely to produce unprecedented situations of social turmoil, chaos and lawlessness. The whole network of police activities and strategies in the crime control area will have to be reworked, reoriented, strengthened and refurbished. Systemic and functional alterations and improvements will become inevitable. With the ever-growing pace of breakdown of family norms and bonds, which constituted a unique ingredient of Indian civilization and way of life, the invisible but powerful positive societal links with the individual have snapped. In the event, deviant behaviour and violations of socially accepted values have become the rule rather than the exception in our fast growing metropolitan areas. The unchecked and unplanned growth of these urban conglomerates has also generated many other related issues and difficulties. The runaway expansion in the volume of motorized traffic within cities and on some densely used highways has given rise to a host of problems for the police and civic authorities. The daily influx of hundreds of thousands of travelers, tourists, workers and other people in search of jobs or for other purposes throws the established system of police surveillance into utter confusion. All these various problems and crisis situations will continue to proliferate in the new century. The critical question is whether the Indian Police and the state governments are fully equipped and willing to face, or are even aware of the rapid march of events, which will soon render the mid-nineteenth century mindset of our police forces totally and unambiguously irrelevant and non-functional. From all available evidence, which a perceptive individual can garner, the answer seems to be a resounding no. Even the modest recommendations made by the national Police Commission a decade and half ago eminently pertinent as they were to our social defence system then, may soon become out of date in the context of the policing needs of the twenty-first century Indian society. Since it is not possible to reverse the course of events, a modern society has to pull its act together in time to effectively tackle newer and more complex situations threatening social cohesion and harmony.

Recently, Indian judiciary has adopted an activist role in many areas of governmental activity. Their pronouncements and decisions have helped many a moribund government agency to come to life. Mostly the courts have concerned themselves with human rights and environmental areas alone though the Supreme Court has lately lent considerable strength and stature to the Central Bureau of Investigation in their enquires relating to large scale political corruption in handling matters of state. Indictment of several powerful politicians and bureaucrats, even governors of states, and chargesheeting of former senior ministers for offences of murder and sheltering hardened criminals, where the police were earlier afraid of even conducting sustained investigations, brings a new reassuring element to a situation of utter interia and venality in governmental working. It has kindled a new ray of hope in the oppressed Indian masses. However, judiciary cannot ever be a substitute for a good government and they can only play a limited role in a few areas that are brought to their notice by public bodies or individuals. Police reform is a complex process which can, in the final analysis, be brought about only by public awareness of their rights and powers in an enlightened but assertive manner. Till then the Indian Police will continue to be governed by its twin legacies of servility and oppression. Half a century of freedom and democratic pretensions have made no difference except for the worse. The question whether radical police reform will ever occur through governmental or parliamentary initiative in India, remains steeped in deep doubt.

CHAPTER 4

Maintaining Social Order

R.K. RAGHAVAN

A staggeringly populous nation—with a low literacy rate (52.2 per cent) and a high unemployment level, both of which are compounded by sharp religious, political and regional differences—India offers a fertile ground for social conflict that frequently manifests itself in the form of riots in public places. The crucial test of police effectiveness in any society is how sensitive the police are to matters affecting the preservation of public peace. This is an area of responsibility and reputations are either made or marred by the ability with which the police handle group violence in the streets. Moreover a failure to act quickly for the purpose of neutralizing anti-social elements who tinker with the day-to-day peace in society, reflects poorly on police professionalism. In India, inter-religious riots, especially those between Hindus and Muslims, often lead to a colossal loss of lives and property at the hands of criminals masquerading as protectors of religion. Similarly, the incapacity and, sometimes, a reluctance to step in to prevent wanton destruction of public property committed by political groups and sectarian organizations for the flimsiest of grievances, is another phenomenon that makes quite a few people cynical of police competence. These in particular raises several issues revolving round police preparedness and ability. But this scenario will have to be viewed against the history of foreign invasions and the long drawn-out struggle for freedom from the British that began during the middle of the nineteenth century and concluded nearly one hundred years later. The nature of political evolution has understandably had a palpable impact on the quality of policing, and the happenings in the political arena continue to strongly determine police perceptions at all levels.

In the eight decades following the promulgation of the Police Act in 1861, till India became free from British rule in 1947, the police were subjected to myriad influences. More than crime, it was in the area of preservation of law and order that they were under tremendous pressure from different sources. There was the ferment in the political arena flowing from enhanced political awareness and a desire to break away from the shackles of the foreign power. This was exacerbated by pronounced bitterness between religious groups, a development traceable to the deliberate British policy of 'divide and rule'. Altogether, it was an important phase of evolution of the Indian Police as a vital arm of government for establishing stability in society. This was again a period in which certain traditions, which even now characterize police attitudes, were established.

A long-winded account of the freedom movement is not warranted here. Suffice it to say that this prolonged struggle posed many problems to the policeman in the field. Different strategies were required to tackle three aspects of the native fight against the British.

First, there was a non-cooperation movement which took the form of abstention from all obligatory responses to government activity, such as attendance at courts, participation in military service, etc. This was followed by a phase of civil disobedience, which essentially took the form of massive public demonstrations when such large congregations in public were prohibited by law. While non-cooperation, by its nature, was passive and therefore non-violent, civil disobedience led to violence against public property and public servants. There were mob attacks on police stations in Bihar, Bengal and United Provinces. In one such instance (February 1922), 22 policemen were killed at Chauri Chaura Police Station in the United Provinces.

Police reaction to such impulsive mob violence was uniformly restrained. Griffiths (1971: 255) wonders whether 'anywhere else in the world, so widespread and dangerous a movement, either could or would have been controlled with so little display of force'. An unfortunate off-shoot of the civil disobedience movement was the terrorism that was employed by overzealous nationalist elements, some of whom had gained more than a foothold in the Congress party that was spearheading the freedom struggle (Curry, 1932). This posed a problem which called for qualities different from those needed to counter an open movement, such as civil disobedience.

There were several instances of terrorist violence directed against the British officials, such as the 1897 murder of two officials of Poona (Bombay Province) and the 1909 murder of District Magistrate Jackson of Nasik. The raid on the Chittagong (now in Bangladesh) Armoury and two attempts on the life of Calcutta's police commissioner in eastern India and a series of bomb explosions in UP (central India) were all indicative of the terrorist might. During 1907–17, in Bengal Province alone, revolutionary parties were responsible for more than 200 outrages and the murder of 20 police officers (Curry, 1932).

While the initial police response was defensive and tardy, a degree of professionalism was acquired in course of time. This was clear from the number of prosecutions launched and convictions obtained, particularly in the Punjab (Griffiths, 1971).

Another area in which the police found themselves in a tight corner was the delicate state of Hindu–Muslim relations. Antagonism between the communities was historically deep-rooted, traceable to the Muslim invasion of India, centuries before the British came in. There was, however, only a limited opportunity for it to explode into an ugly day-to-day confrontation. This was partly explainable by the fact that there were well-defined pockets of influence for each of the two religions, where the weaker group had to necessarily assume a low profile (Griffiths, 1971).

To begin with, the British adopted a neutral stance. In course of time this yielded place to a sly support of Muslims. Some historians believe that this was not deliberate, a perception common to some former British civil servants like Griffiths (1971). There is, however, a strong body of opposite opinion that the British were in fact prone to mischief and had evolved a 'divide and rule' policy. It is beyond the scope of this paper to scrutinize the merits of the rival viewpoints. It is enough to observe that there was a marked rancour between the religionists, to which the district administration had to be sensitive. Even a trivial incident could degenerate into mindless violence.

One of the first major riots under British India was in the western city of Bombay in August 1893, when a large Muslim mob coming out of a mosque attacked a Hindu temple. (This was in reaction to incidents that had occurred in Kathiawar earlier during the Muharram celebrations.) In the violent exchanges, about 50,000 people fled the city, 100 were killed and 800 injured (Curry, 1932; and Gupta, 1979).

Tension during the annual Muharram festival of Muslims and the Ganpati festival of Hindus was to become a regular feature. It was only some 'firm but judicious action' the police that helped to check violence (Griffiths, 1971).

Two riots in the Madras Presidency (now the state of Tamil Nadu) of southern India in 1912, at Tirupattur and Berhampur, saw an orgy of violence that required the use of force by the police (Griffiths, 1971). The 1916 Lucknow Pact brought some temporary peace. This received a setback following the Moplah (a Muslim farming community) rebellion of August 1921 in the Malabar district of Madras Presidency.

The period 1921–40 may especially be looked upon as an era of communal discord that posed major difficulties to the police. The year 1926 was a particularly bad one. Almost the whole of India was affected by Hindu–Muslim conflict. The disharmony was most visible in Bengal, Bihar, the Punjab and United Provinces. In July that year, Muharram celebrations in Calcutta led to 28 deaths and injuries to 226. There were 71 communal riots during 1926 in Bihar and Orissa (Griffiths, 1971). The next marked phase of communal violence was in 1929, when, in the Bombay Province alone, 149 people lost their lives and property worth half a million rupees was stolen. Discussing the police role around this period, Curry (1932: 304–5) says: 'It was only the staunchness of the Indian Police which prevented India from falling into a bottomless pit of disaster and chaos.'

The completeness of the communal divide was obvious from the unprecedented violence that one saw during 1946–7 on the eve of the transfer of power from the British to India and to the newly carved out Muslim nation of Pakistan. There was senseless violence in Bengal, Bihar and the Punjab, which took the form of mass killing, abduction and rape. Police forces were totally stretched, and it was a measure of their discipline and determination that they did not break down totally.

POST-INDEPENDENCE SCENARIO

Since attaining freedom, India has gone through several traumas on the law and order front. The first problem that faced the infant nation was one of political consolidation. This called for establishing control over some of the Princely States whose rulers were anxious to retain their autonomy even after the British departed. Kashmir and Hyderabad were two such states.

While the Indian Army tackled the problem in Kashmir by throwing out the raiders (a group comprising armed tribals and members of the Pakistan Army) sent by Pakistan to pressure the ruler (Maharajah) into opting for Pakistan, it was the police that was employed in Hyderabad. The Muslim ruler of Hyderabad, the Nizam, in total disregard of all logic and geography, wanted to accede to Pakistan. Responding to popular sentiment which favoured India, the central government sent a police force which swiftly brought about a surrender of the Nizam forces. This remarkable operation, remembered even today as the 'Hyderabad Police Action', highlighted the professional skills and discipline of the Indian Police.

The next test of police efficiency came during 1947–51 from the same area in the south in a cluster of districts called Telengana. Uneven distribution of land and gross ill-treatment of farm workers by landlords had generated a strong leftist movement there. The peasants, under the aegis of the Communist Party, indulged in large-scale violence against land-holders. Since the police force sent from Hyderabad were unequal to the task, large contingents were requisitioned from the neighbouring Madras State (now Tamil Nadu). The movement was contained in course of time, although the methods employed by the police were denounced by some as brutal and illegal.

DEVELOPMENTS SINCE 1950

Generally speaking, democracy, in its most liberal sense, has survived in India, notwithstanding the few phases of authoritarian rule at the centre and in some states. These phases have, however, been short, thanks to the sensitivity of the fundamental organs such as the judiciary, legislature and press. An undisputed fact also is the stability lent by a well-oiled civil service machinery. The police remains a vital segment of this mechanism and the mainstay of successive governments in their endeavour to maintain law and order.

The use of the police has been frequent and extensive, and the force has been criticized widely for functioning as the handmaiden of the political party in power. This impression has unfortunately become stronger over the years, because the campaign to promote the nonpartisan character of the police has remained feeble. On the other hand police has been facing new types of problems in a new situation.

The problems faced by the police on the law and order front since 1950 fall into the following broad categories:

(i) Violent agitations by linguistic groups for re-drawing the political map so as to earmark one state for each language;
(ii) Similar tactics of tribal groups, particularly those in the north-east region;
(iii) The demand for the re-distribution of land ownership, voiced initially by the Communist Party, and subsequently by extremist groups born out of the Indian communist movement, leading to the liquidation of 'class enemies' and police informants;
(iv) Violent agitations engineered by political parties, ostensibly in support of some live economic or social issue, but mainly to bring down lawfully elected governments;
(v) Terrorism by groups wanting to secede from the Indian union, such as in the Punjab and in Kashmir;
(vi) Violent clashes arising out of the unconcealed fundamentalism espoused by some staunch groups among Hindus and Muslims, a few of the latter aided and abetted by Pakistan from across the border;
(vii) Endemic caste clashes in the rural hinterland, often centring round antagonistic land and related problems between the landlord and agricultural workers; and
(viii) The emergence of a sharp division between the 'forward' and 'backward' classes following introduction of a quota system for distribution of seats in educational institutions and for government staff selections, leading to public violence.

THE POLICE RESPONSE

In view of the above situations the police has remained under tremendous pressure. In the absence of proper training, orientation, sufficient man power and autonomy, the police response has remained. Basic aspects of police response can be mentioned as under:

(a) Substantial sections of the country suffer from attempts by various groups to tinker with public order. Violence varies only quantitatively. As a result, police forces have to be in a perpetual state of readiness.
(b) Almost every state, at sometime or the other, seeks the central government's help to provide police forces, such as the Central Reserve Police Force or Border Security Force, to bring a dis-

turbed situation under control. Requisitioning the police of a neighbouring state is also common.

(c) Police resort to firearms to quell riots is the order of the day. Very often, this is followed by a popular demand, backed by political parties in the opposition, for a judicial inquiry to find out whether such use was justified by the circumstances of an incident. Except in a very few cases, such an inquiry always ends in favour of the police.

(d) Police intervention in clashes involving rival religious or caste groups is assailed frequently as biased. This is particularly true of a Hindu–Muslim confrontation in communally sensitive states, such as UP and Bihar, where a division of the constabulary into Hindus and Muslims is often alleged.

(e) In clashes pitting the ruling political party against the opposition, the police invariably tends to side with the former, particularly in the matter of arrests.

The following three areas are of contemporary relevance to police operations:

(a) Terrorism;
(b) Inter-religious riots; and
(c) Physical protection of dignitaries (VIP security).

As this volume is primarily concerned with police's dealing with minorities and in communal situations, we only can discuss the relevant one from the above.

HANDLING OF INDIA'S INTER-RELIGIOUS RIOTS

One major criticism of the Indian Police during the past three decades has been its inability to handle clashes between members of different religions, popularly referred to as 'communal riots', especially of the Hindu–Muslim variety, in a professional manner. A bias in favour of the Hindu rioters, and the delayed and excessive use of force are two specific complaints.

Commissions of Inquiry in different parts of the country have gone into the causes of many riots, apart from fixing responsibility for failures of civil servants, especially the police. Reports of these commissions are valuable for their observations on police performance. This is notwithstanding the fact that commissions are seldom appointed in quick time, and the evidence placed before them is very often garbled, leading to certain untenable conclusions (Rajgopal, 1987). The gravamen of the charge by many commissions is the initial lack of police firmness against rioters. The Jaganmohan Reddy Commission—which looked into the September 1969 riots in Ahmedabad and other Gujarat towns in which 524 lost their lives—said: 'The Police lost the initiative and, once the situation got out of control at the very commencement of the riot, they were overwhelmed by the situation which confronted them.'

A lack of judgement of a developing situation is another shortcoming. The district authorities, police and the magistracy, very often ignored evidence in the form of isolated incidents that could ignite religious feelings. As a result, in a short time, they were faced with a situation that required action which was beyond their capacity.

There have also been occasions marked by an utter lack of coordination between the police and army units called to assist them in grave disturbances. This pointed to mutual suspicion, rivalry and an inability to overcome ego considerations when dealing with major religious conflagrations. One of the commissions also referred to an unwarranted interference from the higher echelons of the government. This greatly cramped the style and autonomy of field officers and thereby affected their ability to contain riots (Rajgopal, 1987).

Possibly the most serious complaint is the alleged police failure to project a neutral image. The Justice Jitendra Narayan Commission—which looked into the 1979 Jamshedpur (Bihar) riots—was scathing on the pro-Hindu action of the Bihar Military Police. In the Aligarh (1979) and Moradabad (1980) riots in UP, a similar impression of police bias against the minority community was dominant among the public (Rajgopal, 1987).

Deeply concerned over the impact of repeated clashes between religious groups on the social fabric, the central government maintains an active dialogue with state governments. One significant move is the identification of trouble-prone 'communally sensitive districts' in every state which require special attention, so that there is a continuous monitoring of inter-religious relations. Another is the move to pin down responsibility, for swift action to contain trouble, on the district magistrate (collector) and the superintendent of police. In cases of failure on their part, governments have initiated disciplinary action, such as suspension from service.

Perhaps the most positive of the moves initiated so far to tackle communal riots is the creation of a Rapid Action Force (RAF) within the Central Reserve Police Force. The RAF is a crack force that is normally airlifted to scenes of trouble so that quick action is initiated to contain explosive situations. The RAF performance till now has been satisfactory, though no serious study of its effectiveness is available to facilitate a meaningful public debate. Let us have a look how the police is prepared to handle situations of disturbances.

DRILL FOR HANDLING PUBLIC DISORDER IN INDIA

It is the police station, as the basic unit of administration, that first receives a complaint/information of apprehended breach of peace or about an incident that has already taken place. In the rural areas, this is often handed in personally by an interested party. In the semi-urban and urban police stations, there is a telephone—other than the dedicated internal radio telephone—accessible to the citizen and by means of which, news of an incident is very often received from the public. There are also instances of patrolmen alerting a police station. In the larger towns and metropolises, police control rooms receive calls from the public and activise police stations or patrol vehicles.

Police stations respond by dispatching small parties of policemen who may not always carry any arms with them. This is normally adequate in a majority of cases. In more serious incidents, where rival parties have employed weapons, police stations invariably depend on the Armed Reserve, which consists of personnel trained to disperse mobs through the use of tear-gas shells or firearms (usually .303 rifles). Police stations do have similar firearms which are, however, used only in extreme emergencies, such as a mob attack on the station premises. In graver situations, when even the Armed Reserve is unequal to the task of restoring order, the State Special Armed Police steps in on the DGP's specific order.

PREVENTIVE ACTION BY THE INDIAN POLICE

There is a reasonably sensitive and focused machinery down to the level of a police station or a group of stations (called the Circle), which is responsible for keeping track of trends on the ground, so as to facilitate timely preventive action whenever a breach of peace is anticipated. This takes the form of an Intelligence Branch, both at the State Police and the District Police Headquarters. The former is supervised immediately by an IG/ADGP. It has staff up to the level of a district. In addition, every district superintendent of police (SP) has an intelligence or special branch inspector (in some states, of the rank of deputy superintendent) who acts as his 'eyes and ears'.

The task of the Intelligence staff is to keep track of trends which point to dissatisfaction over any act of commission or omission by the government, or that of any individual/group, and is likely to inflame public opinion and affect public peace. Issues as disparate as the non-availability or short supply of essential articles of daily consumption, such as food, water or fuel, misconduct of a civil servant towards the public, showing dishonour to religious symbols, or a wage dispute between the management and labour in an industry, are all capable of snowballing into major conflicts which need close monitoring.

Information on a developing situation, of the kind described, is promptly passed on by Intelligence to the civil authorities. The latter initiates appropriate steps to redress a grievance through negotiation or administrative measures. When such action fails to assuage feelings, and there are individuals determined to embarrass the government by resorting to unlawful modes of agitation, the civil administration normally draws on the authority conferred on it by statutes and sets in motion swift preventive action.

Two important provisions of the Criminal Procedure Code (CrPC) are relevant. First, under Section 144, the administration may direct an individual or persons living in a particular area or the public in general to desist from an act that is likely to disturb public tranquility. This enables the administration to ban a public gathering of five or more persons for a specified period. Section 145 gives similar authority in respect of a dispute over land or water that threatens public peace. Orders under the two sections are promulgated by the executive magistrate on a recommendation from the police or otherwise.

Some provisions of the Police Act 1861 also come in handy to the police. One of these is Section 30, whereby a district superintendent of police or his assistant/deputy may regulate public assemblies and processions by insisting on their organizers to obtain a prior licence which imposes certain conditions, such as the specific route along which a procession may be taken. Violation of licence conditions invites penal action.

Additionally, the police can make preventive arrests under Section 151 of the CrPC. It has been the police experience that such arrests sometimes lead to further trouble, and hence these could only be the last alternative. Section 107 permits a magistrate to bind over rival parties, locked up in a dispute, to good behaviour for a specified period. This has also been found useful in maintaining peace.

In India, riots involving a direct Muslim confrontation with the police and those pitting the former against the majority community of Hindus have no doubt been many, especially in the pre-Independence period. It is, however, reasonable to estimate that these now constitute much less than 50 per cent of the total number of riots, even in the most sensitive geographic area. Riots arising from political demonstrations, labour disputes, and linguistic and inter-state controversies outnumber those arising from religious differences (otherwise known as communal clashes).

In the Indian setting, incidents involving the minority group of Muslims are almost invariably a confrontation with the majority Hindu community. The attack on the police is only a sequel. But once police—Muslim exchanges begin, there is a strident propaganda that the police are biased and are acting at the behest of Hindus. This is analogous to the black belief of a racist slant in the American Police, except that, there is no charge that this is the result of a link-up with any organized white group. In India, the strong presence of well-organized and active Hindu fundamentalist bodies almost always lends basis to an allegation of police nexus with Hindu bigots.

The excessive use of force, when strictly not warranted, and a failure to maintain a posture of neutrality between communities, are two distressing features of the scene in many communal riots. In dealing with police–government relationship, non-implementation of the National Police Commission (NPC) recommendations is one major reason for police subordination to the political executive instead of the law of the land. Current trends do not augur well for the future. The police will continue to be assailed for acting as the handmaiden of the ruling party. This will remain so unless certain basic reforms of the system are brought out. A judicial fiat on the subject could help. It alone will not, however, do the trick. There has to be a sea-change in the perceptions of the politician vis-à-vis the police. As long as he looks upon the police as a tool to settle political scores with his adversaries, nothing will alter. As things stand, hopes of police reform are bleak because there is near unanimity—as with regard to corruption—cutting across party lines, that the status quo should remain, and that the police should not be conferred operational freedom, but actually controlled as closely as possible.

REFERENCES

Curry, J.C., *Indian Police*, London: Faber and Faber, 1932.

Griffiths, Sir Percival, *To Guard My People: The History of the Indian Police*, London: Ernest Benn, 1971.

Gupta, Anand Swarup, *The Police in British India 1861–1947*, New Delhi: Concept, 1979.

Rajgopal, P.R., *Communal Violence in India*, New Delhi: Uppal, 1987.

Raghavan, R.K., *Policing a Democracy*, New Delhi: Manohar, 1999.

CHAPTER 5

Place and Role of Police in a Plural Society

PRAKASH LOUIS

In the recent past the police force has come under serious scrutiny by the general public as well as the civil society. The Gujarat pogrom has exposed the communal bias the police force has come to acquire in course of time. It is not argued here that the entire police contingent has become communal. But a major segment it seems can be easily aroused by communal passions. Motivated by such passions, they engage in communal violence, or could remain uninvolved or indifferent, and even shield the culprits. All this has come as a shock to the general masses of this country. Further, it is a known fact that casteist, feudal and patriarchal tendencies are a part of the police force as these aberrations are prevalent in society. But the manner with which these attitudes colour the actions, inactions, and biased behaviour of the police force is a cause for concern today. It is the expectation of common masses of this country that with the evolution of the Indian social order and political system, the performance of the law enforcers would also change and acquire a positive-proactive role. But this aspiration of the citizens of this country seems to be belied by the politicians who continue to manipulate the role of the police force for their advantage.

The National Police Commission (NPC) which was appointed on 15 November 1977 submitted its report on 7 February 1979, made the following observation in its Preamble.

> Police performance in India today is under close review and critical assessment by a demanding public in far greater measure than at any time in the past. Increasing crime, rising population, growing pressure of living accommodation, particularly in urban areas, violent outbursts in the wake of demonstrations and agitations arising from labour disputes, agrarian unrest,

problems and difficulties of students, political activities including the cult of extremists, enforcement of economic and social legislations, etc., have all added new dimensions to police tasks in the country and tended to bring the police in confrontation with the public much more frequently than ever before. Functioning under the constraints and handicaps of an outmoded system, police performance has undoubtedly fallen short of public expectation. (NPC, 1979: 7)

During the Gujarat carnage, there were two slogans about the place and role of police in Gujarat. These slogans represent two widely held perceptions about the police. Video footage seen by the fact-finding team showed slogans like *Yeh andar ki bat hai, police hamare saath hai* (The inside story is that the police is on our side) written boldly on the walls of gutted Muslim homes. The other slogan was *Yeh to hinduon ka police hai, aur hamare virudh hai* (This is a Hindu police and against us) (*The Survivors Speak*, 2002: 17, The first slogan represents the belligerence of the perpetrators of crime. who were sure that the police were on their side and they could with impunity engage in violence. The other slogan speaks about the perception of the victims of communal violence who perceived police to be against them. These slogans drive home the message that the police have become partisan in its attitude and operation.

Some of the major questions that have emerged about the police force today are: what is the task of the police? Is it to be protective, detective or repressive? Does it protect the interests of the citizens or of the ruling establishment? Or, isn't it the job of the police today to be promotive of the rights and dignity of all the citizens irrespective of their caste, creed, religion and region? But since the police force itself is part of the wider social order, it is appropriate that one examine the place and role of police in that broader context. Increasingly one hears of men in police force who either commit suicide or kill their higher officers. This emerging trend should be seriously paid attention to, since this development indicates the low self-worth that is sweeping across the police force. This essay attempts to analyse the place and role of the police in the plural context of India.

PLURAL SOCIETIES

The framers of the Indian Constitution opted for a socialist, secular and democratic form of governance for this country. By opting for a secular state, the architects of the Constitution envisaged that the State will not espouse or establish or practice any religion and that every citizen of this country will have equal right to freedom of conscience and religion. While these ideals exist in principle, in practice the last fifty years of independent India are ridden by conflicts of religious interests bordering on communalism. While secularism remains a far cry, it is the communal forces that have come to occupy the centre stage of Indian society and polity. Moreover, for the vast masses of India, secularism often means denial of religion. Hence, there is a strong move to advocate the principles of pluralism today.

It is pertinent at this juncture to examine the basic features of plural societies so as to locate the place and role of police in such a pluralistic society like India's. Pluralism in its basic meaning refers to the existence of multiplicity of modes and methods, thoughts and ideas, culture and political forms, and of identities. It is deconstructive of any form of monism and uniformity. In the context of social relationships, political forms and principles, pluralism has a special appeal in a diverse society. The meaning and context of pluralism has not, however, been uniform throughout its course of development. With shifting emphasis and focus, pluralism as a concept has been conceived, used and articulated differently. In the contemporary usages, especially in the context of post-modernism and post-colonialism, pluralism indicates amongst other things: a suitably humble and relativistic acceptance that there is a range of cultural values; opposition to all forms of cultural imperialism; release from the dead ends of scientism and rationalism; fruitful methodological diversity; endorsement of different ways of knowing and of being; creativity and openness in theory; and embrace of a wide range of social interests and interest groups in the modern political ambience, none of which are 'primary' in any demonstrable sense; affirmation of democracy as an end in itself; attention to the complexities of political allegiance; the sense that our social and political identities are now chosen rather than inherited; anti-utopian political horizons; enshrinement of the principle of 'equal but different' (McLennan, 1995: 2–3).

In his analysis of pluralism in India, A.P. Vijapur observes:

> Pluralism provides framework of accommodation in a multi-ethnic, multi-cultural, multi-lingual, multi-regional, multi-religious, multi-caste plural society. It is essentially non-homogeneous and non-hierarchical corresponding to the two basic values of equality and liberty. In such a society it is not merely a question of choice but also an existential condition of peace and harmony. It recognises and respects diversities in a given society and provides social and political space for the expression and articulation of multiple identities.

As a principle, pluralism promotes inter-community understanding and in such a condition it appears both a social fact and a value. It is found to be independent of individual's will and volition and in this sense it constitutes a social fact. It appears as a value in a plural society where it reduces the possibility of conflict to the minimum, and thus it is considered to be just, legitimate and desirable (Vijapur, 1997: 4).

Thus, it can be stated that in a plural society, there is a sense of shared identity and destiny irrespective of many differences that are internal and external. India has been trying to maintain this oneness of purpose, though the ruptures have been witnessed right from the beginning. Any attempt to move away from plural cultural, social and communitarian structure to mono forms would result in the hegemony of a ruling elite, who would continuously exploit the discontinuities for their benefit. Let us move on to examine the place and role of police in a plural society.

PLACE AND ROLE OF POLICE

With regard to the Indian police two interrelated issues can be stated:

1. Like any other police force in the world, Indian police is also part of the existing social order. This statement is in no way aimed at reducing the responsibility of the police towards nation-building. But this demands that the society and polity need to take serious note of the colouring of the police force by the social milieu.
2. Due to the existing socio-political, economic and cultural system the police force is treated with callous apathy and animated hostility. This leads to a low status of the police force and even ill treatment in the hands of the political establishment, bureaucrats and the general masses. Further, since most of the lower rung of the police force comes from the lower strata of the society, it does not receive the credit that it is entitled to. This may not be the case with the National Security Guards who could be airlifted to 'liberate' Akshardham. But for the majority of policemen at the lower order of the force, life is a drudgery not only on duty but off duty too.

While analysing the evolution as well as the functions of police system, P.D. Sharma argues, 'Here is an organization which cannot militantly negotiate at a bargain counter. But, if kept as it is, in its historical role of colonial past, it can perpetrate an imperial fallacy that the maintenance of order is synonymous with the preservation of law of the land. In a democracy where this law and the lawmakers change too frequently and several kinds of disorders reflect and measure peace and goals of social change, the professional universe of the policeman is riddled with political problems, which he can neither overcome or suffer' (Sharma, 1981: 2). An examination of the last five decades of police function and reform indicate the fact that there have been less of reform and more of direct and indirect control of police by the ruling elite.

About the origin and structure of police in India there are two views: One, some people claim that the police of present day India are essentially Akbar's creation and that, despite the Police Act of 1861, the same basic police system has persisted through the ages. This undermines the innovations in forms and functions during the colonial rule. Two, the more common assumption—that the reform of the police force was a direct consequence of mutiny—errs in the opposite direction by neglecting the previous fifty years of colonial experimentation and search for an effective police agency (Arnold, 1986: 237). Interestingly, even if this was the legacy of police force in India, the last five decades have not altered the structure, function and interference by the ruling classes in any significant way.

Further, it has been argued that the colonizers not only created two branches—armed and unarmed—but they also kept both these under the provincial list. Under the provision of the Government of India Act 1935, 'peace and tranquility of India or any parts thereof was kept as a special responsibility of Governor-General. His counterpart, the Governor, also had a similar responsibility for his province. This drained out the state resources but also forced the central government to raise and maintain specialized agencies of police to supplement the armed wings of the state. But in fact the cost of armed police should rest with the central government' (Sharma, 1981: 20).

Even a cursory glance at the manner in which the police as an agent of state machinery has evolved points to the fact that the muscle power seems to have dominated the police force. They were also paid very low amount as remuneration and thus were forced to fleece the common masses.

Prior to the organization of the new police in 1861, the investigating officers were the *darogas* in charge of police stations, whose minimum pay was fixed at Rs. 50.00, rising in a few cases up to Rs. 200.00, between 1845 and 1857.

The grassroots perversion of the existing system, which was perpetuated in 1861, took place as the police stations were placed in the charge of mostly illiterate Chief and Head Constables promoted from Constables and paid mere pittances as salaries on purely financial considerations. This arrangement, along with the criminal laws, ensured that the primary police functions would be performed with brute force and by installing in the people a fear of the police. The inefficiency and bad reputation of the police and the abuses in the functioning in the police stations increased over the years (Gupta, 1979: xiv).

Going further, one can also identify historical deficiencies in the development of police force over the centuries. The police organization in Indian states is primarily governed by the Police Act V of 1861, which was based on the recommendations of the Police Commission of 1860. This act prescribed a single and linear police bureaucracy from IGP to the constable. It is expedient to note here that the Sepoy Mutiny in 1857 led to the distrust of Indians. This ultimately led to police reorganization. But even after 140 years, the Indian political establishment has not evolved its own structure and process of police order. The Police Commission of 1902 reviewed the state of police at the end of this period and reached the conclusion that the 1861 system had failed. But the recommendations of 1902–3 as well as many other recommendations could not be put into practice due to considerations of economy. Interestingly, in the so-called naxalite infested regions, there seems to be no dearth of money to deal with the 'terrorist elements' while in ordinary situations even providing the basic infrastructure to the police force becomes an financial constraint.

The development of law and order machinery in post-independence era has introduced four major features in the organization of Indian police:

1. Expansion of Police Tasks

According to the *Crime in India* 2000 records, there were over 17.7 lakh crimes related to IPC alone. It was also reported that there had been over 64 per cent increase in importation of girls. Punjab reported 19 per cent increase in sexual harassment, etc. (*Crime in India*, 2000: 1). If one proceeds further, one would realize that these are only those that are reported and recorded. There are many more incidents criminal in nature which call for the attention of the police.

2. Proliferation of Police agencies of the State and the Union

In 1970 there were about 8,000 police stations in India covering about 50,000 urban and 70,000 rural habitations. But this has grown beyond manageable limits. From Table 1 it can be gathered that the police stations have grown from 8,000 to 19,228 by the year 2000.

TABLE 1. PROFILE OF POLICE FORCE

	Area	Quantity
1.	Zones	64
2.	Ranges	157
3.	Districts	635
4.	Sub-Divisions	1,481
5.	Circles	2,452
6.	Police Station	12,248
7.	Police Outposts	6,980
8.	Police Force—Total	14,79,024
9.	Women Police	24,713

Source: Bureau of Police Research & Development, Ministry of Home Affairs, Government of India, 2001.

3. Emergence of Quasi-police Structures in Non-Police Departments

Along with regular police force, there have also developed departments like the Railway Police, Forensic Science Laboratories, Inspectorate of Explosives, etc.

4. Dysfunctional Organization of Rural Police

In the past, the *chowkidari* system [village-police mediator] functioned to promote law and order and to provide information. But with the decline of the *chowkidari* system the pressure on the police force has increased.

At this juncture it is expedient to examine briefly the reality of the police force and its infrastructure. Sharma identifies the following five characteristics when it comes to the infrastructure related to the law-enforcing agency: (1) the democratic philosophy of the Constitution does not get reflected in the concept and organization of the Indian

Police which, when the chips are down, means the *de facto* government. (2) The penal provisions do not imply a decent society and an honest police. The post-mutiny hangover distrusts the police and the society in preference to civilian magistracy which was, and which has been, the lynchpin of the administrative system in the past as well as the present. (3) The political executive in the federal system in India, with police as a state subject, has asserted its executive character through the political exhibition of police power. The dangers of political instability and the lust to hang on to political power have further rendered the paramilitary police as quasi-political, which is inimical to the democratic objective of the polity. (4) The people in India, who have been brought up in colonial traditions of police hostility and the official police violence during freedom struggle, remain ignorant about the hazards, dilemmas and limitations of policing as a profession. They blissfully believe in the authorship of police excesses, without delving deep into the causes of police misbehaviour or neurosis which emanates from the anomalies of the infrastructure. (5) The political parties, the vernacular press, the opinion makers, the agencies of mass media and voluntary associations, who have the role of building bridges, have by and large done very little to build an ethos which can make the Indian Police efficient, effective and still more responsible (Sharma, 1981: 3–4). All these further complicate policemen's perception about their place and role in the Indian polity.

Before we proceed to examine the interaction between police and the society, it is appropriate to identify the problems of police personnel:

Generalism or Lack of Specialization in Police Cadres

It is common knowledge that most of the lower rung policemen do not even undergo the basic induction level courses which are supposed to enable fresh recruits to get inducted fully with the police contingent. If even basic training was not made available for the lower rank policemen, their performance would not be up to the mark.

A Big Hiatus Exists between IAS and IPS and the State Police Services

The IPS cadres are considered to be bureaucrats and are respected, but the lower rank policemen are seen with contempt. Within the general administrative system, the IPS is considered to be secondary to IAS. The disparity in recruitment methods, promotional avenues, service conditions also clearly show the differences. If this is the case with the higher-ranking officers, what would be the state of lower level policemen is anyone's guess.

Police Training and Legacies of Para-militarism

Each state is supposed to plan its own training facilities for the constabulary, sub-inspectors and deputy superintendents. Even at the level of training the policemen at the lower order are not provided with basic training facilities, while the higher-ranking officers are provided with pre-promotion, refresher and specialized courses. This creates a vast gap between the two segments.

Hazards and Risks in Police Job and Inadequate Compensation

It is a well-known fact that police force is regularly exposed to risk and hazards. While compensation in general has been inadequate, in the recent past there has been clear bias in favour of those who are killed or wounded in the so-called 'terrorist operations' than those who are killed or wounded in ordinary law and order enforcement situations. This becomes a demoralizing phenomenon.

Outdated Service Conditions

The Third Pay Commission had categorically stated that the remuneration provided to the police personnel is inadequate and not commensurate with either their duties and responsibilities or the specially arduous conditions of their work. A policeman's pay scale is comparable to a semi-skilled labourer.

Low Morale and Corrupt Image

The above stated facts lead to low morale and some of the policemen engage in all kinds of dubious ways of getting money. This further presents a corrupt image about the police order.

Disciplined Services and Absence of Grievance Redressal Mechanism

While the police personnel are engaged in a disciplined service, it has often been observed that they themselves are indisciplined. In case of grievances, there are no mechanisms for redressal of grievance.

POLICE AND SOCIETY

Ensuring the safety, security, dignity and property of every citizen of a country is the task of the government. In all the countries this task is mostly performed by the police force. Both individual and collective safety is ensured by the functioning of the law and order machinery, which is the police segment of the administration. But due to the qualitative and quantitative changes that have occurred in the law and order situation, policing is becoming more and more conflict ridden.

Further, due to the form of society and polity that has evolved in India over the years, power vests with a small minority. While this minority enjoys all the power, privileges and positions, the vast majority has to labour for the betterment of the minority ruling class. In this skewed and hierarchical and unequal social order, police also becomes the agent of the powerful. This reduces scope for public accountability. The creation of two wings within the police force, that is, one to function with muscle power and the other to gather information and to warn about possible uprising and violence against the ruling class, goes to establish the fact that the law and the order machinery has been viewed as a tool in the hands of the power elite.

It has been regularly recorded that the dominant caste men, feudal landlords, urban elite and rural thugs behave in a manner that denies justice, equality, dignity and liberty to common rural folk, lower castes and women. It has also been observed that the majority of policemen in the higher rank come from the dominant social groups and they treat the common masses in the most disdainful manner. Even those who come from the lower order illtreat the ordinary people since it is at them that they can vent their feelings without fear of being penalized. Moreover, in a skewed and hierarchical social system, maintaining law and order means keeping the status quo intact.

For example, in a state like Bihar, which has credible records when it comes to controlling communal riots, the attitude of the police and the administration towards the common persons is extremely negative and oppressive. In the so-called naxalite infested central Bihar, various operations like Operation Task Force, Operation Agnidoot, Operation Devdoot, Operation Flash, and Operation Clean were carried out by the police and the administration. These operations confer enormous powers on the security forces to carry out raids, search operations, *kurki-jabti* (confiscation of the property of 'absconders') and 'encounters', which is a euphemism for extra-judicial executions. A police officer himself acknowledged that no operation in central Bihar could rejuvenate the sagging credibility of the administration. For about 80 per cent of the masses here, the police and the administration mean 'enemies' (Louis, 2002a: 255).

In Bihar, proximity of the police to the landlord and sympathy for the *senas* or the private caste militia is well known. The DIG of police, Shashi Bhushan Sahay, in his report 'Extremists in Bihar and Bhumi Sena' acknowledged that whenever they had to take action, the police generally took the side of the Bhumi Sena (caste militia). For instance, nine landless labourers were massacred in front of the police camp at Lahasuna by the Bhumi Sena, but apparently, the police did not know of the outrage. In Narayanpur, when the people informed the police after the massacre, the police chose not to take action, because 'the village was outside their jurisdiction' (Louis, 2002a: 169). These data go to establish the fact that in a semi-feudal social order, the law enforcing machinery becomes the agent of the dominant caste.

The evolution of Indian policewomen also provides profound insight into the steps taken to promote women into police sector and also the patriarchal mindset, which is deep-rooted in India. Amarjit Mahajan argues that by 1930, most of the European countries had women in their police force. The negative male attitudes towards women in law-enforcement have been a hindrance. In India women police were appointed in Kanpur in 1939 when the labourers were to be physically lifted. The State of Travancore also experimented with the appointment of women as Special Police Constables in 1938. During the Partition the need was felt to have women in police force. A woman sub-inspector and a few constables were appointed in Delhi. In addition to providing security to prime minister against women intruders, the Ministry of Relief and Rehabilitation also needed women police for recovering abducted women at that time (Mahajan, 1982: 38–9).

The Delhi Police Commission (1968) had suggested the enlargement of the field of activities of policewomen, but struck a cautious note about their duties. It recommended: 'Policewomen's work should start with looking after children and women and gradually they may be utilised for public relations work on behalf of the police'. The bias could be further seen: 'Organizationally the women police must be kept under the direct control of one single officer and he should be the DC of Old Police Lines. The DC will have under him one young ACP (married) in-charge of women police. His wife should also be interested in social service work' (Delhi Police Commission Report 1968, p. 323, quoted in Mahajan: 1982: 41).

The above stated facts and figures document the fact that the police contingent is part and parcel of the Indian social order. Moreover, it also states forcefully that the pressure on the police takes a variety of forms and shades. But the infrastructural facilities as well as economic benefits made available to them are far from satisfactory. From this socio-historical background, let us examine the role of police in communal riots.

POLICE AND COMMUNAL RIOTS

As has been argued throughout in this paper, the police force is an integral part of the society and in India, which is founded on plural socio-cultural principles, the role of the police in ordinary times as well as during communal riots becomes all the more crucial. Asghar Ali Engineer, who has been analysing the role of the police in communal riots argues,

> The role of the police in communal riots has always been a highly controversial issue. Victims of riots generally complain that: (1) The police did not come to their rescue; (2) Police forces were themselves instrumental in the killing; (3) They led the mob in looting and burning; (4) They arrested innocent persons and tortured them inside the lock-up and false charges against the arrested persons, (5) Encouraged the culprits to do whatever they liked by preventing the members of one community to come out during the curfew and allowing to do so with impunity. (Engineer, 1994: 835)

While this perception may be contested, it is the reality that needs to be brought under severe scrutiny.

> Amongst all the state machinery, it is the police force that comes in direct contact with the victims and is the most visible part of it as far as the general public is concerned and hence it is the police which is condemned most by the people. . . . Police can act much better if there is political will. The politicians, administration and the police all play their roles in the event of an outbreak of communal violence. If the ruling politicians are determined to prevent violence, the administration and the police machinery can act with much greater determination and efficiency. For example, when communal violence broke out in Sitamarhi in early 1992. Laloo Prasad Yadav immediately reached the town and took command and brought the situation under

control, though many lives were lost by then. Had Laloo Prasad Yadav not taken the control, much more damage would have been inflicted.(Engineer, 1994: 835–6)

The Gujarat pogrom poignantly brings out the malice that is engulfing police in a communally charged country. During the continued communal violence in Gujarat, Chief Minister Narendra Modi is reported to have said: 'I am absolutely satisfied with how the police and the government has handled the backlash. I am happy the violence has been largely constrained' (*Times of India*, 1 March 2002). But the violence that continued unabated proved the Chief Minister wrong. Consciencious civil servants say that any riot like situation can be stopped within three hours if there is political will among the civil and political administration. It is also significant to note that while there were both higher and lower police officials who functioned like communal agents, there were also other police officials who tried to uphold the law. But they were penalized by the political establishment. Rahul Sharma, the DSP of Bhavnagar, and Rajiv Ranjan, DSP of Patan, tried to protect the minority community and its establishments. The ruling class of Gujarat harassed them. Officers in those districts where communal carnage did not take place were presented with bangles to tell them that they were not men but women. It is alleged that the members of Sangh Parivar instigated this (Louis, 2002b: 241–57).

In a democracy the numbers game is very crucial. A careful analysis of the proportion of Muslims in 1917 in the total strength of the police, the number and vacancies (Table 2) reveals that a high proportion of Muslims were recruited in police. This was due to the fact that the Muslims were considered to be more loyal to the colonial

TABLE 2. PROFILE OF POLICE FORCE IN 1917

Category	Strength	Vacancies	Muslim	%
Military Police	21,509	281	2,664	12.38
District Police	1,65,654	10,470	87,953	53.09
Presidency and Rangoon police	11,254	1,029	2,132	18.94
Special Armed Forces	12,191	270	2,491	20.43

Source: Anandswarup Gupta, *The Police in British India 1861–1947*, New Delhi: Concept, 1979, p. 340.

administration. Whether this is a fact or not is another matter for investigation. But what is real today is that the Muslim presence in police and army has been reduced below their proportion.

In his perceptive analysis of the Gujarat police, Yogi Aggarwal has observed:

> The form and the direction of the politicisation among the police is indicative of what lies in store. It needs to be remembered that the police in Gujarat are thoroughly corrupt, with the misguided prohibition policy being a major source of corruption. In line with the important sections of Gujarat society, the police are often communal, and play a decidedly partisan role in times of conflict. It is attracted to and responds to middle class causes and to political parties such as the BJP which represents these causes (Aggarwal, 1988: 1611).

It would be fundamentally wrong to label all the police officials as biased against the minority. Asghar Ali Engineer in this regard has observed.

> Among the top officers there are two types: those who fight for their convictions and even suffer and those who surrender to the whims of political bosses. The picture radically changes when it comes to lower officers and the constabulary. They are much more communalised. It should also be said that they behave harshly with the weaker sections of the society, including the poor of the upper castes and of course, dalits. There is something fundamentally lacking in their training. It is also partly because of the whole corrupt political atmosphere in the country. There is no value of human life and specially for weaker sections of society. But one should also try to understand some of the problems of the lower officers and constabulary. They are terribly over-worked during communal disturbances. They are often required to perform round-the-clock duty on such occasions. They hardly have time to go home. Also, they perceive danger to their life. It is not easy to work in such conditions. Such tensions make them highly inflammable, and they tend to overreact to any situation. They take revenge on innocent persons. Also they are deeply affected by communal propaganda and caste prejudices like other sections of our society. (Engineer, 1994: 839).

The increasing bargaining power of the police before elections or before festival seasons has come to haunt the rulers. Aggarwal in his analysis of the police strike in Gujarat maintains the police strike was tamed but not crushed. The distinction is important, for the police are too important an arm of the state for it to be crushed.

With the general elections less than 18 months away, it was important to have the police on the side of the ruling party by the time elections were held. A senior Congress leader made this plain, explaining why the action against the police indiscipline could not have been taken earlier, why it was now necessary, and could not be further postponed. The form and direction of the politicization among the police is indicative of what lies in store. It needs to be remembered that the police in Gujarat is thoroughly corrupt, with the misguided prohibition policy being a major source of corruption. In line with important sections of Gujarat society, the police are often communal, and play a decidedly partisan role in times of conflict. It is attracted to and responds to middle class causes and to political parties such as the BJP, which represents these causes. And in former Baroda police commissioner Jaspal Singh, the politically inclined among the police have a symbol and a model. (Aggarwal, 1988: 1611)

To understand this phenomenon, it is imperative that we review the perception of the Muslim community about the police administration. Moin Shakir has observed:

There is general feeling among the Muslims that during the communal clashes, the police and administration do not protect them. The police personnel betray the worst kind of communalism. They fail to bring to heel known preachers of communal hatred. They are unwilling to employ all the administrative measures available to them. The Hindu communal elements are given free hand to propagate communal hatred without any objection from the administration, as for instance in the Rourkela riots of 1964. The demolition of mosques had been allowed to continue for hours in Aligarh, with the connivance of officers. No preventive measures are adopted, with the result that the Muslims suffer irrecoverable losses. (Shakir, 1991: 96).

These acts of omission and commission lead to distrust of the police force by the common masses and further alienates them from the law enforcing machinery.

NHRC'S VIEWS ON GUJARAT ADMINISTRATION

Before we conclude this analytical piece, let us briefly examine the views of National Human Rights Commission (NHRC) on the failure of the Gujarat administration in general and of the police in particular in protecting the victims and in penalizing the culprits. The NHRC identified the following as the failures of the Government of Gujarat: failure to protect right to life, liberty, equality and dignity; failure of intelligence; failure to take appropriate action; failure to identify local factors and players; pattern of arrests; uneven handling of major cases; distorted FIRs: 'extraneous influences', issue of transparency and integrity; pervasive insecurity. For instance, if the High Court Justices Kadri and Divecha could not be protected, the fate of the common masses is anyone's guess.

A brief analysis of NHRC's perception of police during the Gujarat pogrom is called for here. Taking cue from the earlier commission reports in clear and categorical terms, NHRC identified the mistakes of the police. And then, quoting from the 'Guidelines to Promote Harmony' it recapitulated the grave issue of communal riots in great detail. It also reiterated the fact that these guidelines have a high degree of relevance to what occurred in Gujarat recently.

NHRC went on to argue that the Second Report of the NPC recalled and examined the work of previous Commissions of Inquiry to look into major incidents of communal violence, including *inter alia* the Raghubar Dayal Commission (Ranchi–1967), the Madon Commission (Bhiwandi–1970), the Jaganmohan Reddy Commission (Ahmedabad–1969) and the Balasubramanian Commission (Bihar Sharif–1981) and reached the conclusion that there was a 'pattern in the failures' to deal effectively with the outbursts of communal violence. The 'pattern' pointed to the following 'failures' (paragraphs 47.6–47.16):

- A failure in timely and accurate gathering of intelligence;
- A failure to make a correct assessment of the intelligence reports;
- A failure to anticipate trouble, and to make adequate arrangements on the ground;
- A failure to deploy available resources adequately and imaginatively in vulnerable areas and a tendency to disperse the force in penny-packets without sufficient striking reserves;
- A failure by the DM and SP to take 'quick and firm decisions' and a 'growing tendency among the district authorities to seek instructions from higher quarters, where none are necessary';
- A failure of police officers and their men to function without bias—in fact, a pattern showing 'unmistakable bias against a particular community';
- A failure of officers to take responsibility in dealing with a situation, 'to avoid to go to a trouble spot, or when they happen to be present there, (to) try not to order the use of force when the situation demands, or better still slip away from the scene leaving the force leaderless';

- A failure to post district officers on 'objective considerations' or for 'long enough tenures'; instead, officers 'being posted and transferred due to political pressures,' adversely affecting the discipline and morale of the force, the 'spate of transfers' undermining the 'credibility of the administration.'
- A failure to be transparent in respect of a situation and a tendency to 'hide the true-facts,' even among senior officers. The tendency to 'minimize' the number of casualties often resulted in rumours, the populace then choosing to believe 'sources other than the administration and the government media'.

The Second Report of the NPC then went on to make a number of powerful recommendations, many of which were subsequently used in the Guidelines of 1997, referred above. Among the more relevant of the NPC recommendations, specifically in respect of communal situations, were the following:

- The administration should disseminate correct information to the public through all available means. In cases of mischievous reporting, the state government and local administration should use every weapon in the legal armory to fight obnoxious propaganda prejudicial to communal harmony (paragraphs 47.28, 47.29).
- The authorities in dealing with communal riots should not be inhibited, by any consideration, to adopt lukewarm, measures at the early stages; a clear distinction must be made between communal riots and other law and order situations and 'the most stringent action taken at the first sign of communal trouble'.
- Officers who have successfully controlled the situation at the initial stages with firm action should be suitably rewarded. Immediate and exemplary action should be taken against officers who wilfully fail to go to the trouble spot or who slip away from there after trouble has erupted.
- The NPC Report 'strongly disapproves' of 'the practice of posting and transfers on political pressures'. Only specially selected experienced officers with an image of impartiality and fair play should be posted to communally sensitive districts.
- There should be a control room in all of those places which have been identified as prone to communal trouble. Even though some information passed on to the control room may not be

useful . . . every bit of information passed on to the control room should . . . be acted upon as if it were genuine.

- Unless crimes committed are registered, investigated and the criminals identified and prosecuted, the police would not have completely fulfilled its role as a law enforcement agency. . . . The police should realize that the task of investigation is a mandatory duty cast upon it and any indifference to this task can attract legal sanctions.
- In a riot situation registration of offences becomes a major casualty. 'It is futile to expect the victim of the crime to reach a police station risking his (her) own life and report a crime to the police.' The police should therefore open several reporting centres at different points in a riot-torn area.
- The police forces of the various states in the country should truly represent the social structure in the respective states.

In drawing attention to the circulars, guidelines and reports mentioned above, the Commission would like to underline its sense of anguish that, despite the existence of such thorough and far-reaching advice on how to handle incidents of communal violence, the Government of Gujarat has conspicuously failed to act in accordance with the long-standing provisions of these important instructions and that, measured against the standards set by them, the performance of the state appears to be severely wanting. The Commission believes that there is need for careful introspection within the state government in this respect; the shortcomings in its performance need to be analysed, *inter alia*, in the light of the statutory provisions, circulars and guidelines referred to above, and a detailed report based on that analysis should be made available by the state government to the Ministry of Home Affairs, Government of India, and to this Commission for their consideration. The report should indicate the precise conclusions that the state government has reached, and the steps that it intends to take, to prevent the recurrence of the type and range of failures that have marred the performance of the state in the handling of the tragic events that occurred recently. The report should also indicate clearly what steps the government intends to take against those who are responsible for these multiple failures, identifying the delinquent public servants, and others in authority, without equivocation. (*The Gujarat Pogrom*, 2002: 29–47)

Taken together, it needs to be stated that in a democratic polity, in normal circumstances and more so during the period of heightened tension and violence, it is the police which is supposed to ensure law and order. But, riot after riot, it has been established that the police itself is becoming more and more communal, casteist and a practitioner of corrupt practices. There are many factors which contribute to this downward trend. Like in many other issues, extraordinary political will is needed with regard to ensuring the rightful place and role of police in a democratic form of government. Is the Indian society and polity willing to engage in this exercise is a question that knocks at the door of the conscious and conscientious citizens of the country.

REFERENCES

Aggarwal, Yogi, 'Gujarat Police Strike', *Economic and Political Weekly*, 23 (32), 1988.

Arnold, David, *Police Power and Colonial Rule: Madras 1859–1947*, New Delhi: Oxford University Press, 1986.

Crime in India, New Delhi: National Crime Records Bureau, Ministry of Home Affairs, 2000.

Engineer, Asghar Ali, 'Communal Violence and Role of Police', *Economic and Political Weekly*, 29 (15), 1994.

First Report of the National Police Commission, New Delhi: Government of India, 1979.

Gupta, Anandswarup, *The Police in British India 1861–1947*, New Delhi: Concept, 1979.

Louis, Prakash, *People Power: the Naxalite Movement in Central Bihar*, New Delhi: Wordsmiths, 2002a.

—— 'Gujarat Carnage: Protectors have become Predators', *Social Action*, vol. 52 (3), 2002b.

Mahajan, Amarjit, *Indian Policewomen*, New Delhi: Deep & Deep, 1982.

McLennan, George, *Pluralism*, Buckingham: Open University Press, 1995.

Police Organisation in India, New Delhi: Commonwealth Human Rights Initiative, 2002.

Shakir, Moin, 'An Analytical View of Communal Violence', in *Communal Riots in Post-Independence India*, ed. Asghar Ali Engineer. New Delhi: Sangam Books, 1991.

Sharma, P.D., *Police, Polity and People in India*, New Delhi: Uppal , 1981.

The Gujarat Pogrom, *Indian Democracy in Danger*, New Delhi: Indian Social Institute, 2002.

The Survivors Speak, *How Has the Gujarat Massacre Affected Minority Women*? Ahmedabad: Citizen's Initiative, 2002.

Vijapur, Abdulrahim P. (ed)., *Pluralism, Minorities, National Integration Problems and Prospects*, New Delhi: South Asian Publishers, 1997.

CHAPTER 6

Police and the Minorities in India

PREM DHAR MALAVIYA

Respect for the rights of all is said to be the litmus test for democracy, but even as we pride ourselves on being the largest working democracy in the world, serious doubts have been expressed over the will and the capability of one of the main organs of the State, namely the police, to protect the life, property, and dignity of the weaker sections of the society, including religious minorities.

POLICE BIAS

The question of police bias against religious minorities gained centrality in the 1970s when the UP PAC were accused of shooting only at the Muslims during communal riots, so much so that PAC units were replaced by CRPF/BSF units at some places in Aligarh, during the riots of 1978. At a later date, the Delhi police were bitterly criticized for remaining mute witnesses to the brutal attacks on the Sikhs during the riots of 1984. Recently, the Gujarat police have been condemned for allowing 'the gruesome massacre of innocent and hapless Muslims' in 2002. It is a notorious fact that few miscreants have ever been convicted of the horrible offences committed during the riots, raising doubts about the sincerity of the police investigations. The Delhi police added another sorry chapter to this sad tale when they failed to register even FIRs in respect to all the heinous offences committed during the 1984 riots. Quite recently, the Supreme Court has ordered a review of all the riot-related cases which were Finally Reported by the Gujarat police, suggesting wilful negligence in the investigations of these cases.

In response to accusations of police bias, the central government established a special force called the Rapid Action Force (RAF) within the CRPF in the 1990s, which comprised designated numbers of persons belonging to different religious denominations, to deal with communal conflicts in the country. However, since the number of RAF units is quite small, it cannot possibly cover all the hot-spots during a communal flare-up. So the big question remains as to what should be done to ensure that the police forces of the country remain unaffected, despite their Hindu character, by the 'rising tide of communal Hindu politics' and give due protection to all manners of people in all situations.

THE CAUSES

Religious sentiments have been systematically exploited for political purposes in this country, at least for the last 100 years. When post-partition riots subsided, there was a hope that communal riots would be a thing of the past, but this hope has been belied and the number of incidents as also the virulence has been rising, decade after decade. As Rafiq Zakaria notes (*Communal Rage in Secular India*), 'Before 1947, the rage had gripped the communal Muslims in the name of Islamic nationalism; now the communal Hindus have taken to it and use it against the Muslims in the name of Hindu nationalism'. Since the police are very much a part of the civil society, the policemen are as much exposed to the communal virus as anybody else; in fact, since hordes of policemen are deployed at every political rally, every meeting, every demonstration, for hours on end, and since they listen to the politicians (even if with only half the ear) spouting forth against each other and since politics—from national level down to the panchayat level—now seems to be centred around not developmental issues nor governance issues but only around some communal incidents of the past, the policemen are exposed to communal speeches of the worst kind and inevitably, some of them are touched by the communal virus. Moreover, despite all the obfuscations by the politicians, the policemen know how many religious structures have come up in the sensitive areas without the requisite permissions and what exactly is taught to the youngsters in the name of religious purity and cultural identity and why nothing is done to put a stop to such activities. This makes the policeman susceptible to the idea that in giving protection to these people, he is somehow betraying his own community and this induces a sense of guilt in him. So, when an opportunity arises, as during communal riots, he gives vent to his pent-up feelings by inflicting pain and indignities on the community 'in the wrong'; since the luxury of such a catharsis is available only to the men belonging to the majority community, the minorities suffer at the hands of such policemen.

The second cause of police bias is corruption and indiscipline in the police forces. It is well known that when a communal situation is developing, criminal gangs are often commissioned to carry out attacks on the 'other' community, to set fire to shops and houses, and so on. It is also well known that all organized gangs have a number of police officers in their pay. So, when a gang is carrying out its commission, these police officers look the other way. If their supervisory officers ignore such dereliction of duty or readily accept the staple excuse of lack of actionable intelligence or of adequate force and if they do not pay serious heed to complaints that the people who approached the police for help were abused or ill-treated instead, it not only emboldens the bad-eggs, but it legitimizes their actions in the eyes of their colleagues; their gang grows in size and influence until it colours the thinking of the whole unit.

The third, and the most important, cause of the lack of will on the part of the police is the domination of the ruling political elite over the police force. It is widely believed that the anti-Sikh riots in Delhi continued for so many days because some influential politicians did not want them stopped earlier and FIRs were not registered in so many heinous cases because they did not want the offenders to be seriously pursued by the police. A similar thing is believed to have happened in Gujarat in 2002: senior officials of the day have deposed before the Nanavati–Shah Commission that police officers who were handling the riots efficiently were transferred out on the instructions of the chief minister.

THE POLITICAL TANGLE

The emergency had forcefully brought home to the people how the police could be misused by the ruling political elite and when the National Police Commission (NPC) was set up in 1977, one of its terms of reference was to recommend measure to 'prevent misuse of police by administrative or executive instructions, political or other pressures, or oral orders of any type which are contrary to law'. In their second report (1979), the commission said that the superintending role of the state government should be limited to ensuring that police performance is in strict accordance with the law, and to 'help' the government to discharge this responsibility in an open manner, the commission recommended the establishment of State Security Commissions comprising six to nine members each, with the Minister in charge of the police as chairman. They also recommended that two of the members be members of the state legislature (with one being from the opposition benches). The commission said that the investigative tasks of the police shall be beyond any intervention from the executive or the non-executive, though in the performance of preventive tasks (which include prevention and suppression of riots), the police should be subjected to overall guidance from the government, but there should be 'no instruction in regard to actual operations in the field'. These recommendations have been enthusiastically welcomed by most of the police officers though, looking to the capacity of the politicians to strike deals and to get round all kinds of institutional safeguards with the help of tame bureaucrats, there is some doubt whether State Security Commissions would be really effective. Shri Mulayam Singh Yadav once told the media (*Indian Express*, Hyderabad, 12 August 1991, p. 11) that he had bailed out a BJP leader who was accused of murder, on the recommendation of one of his own MLCs: he had managed to get a Final Report filed against the gentleman, who went on to become a minister in the Kalyan Singh ministry. The commission's recommendation about police being subjected to overall guidance from the government in its preventive tasks is also somewhat ambiguous. In the early 1960s, when illegal immigrants from East Pakistan started trickling into Assam, they were liable to arrest and detention under the Foreigners' Act, 1946. But the government advised the police to refrain from arrests, leading ultimately to prolonged agitations and untold miseries for the people of Assam, the spread of the illegal immigrants to all parts of the country, and the advent of ULFA. In early 1970s, when his influence was still limited, Sant Bhindranwale was allowed by the central government to travel from his headquarters to Bombay in a convoy of trucks sporting machine-guns and other military weapons (for which even the central government was not empowered to issue licences) in clear defiance of the laws and the state governments were advised not to interfere with him; it proved to be a historic journey which led to considerable accretion of power by the Sant, and the whole nation paid the price of such appeasement a few years later. One wonders whether State Security Commissions could have blocked these political decisions and allowed the police to enforce the laws.

One would recall in this context that in 1970, there were anti-Vietnam war demonstrations going on in Australia. In Adelaide, the demonstrators had announced that they would, as part of the demonstration, sit down on the road and block an important traffic crossing. The police commissioner publicly warned them against it. The prime minster of the State advised the commissioner to allow the demonstrators to sit on the intersection for half an hour, but the commissioner refused and the prime minister told the House (then in session) that he had so advised the police commissioner but the commissioner had told him that he would do his duty as defined by the laws!

It is also difficult to visualize that a police officer who is transferred by the government (for being too efficient in the suppression of communal riots) could appeal to the State Security Commission and that the Commission could stay the transfer or that the Commission could convene a meeting without the chairman's concurrence and ask the Army to move in and control rioting when the government is not inclined to do so.

Anyway, whether effective or not so effective, no major political party has supported the recommendations about State Security Commissions. On the contrary, many politicians have argued that the governments must have complete control over the law and order machinery and that the police cannot be allowed to balk at any orders give to them. Their main argument is that the price of communal riots has to be paid by the ruling party, as by the Congress after the 1984 riots and by the BJP after the 2002 riots. Secondly, aggregation and projection of various interests, as indeed negotiations in the case of conflict of interests, are some of the core activities of political parties and only the politicians can tell why rioting has been started and how it can be ended and so, only they can tell what needs to be done and when.

There are several pitfalls in this line of thinking, even if it reflects the present ground reality.

An obvious flaw is that there is no certainty that there will always be a secular government in all the states or that communal riots will not be engineered to settle power-struggle within a secularist party when it is in power: during M. Chenna Reddy's last term as chief minister of Andhra Pradesh, communal riots started in Hyderabad over a very trivial matter, but they continued unabated despite all the efforts of the administration until Chenna Reddy resigned, and then, the rioting simply petered out. The protagonists of the idea, however, skip around this point by saying that they are constantly fighting to keep the communal forces out of the seats of power and they deny that riotous elements are patronized by anyone to strengthen his position in the intra-party power-struggle: they explain away the Hyderabad affair as mere coincidence. The second pertinent objection to the idea is that some of the worst communal holocausts in the past (in which the police had not performed their role properly) had happened in the states firmly under the rule of the secularist parties; this fact is simply ignored by the protagonists of the idea of greater political control over the police.

There are, however, two serious problems even with the existing level of political dominance. In a developing, pluralistic society like ours, where several groups of 'have-nots' are now struggling to establish their political clout, and where social values are in a state of flux, sectional conflicts are inevitable. If the police force handling a conflict is perceived to be biased or acting at the behest of one party, then the other side must act to defend its rights, its honour; so, muscle-men are invited to the fold: to defend the cause. Since the importance of such people is directly related to the degree of tension and the imminence of conflict, they gravitate towards the more recalcitrant elements within the group and constantly work to escalate conflict, leading to greater disharmony in the society in general. Moreover, as the boss of a private army in Bihar once explained, 'if the local police is under the thumb of your rivals and looks the other way when you are under attack, when your crops are being burnt and your house looted, then what option have you but to raise your own army? And, when you have an army, how do you keep it fed except to ask it to poach on the others, while you provide such help as you can (mostly by way of shelter)?' Thus, the excessive domination of politicians over the police is largely responsible for the growth of private armies and for legitimizing the presence of muscle-men in political parties and the consequent break-down in law and order in Bihar and elsewhere.

The second problem with the present scenario is that when there is too much of back-seat driving, the front-seat driver loses all initiative; in such a scenario, the police is slow to react to any situation, be it a communal riot (as in Bhagalpur) or be it a burgeoning fraud (as in the Telgi case). More, it has given scope to the politicians to play with the internal discipline of the police; subordinates dismissed for misconduct or indiscipline of the gravest kind have been reinstated at the behest of their political patrons, subordinates transferred out for failure to perform have been restored to the post and superior police officers asked to eat the crow, and adverse remarks have been expunged on the flimsiest pretext, all at the behest of politicians. So, the senior police officers are mostly chary of looking too closely at the doings of their subordinates, supervision and enquiry have lost their meaning, discipline has been badly eroded and combined with the fact that they must bend the rules and sacrifice the interest of their subordinates to placate their political masters and save their own positions, it has led to complete loss of moral authority of senior police officers; the sub ordinates neither respect nor fear their superiors, as a result.

The constitution provides for the superintendence of High Courts over the lower courts and the Supreme Court has ruled that this word shall have a limited meaning: the High Courts are only to ensure that the lower courts do all that law enjoins upon them and that they act at all times strictly according to laws. Based on this judgement, the NPC had said that the superintending role of the state governments under the Police Acts should be similarly limited. But, in the Saldhana case (AIR SC 1980) the Supreme Court has allowed full latitude to the state governments in exercising the powers of 'superintendence' and few police officers have ever got relief from the courts against 'arbitrary' orders of the state governments, particularly transfers. The result has been that police officers are regularly transferred to accommodate the wishes of the local politicians: some are transferred six times in four months, while others remain in the same station for decades, some are transferred for registering FIRs, some for arresting offenders, some for suppressing riots and some even for executing arrest warrants issued by the courts and such transfers have become so common that they excite no public reactions at all!

Thus, it is difficult to think of a formal arrangement that would reconcile the state governments' powers of superintendence with the police officers' duty to act according to the dictates of law. The NPC have indeed recommended that to 'restore the capacity of the police as an organization to resist such (improper) pressures', the chief of police should be given a statutory term of four years in the office. But apart from the difficulty of finding an officer who would have a mind of his own and yet win the appointment to the chief's post, one must consider that the governments enjoy such vast powers that they can easily reduce an inconvenient chief to a figure-head: they can suspend and order an enquiry against any junior (who has dared to go against their wishes) without the concurrence of the chief (even over his objections, for that matter) and get what they wish done through others, particularly the corrupt and over-ambitious men who are prepared to do 'anything' to win the favours of the rulers and who are to be found in large numbers in any police force. So, even this safeguard may not be as effective as one would like nor make it possible for police officers to work without fear or prejudice of any kind: after all, despite Supreme Court keeping an eye on the appointment and tenure of its chief, the CBI has favoured or dis-favoured L.K. Advani or Laloo Prasad Yadav, depending upon the political complexion of the central government.

It has been noted earlier that there are two other reasons why the police acts in a biased manner towards the minorities, namely, exposure to communal propaganda and corruption and indiscipline in the force. Since everyone reacts to stimuli in his own individual manner, it is difficult to identify in advance the policemen affected by the communal virus, but the spread of the communal virus can be checked if the Station House Officers (SHO) and the first line supervisory officers can be motivated to enquire promptly and thoroughly into complaints of communal bias and mete out condign punishment to the mal-contents. Communal tendencies and corruption can also be curbed if there is effective leadership, *within* the arena, which is seen as sharing the difficulties and frustrations of the common policeman and coping 'successfully'; if the leader is located outside, he is easily dismissed as a do- gooder and his words fall on deaf ears. Unfortunately, the structure of the police is such that there is no effective leadership at the police station level, where it is most required: the SHO is mostly expected only to ensure compliance with orders and not to exercise leadership. While most of the responsibility for results is placed on the SHO, he is but seldom provided with commensurate resources; nor is he given any powers to punish deviance among the subordinate staff. This means that the SHO has to run to his superiors all the time, for resources, for disciplining subordinates, for practically everything. Since this is neither very practical nor much to the liking of the SHOs, most of them resort to short cuts to deliver results in areas of high visibility and they have a tacit understanding with their subordinates that in return for their help in achieving this, the SHO would close his eyes to what the subordinates are doing otherwise. So, the leadership of the SHO becomes very tenuous, and since the other leaders are placed outside the arena, they are neither able to influence individual opinions, nor are they able to influence police culture, with the result that the traditional definition of 'success' for the policeman, namely catching criminals and getting them punished by law, is giving way to the new, namely making money and exercising untramelled powers. The few who epitomize the old values and could still influence opinions and cultural values are, unfortunately, the very people for whom the politicians have not much use and they are transferred so frequently that they are just not able to maintain contact with any set of subordinates long enough to make an impact. All in all then, the option of correcting police bias through the influencing process is no longer viable and the only way it can be done is through discipline, which, as has been noted earlier, is subject to politics!

Before concluding this discussion of police and politics, it may be mentioned that the Indian police forces have not had a very good public image. Way back in 1856, the Court of Directors of the East India Company had said, 'That the police in India has lamentably failed in accomplishing the ends for which it was established is a notorious fact; that it is all but useless for the prevention, and sadly inefficient for the detection of crime, is generally admitted; unable to check crime, it is, with rare exceptions, unscrupulous as to its mode of wielding the authority with which it is armed for the functions which it fails to fulfil, and has a very general character for corruption and oppression' (Anandswarup Gupta, *The Police in British India 1861–1947*). Unfortunately, the police were not able to redeem their image in the period immediately following independence, when there was no political interference in police work and when police chiefs enjoyed complete security of tenure. The result is that, a hundred and fifty years after this was written, a very large number of people feel that it is an apt description of today's police and so, any proposal which smacks of greater autonomy for the police is most unlikely to find favour with the people.

WAY FORWARD

If one wishes that the religious minorities and other weaker sections of the society should receive due protection from the police, irrespective of the political complexion of the government, then the only possibility seems to lie in bringing the weight of public opinion to bear against the misuse of the police by the ruling elite. Such an arrangement seems to be working well in UK where, as mentioned in a Government of India letter dated 3 September 1931, addressed to the secretary of state (reproduced in Gupta, ibid.) 'the constitutional relations between the Commissioner of Metropolitan Police and the Home Secretary in Great Britain give in themselves no guarantee against improper and unwise political interference in the administration of the police'.

For this, there are two pre-requisites: the police should work in an open manner so that people know the truth about their work and should not get confused by half-truths and lies which now seem to surround them; and secondly, and more importantly, people should want to *check misuse of police*, as distinct from wanting to replace the person in the driving seat. The NPC have refuted all arguments against openness in police work and said (Fifth Report, 1980), 'We have considered this matter very seriously and come to the conclusion that all police activities to the extent possible should be open except for four specific areas. These four areas are: (1) operations, (2) the intelligence on basis of which operations are planned and conducted, (3) privacy of individual citizen, and (4) judicial requirements.' To institutionalize openness as also to provide correct information to the public from the primary source, it may be suggested that monitoring committees should be formed at the police-station level which should have statutory authority to seek (as a body, not otherwise) any information from the police, except information falling in the four categories specifically mentioned by the NPC, and to convey public's expectations to the police. They should also have the statutory right to place any matter (including the denial of information on grounds of secrecy) before the higher police authorities, the government and the public, as they deem fit.

Assuming that the people want the misuse of police checked (nothing can really be achieved if people don't want it), this could have several advantages. Since the delivery (or non-delivery) of police service takes place through the police stations, having a monitoring body at that level would have obvious advantage as far as checking or exposing malfeasance is concerned. Secondly, it would help to align police priorities with public concerns and, hopefully, check the misuse of police manpower, which is one of the less visible but very serious problems of the police. Thirdly, it could make the people more aware of some of the real problems faced by the police and most importantly, see how various restrictions imposed by the law on the police make it more difficult for the honest and conscientious policemen to achieve success while unscrupulous policemen are hardly affected by them. For instance, Section 161(2) of the CrPC was amended in 1974 to provide that a witness shall be bound to answer 'truly' all questions put to him by an investigating officer (subject to safe-guards against self-incrimination), but Section 162(1), which provides that no statement made to the police shall be signed by the person making it, was left unchanged, with the result that witnesses continue to lie to the police and not one has ever been prosecuted (under Section 193 of the IPC) in the last thirty years (and none is likely to be prosecuted, ever). So, a conscientious policeman has very little chance of gathering the truth from a recalcitrant witness (which category includes all professional criminals) whereas an officer who has no inhibitions about the use of third-degree can well succeed. The NPC had put the matter very succinctly when it said (Eighth Report, 1981), 'As yet, it is not clear to any policeman how he can investigate a case of dacoity in a perfectly legal manner, and yet secure conviction from a court of law. The same is true of a number of offences.'

CONCLUSION

If the police are to protect the political rights of the minorities and the weaker sections of the society against physical violence, they are more likely to succeed if they are, and seen to be, impartial and not wholly at the mercy of politicians and the politicians are perhaps best checked if the people are able to monitor police work at the cutting edge; without power of command, but with the power to expose suspected malfeasance to universal gaze. At the same time, an overhaul of the Criminal Justice System is absolutely necessary so that ordinarily talented but honest and diligent policemen can bring all manners of criminals to book through the due process of law but with a greater degree of certainty and in real time and thereby discourage putative miscreants. In particular, suborning witnesses as also wilful perjury by witnesses should entail swift and deterrent punishment; trials should be held while the memory of the witnesses are still clear and before the outcome has lost public relevance; and policemen found guilty of malfeasance should face certain dismissal and be liable to pay compensation from their own pockets.

Police organizations can certainly help the reform process if they can discover the reasons why they could not redeem their image when there was no political interference and when police officers had secure tenures and evolve procedures to overcome the problems; particularly, if they could streamline the procedure for enquiries into complaints and if they could pay greater heed to rewards and punishments so that they reflect commitment to public good rather than loyalty to the superiors. They also need to pay much greater attention to intangibles like organizational culture and leadership at the police station and district levels.

CHAPTER 7

Endangered Minorities in India: Understanding the Role of Police

ABDULRAHIM VIJAPUR AND
MD. MOHIBUL HAQUE

One more sad chapter has been written in the history of Indian Police following what we witnessed in Gujarat in 2002. The police has always been put to severe criticism by saner elements in the civil society, for callousness and communal bias. Such criticism is not wholly untrue, as there was open and active complicity of the police in the systematic genocide of Muslims that was perpetrated in Gujarat.

The rights of minorities in India today stand unprotected and when one of the most, visible hands of the state turns against them, the recourse would be one of general disillusionment with the state itself. India, which was envisaged by its great freedom fighters to be a land of no discrimination of any kind on the grounds of creed or religion has not proved itself to be so. Civil-society is communalized to the extent where any untoward incident can lead to a big flare-up. If the police, the protectors of law and order completely withdraw from their role of keeping minor incidents from erupting into full-blown riots, and on the contrary, side with one community, consequences would not be too difficult to foresee. The foundations of our country—democracy and liberty, leave alone secularism—will be shattered if in our concept of the welfare state, the police is allowed to abrogate its responsibility as an unbiased agency.

We will discuss here the role our police has played during the communal riots that have marred more than fifty-five years of our independence. This will implicitly bring out the ways in which the rights of minorities have been violated by it.

Police is an inevitable apparatus of the state. Ironically, it has been created to tackle the same problems that it is now actively promoting by its attitude. It will lead the discussion to another direction if we say that the police in India is increasingly getting criminalized. Suffice it to say that it is a very dangerous situation where police, armed to the teeth with legal measures, turns on the same society which had created it for the protection of its life, rights and properties.

The police, as the official representatives of the government in power can do a lot of things with *de facto* immunity.[1] The general picture of the Indian police is one of fear and disgust, and now increasingly of indifference. And it is not one of a bloated, bumbling, comic figure holding a *lathi* in one hand, with the other extended for a bribe, as is often portrayed in the movies.

The fear is the natural outcome of the knowledge, or more appropriately false knowledge of people that police can act in any way they like. Although checks do exist on its functioning, but long periods of life spent in ignorance makes masses, more often the rural populace, prone to this deep-seated notion about police. The police behaviour towards innocent citizens and crime-doers evokes a sense of disgust. Earlier, some ill-informed policemen believed that they could manhandle people in police custody. They thought that it was a statutory privilege that they enjoyed. As a consequence of this, they resorted to ill-treating or manhandling indiscriminately and therefore there arose a sub-culture in police which approved of all sorts of harassment of public. Petitioners, informers, witnesses, people who stepped into police stations or even onlookers at a scene of crime become afraid of police manhandling, ill-treatment, harassment and verbal abuse.[2] Increasingly, people feel that there is no use in registering complaints to the higher-ups in the authority.[3]

This detestable attitude of police towards the general public assumes a more vicious shape when the very contentious police-minority relations are analysed.

It can be shown by the selective applicability of law as done by the police. The selection of people on whom the law is applied is determined by the deep-seated rancour against the 'other' community.

Terrorist and Disruption Activities (Prevention) Act, TADA, was uniformly misused. According to India's former Minister of State for Home Affairs, M.M. Jacob, a total of 26,915 people had been detained under TADA between 1988–91. Surprisingly, the highest figures were recorded in Gujarat (9,569 people) where the menace of terrorism was very low compared to Punjab, Jammu & Kashmir and Assam. According to Amnesty International's report, TADA was disproportionately used against tribals and Muslims. In Gujarat, three quarters of those held under TADA at the end of 1989 were Muslims.[4]

During riots, a much more abominable face of police comes to the fore. Following incidents of communal violence illustrates this.

In the anti-Sikh riots of November 1984 which followed the assassination of the Prime Minister Indira Gandhi by two of her Sikh bodyguards, the death toll of the Sikhs killed in Delhi was 2,733 or one every 30 seconds. This was one of the most well-organized communal riots in connivance with the ruling party. Despite the submission of reports by three commissions of enquiry—Justice Ranganath Misra Commission Report (1987), Jain–Agarwal Committee Report (1990) and Justice R.S. Narula Panel Report (1994), all of which had indicted 72 police officers, two union ministers and a Congress MP, no prosecution has been initiated against any one of them so far. It is well known that the Delhi carnage was instigated by local Congress party MPs with the passive complicity of the security forces.[5]

After Hindu-Muslim communal rioting in Meerut in May 1987, in which 91 people were killed, over 600 were arrested on 22 May in the Hashimpura area of Meerut by the Provincial Armed Constabulary (PAC)—a predominately Hindu force. According to press reports, 32 of them disappeared and were presumed killed. Aged between 13 and 65, they were reportedly taken by truck to the banks of the upper Ganga canal near Muradnagar by the PAC. Here they are believed to have been shot in secret and their bodies thrown into canal. Two survivors have testified that they were taken to the canal by PAC men. However, the PAC denied the killings. Official enquiries, not made public so far, confirmed the gruesome killings and blamed the PAC for it. Nevertheless, the government has said the ex-gratia payments were made to relatives of 13 people whose bodies had been found and identified, and also to 17 of the other 19 people killed whose bodies had been found. In making these payments, the government did not accept official responsibility for the killings.[6] On 23 May, some PAC men were alleged to have gone on a rampage in Maliana, a village near Meerut, indiscriminately shooting unarmed men, women and children of Muslim community. Some 80 bodies were later found, while 16 Muslims died in police custody.

On 13 August 1980, on the day of Id, the PAC men fired upon a congregation of 50,000 people in Moradabad city who had gathered in the Idgah for offering *namaz* (prayers), killing 50 persons in the process. The exact death toll is not known because the PAC removed some of the bodies. According to an eyewitness, Naseem Ahmed, he helped pick up 24 bodies from the compound of the mosque, including 13 children.[7]

Hundreds of such incidents have been taking place in other parts of the country which reveal direct involvement of law enforcing agencies in the killings of the people of religious minorities. The frequent occurrence of such incidents prompted an Allahabad High Court judge to remark that the 'Police represent the most organized group of criminals in India'.[8] Even the Sixth Report of the NPC, dated March 1981, made an observation: 'In several instances police officers and policemen have shown an unmistakable bias against a particular community while dealing with communal riots'.[9]

During the Bombay riots of December 1992 and January 1993 the adverse role the police played in fomenting violence, leave alone preventing it, says a lot about the erosion of the sense of duty as a neutral maintainer of law and order, in highest as well as the lowest echelons of the police. The *maha-aartis* launched by the Sena–BJP combine from 26 December 1992 in Bombay added to the communal tension, endangering the fragile peace which had been established. Some of the *maha-aartis* were later used as occasions for delivering speeches and; inciting communal passions. The crowds dispersing from the *maha-aartis* indulged in damage, looting and arson of Muslim establishments on the way. The *maha-aartis* continued unabated with no restriction on them being imposed by the police throughout January 1993 and came to an end only by the first week of February 1993. The damage had been done by then.[10]

A detailed reading of the Justice Srikrishna Commission Report is imperative to understand both the rank inefficiency and inbuilt anti-minority bias that has come to dictate the actions of a large section of police personnel. The testimony of Srikant Bapat, the then police commissioner of Mumbai, put to severe scrutiny and cross examination by the judge, is extremely important in this regard. He states on oath not only that he believed January 1993's violence to be the result of the 'Hindu backlash' but compounds this unsubstantiated version with complete ignorance of incidents of brutality from December 1992 until February 1993 that were directed against minorities.[11]

In several areas it appeared that local Shiv Sainiks were guiding the actions of policemen. In the few cases where local Shiv Sena

Shakha Pramukhs were arrested, evidence from police records and testimonies of policemen shows that bowing to political pressure, the supine police subsequently released offenders with no punitive action.[12]

Numerous instances are recorded in Srikrishna Commission Report where police callousness and bias left the minority community without any means of self-defence. One instance, we would particularly draw attention to is recorded in the report. On 18 January 1993, riots erupted at BIT Chawls, Maulana Azad Road, Sakhi Street and Kalapani, which fall under Agripada Police Station in Mumbai. According to the report, the trouble seems to have first started in BIT Chawls no. 11, 12 and 23. Though the police claim that the incident was one of a violent clash between armed Hindus and Muslims. The true picture was quite different, however. According to one of the Muslim victims, Mumtaz Rehman, the trouble in the BIT Chawls started when Hindu residents started pelting stones on a few tenements occupied by Muslims. Mumtaz telephoned Agripada Police Station to complain that Muslim residents were being attacked by Hindus. The telephone was answered by an unidentified person in the police station, who rudely replied, *Landya Bhai Chup Baitho, Abhi Kuchh Nahi Huva* (You circumcised Muslim! Shut up. Nothing has happened till now), [In Hindu fanatic parlance, Muslims of Mumbai are called *Landya*. While milder *Miya Bhai* is used in Gujarat]. The Report further states that the police actively took part in arson and looting, later, in the same area, with rioters.[13]

One Reshma Umar Makki says, when she contacted Senior Police Inspector Vinayak Patil of Antop Hill Police Station for help, after her house was twice attacked by Shiv Sainiks, he refused to come and retorted 'if a Muslim dies, there would be one Muslim less'.[14]

Justice Jaganmohan Reddy Commission Report on the Ahmedabad riots of 1969 is quite revealing. The report says, this commission of inquiry has cited more than half a dozen instances where Muslim religious places adjoining police lines or police stations were attacked or damaged. The argument advanced by the police officers that because they were busy quelling riots elsewhere, these police stations were shorn of adequate strength and hence these attacks on religious places could not be prevented, did not impress the Commission. It was unconvinced because not a single case of damage to a Hindu place of worship near a police station was reported to the Commission.

Justice Joseph Vithayathil Commission Report on the Tellicherry riots, 1971 has underlined the communal bias in the behaviour of policemen in dealing with riots. It will be better to quote some of his observations which need no further explanation:

> The evidence of the deputy SP says that while on patrol duty he had to curb many among his rank and file who could not restrain themselves when they met Muslims on the road. Similar evidence was given by the sub-collector and other witnesses who have testified saying that while chasing away some Muslims many policemen yelled at them to go to Pakistan. At Mattambaram one or two of them got into the mosque and besides beating Usman Kutty Haji, a very respectable person, broke the tube-light and chandeliers in the mosque. There is nothing to show that there was any justification for this action.[15]

Justice Ranganath Misra Commission on the 1984 anti-Sikh riots in Delhi reports thus:

> The riots occurred broadly on account of the total passivity, callousness and indifference of the police in the matter of controlling the situation and protecting the people of the Sikh community . . . Several instances have come to be narrated where police personal were found marching behind or mingled in the crowd. Since they did not make any attempt to stop the mob from indulging in criminal acts, an inference has been drawn that they were part of the mob and had the common intention and purpose. . . . The Commission was shocked to find that there were incidents where the police wanted clear and definite allegations against the anti-social elements in different localities to be dropped out while recording FIRs.[16]

Over to Gujarat, 2002. India and the whole world witnessed a massacre of minorities on a scale which can aptly be called genocide according to Article 2 of UN Convention on Genocide. Gujarat police has left an indelible scar on their own face. Perhaps no sane and sensible person either from the minority or the majority community will ever condone them for what they did (or more rightly did not do) during the Gujarat riots.

When Sangh Parivar cadres openly boast *Yeh andar ki baat hai, police hamare saath hai*[17] (It is inside information, the police are with us), it says a lot about the state complicity and connivance in the organized pogrom against minorities. On 27 February 2002, after the gruesome attack on the Sabarmati Express in the morning, VHP called for a statewide *bandh* for 28 February, a call according to press reports, its cadre interpreted as a call to action. The state support for the *bandh*, apart from an endorsement of VHP/Bajrang Dal stand, also sent a message to the police.[18] A reporter for *The*

Hindu observed, 'In such a situation, the police would always be hesitant to act lest it hurt the interest of the political bosses. And the saffronized police also found a common cause with the criminals to "punish" the minorities.'[19]

Ahmedabad's Commissioner of Police, P.C. Pandey's comments to *Newshour* (Star News) on 28 February, was telecast again on 10 March. He pontificated, 'These people [read police] also get carried away by the overall general sentiments. That's the whole trouble. The police is equally influenced by the overall general sentiments.' This is the police chief in person. It gave sanction to the policemen to act according to 'sentiment' rather than stringently enforce 'the rule of law'.[20]

On 28 February, as carefully planned mass killings were engineered in 30 different locations all over the state, two senior cabinet ministers, Ashok Bhatt, Gujarat State Health Minister and I.K. Jadeja, State Urban Development Minister, sat in the police control room in Ahmedabad and Gandhinagar respectively, and directly influenced the police not to take any action.

Top police officials all over the country, according to *Communalism Combat* (March–April 2002), said it was 'shocking and unheard of that politicians sit in and try to influence the independent functioning of the police. In the case of Gujarat, when the ruling party and members in responsible positions in government actually espouse an anti-constitutional and divisive ideology, such interference in the police control room assumes criminal proportions'.

In Ahmedabad, Gujarat's commercial capital and the site of Human Rights Watch's investigations, many attacks took place within view of police posts and police stations. Human Rights Watch saw several police posts which were less than 50 ft from the site of burnt Muslim-owned restaurants, places of business, and hotels in Ahmedabad. Without exception, the Hindu-owned establishments neighbouring the destroyed structures were unscathed. Gujarat police failed on all counts, be it intelligence gathering, preventive arrests or riot control. But was the failure due to inadequacy of personnel or weapons? Or was it more by design than by default? Similar incidents were also reported from Dahod (near Godhra) soon after the Baburi Masjid demolition in December 1992. Strict and prompt police action then had controlled the situation.[21] With this history, shouldn't the police have kept a strict watch and vigil over the departure and return of *kar sevaks*, especially when the climate in the country was tense and belligerent. But what Ahmedabad witnessed on 28 February puts all doubts to rest about the police not being hand in glove with saffron brigades. On that day, of the 40 persons shot dead by the police in Ahmedabad city, 36 were Muslims.[22] This despite the fact that it was the minority community that was being targeted by huge and well-organized mobs. According to postmortem reports, it came to light that almost all the killed were between 20 and 25 years of age, and were shot in the head and the chest.[23] The policemen, claiming they were controlling huge Muslim mobs, seemed to have blatantly disregarded the rule-book during riots and shot people above the waist.

In the unending saga of the police making victims the target, two more people on 15 April, belonging to the minority were shot dead at Dariapur, Ahmedabad. The police was effectively aiding a marauding mob that was pelting stones on the hapless Muslim residents in the area. Even minors were not spared by these 'criminals in uniform'. The victims included, among others, an 11-year-old-girl in Dudhia village in Vadodara, hit by a police bullet in the head, and a 14-year-old killed in police firing in Kisan Wadi.

Rapid Action Force jawans are alleged to have beaten up and misbehaved with Muslim women and an elderly *maulvi* in Surat. (*The Hindustan Times*, 5 March 2002). While again in Ahmedabad on 22 March, a group of Muslim women gathered for *majlis*—a ceremony before Moharram which is attended by women only—were attacked by policemen, firing indiscriminately, injuring two young girls in the process.[24]

The carnage in Gujarat is the culmination of years of unabated communal violence. Every time communal violence takes place in Gujarat, it surpasses itself, in brutality from previous instances of violence.

The dirty alliance between an institution for maintaining law and order (which should definitely mean communal harmony) and an ideology for creating communal hatred (and thus anarchy) puts a big question mark on the conscience of the whole country. All vital and sensitive postings in the Gujarat police were systematically politicized and saffronized by the BJP immediately after coming to power. Months before rioting started, the then Home Minister in Gujarat, Haren Pandya, widely reported to have personally led the marauding mobs against Muslims, completely reshuffled the police inspectors and sub-inspectors in Ahmedabad and Vadodara, sidelining the PCs and the DGP.[25]

Moreover, the few Muslim officers in the state force have been systematically sidelined. In fact, in the last seven years, none of the eight Muslim IPS officers in Gujarat have been given an executive posting that has any jurisdictional authority and deals with crime and law and order functions.[26]

Gujarat state police has done serious harm to its credibility. It has proved to be the fuel to the already raging fire of hatred. The role of police is to protect the life, the rights and property of all citizens in an impartial manner. The partisan behaviour of police undermines the fundamental right to equality of the citizens. Rights to life and property of minorities was 'temporarily suspended' by the Hindu fanatics in Gujarat and all through, the state police actively connived with and aided these divisive proponents of saffron terror.

The Indian State may pass into a phase of total anarchy if the communalization of its 'most visible hand' goes on like this, undermining the thousands of years of effort put into building a civilization. Wasn't India looking like the most uncivilized nation in the contemporary world for this protracted period of fascist violence?

Can we ignore the words of Mahatma Gandhi, a Gujarati by birth who once said, 'a civilization can be judged by the way it treats its minorities'?[27] It is time to reflect on these critical issues and take corrective measures to civilize our police force.

NOTES

1. Vadackumchery James *Indian Police and Miscarriage of Justice*, New Delhi, 1995, p. 2.
2. Ibid.
3. Ibid., p. 3.
4. Amnesty International, *Amnesty International Report 1991*, London: Amnesty International, 1991, p. 114.
5. See People Union for Democratic Rights and People Union for Civil Liberties. (PUDR and PUCL), *Who are the Guilty*? Report of a Joint Enquiry into the Causes and Impacts of the Riots in Delhi from 31 October to 10 November 1984, New Delhi.
6. *Human Rights in India—The Updated Amnesty International Report*, New Delhi: Vistar/Sage, 1993, p. 44.
7. For a detailed report see M.J. Akbar, 'Id day of Death', *Sunday*, Calcutta, 24 August 1980, pp. 6–11. See also his *Riot After Riot*, New Delhi: Penguin, 1988.

8. Cited in *Amnesty International Report*, p. 76, n. 6.
9. Cited in Javed Anand, 'Minority Rights in India: Constitution and the Reality', in Sumanta Banerjee (ed.), *Shrinking Space: Minority Rights in South Asia*. Kathmandu: South Asia forum for Human Rights, 1999, p. 157.
10. *Damning Verdict* (Report of the Srikrishna Commission appointed for inquiry into the riots at Mumbai during December 1992–January 1993 and the 12 March 1993 bomb blasts), Mumbai: Sabrang Communications and Publishing, 1998, p. xxiii (Introduction by Teesta Setalvad).
11. Ibid., p. xxxix.
12. Ibid., p. xxix.
13. Ibid., pp. 48–9.
14. Ibid., p. 56.
15. Cited in ibid., p. vii.
16. Ibid.
17. *Communalism Combat*, March–April 2002, p. 114.
18. Sujan Dutta, 'When Guardians of Gujarat gave a 24 hour License for Punitive Action', *Telegraph*, 9 March, 2002.
19. Manas Dasgupta, 'Saffronized Police Show their Colour', *The Hindu*, 3 March 2002.
20. *Communalism Combat*, March–April 2002, p. 118.
21. Ibid., p. 114.
22. Ibid., p. 116.
23. *Indian Express*, 23 March 2002.
24. Ibid., 22 March 2002.
25. *Communalism Combat*, March–April 2002, p. 118.
26. Bunsha Dionne, 'Gujarat's Shame', *Frontline*, 26 April 2002.
27. Cited in John P. Humphrey, *No Distant Millennium: The International Law of Human Rights*, Paris: UNESCO, 1989, p. 46.

CHAPTER 8

Police and the Minorities: A Study of the Role of the Police during Communal Violence in India

K.S. SUBRAMANIAN

In the Indian context, 'communal violence' has come to mean violence against the minority Muslim community by members of the majority Hindu community. For a variety of complex reasons, this has been an endemic problem throughout the post-independence period and has assumed very serious proportions in recent times particularly because of the politically motivated electoral calculations behind whipping up communal sentiments. Violence against other minority communities such as the Sikhs and the Christians too has not been rare—as the anti-Sikh riots of 1984 and the more recent violence against the Christians in different parts of India has shown. There has also been serious violence against the scheduled castes and scheduled tribes as well, in several parts of India. In this paper we are mainly concerned with violence against the Muslim minority although reference will be made to socio-political violence in general.

The paper is organized as follows. It begins with a brief review of communal violence during the post-independence period. Second, it looks at some major instances of communal violence in recent times and the role of the police in this regard. Third, it examines the historical background of the Indian administration and the Indian police. Finally, a brief conclusion is drawn.

Scholars and analysts have gone into the nature, causes, patterns and implications of socio-political violence and their cures in South Asia. In the context of India, it has been generally accepted that the country's liberal democratic institutional arrangements are more adaptable and resilient than their counterparts in the other South Asian countries and that India has in place institutional mechanisms of conflict resolution which makes sure that the existing socio-political set up is not disrupted. It has also been accepted that while there is no shortage of socio-political violence in India, the country's social and political heterogeneity would ensure that pressures of social violence do not build up for far too long or to an intolerable degree along any single fault-line.

Developments over the last decade and more may have put paid to such hopes and expectations. The emergence and consolidation of political and social forces of a 'Hindu nationalist' kind, has exposed the fact that the major fault-line of socio-political violence in India today runs along the lines of the historically inherited Hindu-Muslim divide and may even result in a *de facto*, if not *de jure*, transformation of the Indian polity towards a 'Hindu nationalist' direction in contrast to the secular, socialist, pluralist and democratic arrangement arrived at independence.

According to official reports, in the aftermath of the partition, the communal situation in the country remained relatively calm. During 1950–63, a total of 1,141 incidents of violence took place. In 1964, a significant year, there was a total of 2,115 incidents. From 1964 to 1970, there was an average of 1,025 incidents a year, as against an average of 81.5 per year during the preceding 14 years. A substantial increase in the number of incidents took place during the 1960s and 1970s owing to a variety of factors such as material interests, inherited prejudices and so on. During this period, an increasingly explicit anti-Muslim and pro-Hindu bias on the part of the administration and the police began to be manifested in these incidents. Further, a climate of business competition in riot-prone towns such as Meerut, Moradabad, Aligarh and Jamshedpur was said to be one of the factors which led to riots (Roy, 1987). Cynical politicking by national leaders of the ruling Congress to woo their 'vote banks' led to many conflicts and tension between Hindus and Muslims. Several commissions of enquiry went into these incidents of violence (Ansari, 1999).

II

From the mid-1980s to the 1990s and thereafter, an aggressive form of Hindu communalism has been at work in Indian politics seeking to hijack the Indian polity in a direction opposed to that established at independence. An official report mentions that 40 major communal riots took place during 1990 in the states of Uttar Pradesh, Bihar, Madhya Pradesh, Gujarat, Karnataka, and Maharashtra (GOI, 1990–1). Since then, communal violence has been one of the main features of internal disruption and disorder in Indian politics. The rise of 'Hindu nationalist' political forces under the rubric of the Sangh Parivar (the BJP, VHP, RSS and the Bajrang Dal) and their acquisition of state power in New Delhi in the late 1990s, appears to have strengthened the 'institutionalized riot system' in certain cities (Brass, 1997). This system was clearly perfected in the Gujarat carnage of 2002.

The violent scenario in Gujarat during the period 1987-2002 needs to be taken note of. As noted by many scholars, communal polarization between Hindus and Muslims in the state has had a history and background. The 'Rath Yatra' originating in Gujarat and led by a 'Hindu nationalist' stalwart, culminated in the demolition of the Baburi Masjid in Uttar Pradesh in December 1992. It was a defining moment in the post-independence history of the country. The demolition was also followed by large-scale communal violence in several states, including Gujarat. Statistics from the Gujarat police show that between 1987 and 1991, 106 major incidents took place in the state. From 1996 to 2000, 88 major and 125 minor incidents took place. The year 2002 witnessed 17 major and 18 other incidents. The final communal carnage of 27 February 2002 and thereafter has by now been richly documented.

In this context, it has been argued that there is a close linkage between anti-Muslim violence in India and the way Pakistan, as a 'perfidious' Muslim neighbour, is perceived by sections of the Indian public and politicians. It has been argued that in a communal movement, the government is thematized, but in an ethnic movement, the 'ethnic other' is thematized as an enemy of the nation state. In the latter case, there is a clear majority and a clear minority, which is portrayed as anti-national. After the partition of India in 1947, the idea of the nation state was etched clearly in the Indian consciousness (Gupta, 2002). Pakistan as an enemy state figures prominently in India in moments of ethnic strife. The tendency in ethnic movements is to pillory the minorities as traitors to the nation in response to the call of hostile countries. Some leaders of the recent anti-Muslim violence in Gujarat went to the extent of calling for the dismemberment of Pakistan. Such calls aggravate the serious tensions between the two nuclear-armed neighbours.

The term 'ethnicity' has been used quite flexibly in the Indian context. The current approach appears to regard Hindus and Muslims as 'ethnic' communities although there are considerable internal variations and many sub-communities within these communities, each of which may, by ascriptive criteria, qualify for the term 'ethnic' community. The People of India project undertaken by the Anthropological Survey of India has identified over 4,600 communities in India, all of which may be regarded as 'ethnic' communities (Singh, 1992). The term 'ethnicity' has been prominent in academic studies for over two decades. Increasingly, social-psychological factors have taken precedence over bio-cultural factors in defining and understanding ethnicity (ibid., 1992). The Indian Constitution does not mention 'ethnicity' but recognizes five social categories: the 'scheduled' castes, the 'scheduled' tribes, anglo-Indians, 'backward classes' and religions and linguistic minorities (ibid.). Increasingly, the understanding of Hindu–Muslim conflicts in India has been couched in ethnic terms (Varshney, 2002).

Several reports, official and non-official, have brought out the basic malaise that afflicts Hindu–Muslim relations in India, leading to violence between the two communities and remedial measures have been suggested (Das, 1990; Manor, 1988; Engineer, 1984, 1989; Ansari, 1997; Rai, 1999; Desai, 2002; Ahmad, 2002; Minorities Council, 2002; Government of India reports, including those by the National Police Commission, 1978–81, the Srikrishna Commission on the Hindu–Muslim violence in Bombay 1992–3 set up by the Government of Maharashtra and so on). The most recent instance of violence against the minority community in Gujarat in 2002 was investigated by an eight-member Citizens' Tribunal headed by Justice V.R. Krishna Iyer of the Supreme Court of India which submitted a three-volume report on the subject.

Hindu–Muslim violence is not only bad for governance from the Indian point of view but carries unhealthy portents and signals for the rest of South Asia, where developments in India have important repercussions. This lends relevance to the present analysis.

In this context, the observations and recommendations on Hindu–Muslim violence in India made by different official reports by the National Police Commission (1978–81) of the Government of India are noted in volume VI of the Commission's Report. Other important reports on Hindu–Muslim violence in the recent period with governance implications are: (i) the Srikrishna Commission Report,

1998; (ii) the report on 'Combating Communal Conflicts: The Perception of Police Neutrality during Hindu–Muslim Riots', by Vibhuti Narain Rai, 1999; and (iii) reports on the Gujarat violence, 2002. The Srikrishna Commission was appointed by the Government of Maharashtra to inquire into the Hindu–Muslim violence in Mumbai during December 1992 and January 1993. The report of the Commission was published in 1998 in two volumes. The violence took place in the immediate aftermath of the demolition of the Baburi Masjid in the state of Uttar Pradesh by 'Hindu nationalist' forces. The terms of reference and basic findings of the Commission are extremely important from the policy point of view. It is part of the governance crisis in India that neither the recommendations of the National Police Commission nor those of the Srikrishna Commission, both government-appointed Commissions, have yet been implemented.

While there are a number of useful studies on Hindu–Muslim violence in India (see especially, Engineer, 1984 and 1989), the report of Vibhuti Narain Rai is important as the author is a serving senior police officer in Uttar Pradesh, the most populous state of India with a record of persistent Hindu–Muslim violence. The author studied the role of the police in the Hindu–Muslim violence during the pre-independence and post-independence periods in the following places: Kanpur (1931); Ranchi (1967); Ahmedabad (1969); Bhiwandi and Jalgaon (1970); Banaras (1977); Jamshedpur (1979); Meerut (1990); Bhagalpur (1989); Ayodhya (1992); Bombay (1992–3). His main findings with respect to the role of the police in these cases are as follows:

(i) Police function in a partisan manner during most riots. In all the riots discussed in the study, the police did not act as a neutral law enforcement agency but more as a 'Hindu' force.

(ii) Perceptible discrimination was visible in the use of force, preventive arrests, enforcement of curfew, treatment of detained persons at police stations, reporting of facts and investigation, and detection and prosecution of cases registered during riots. Muslims suffered in all the above-mentioned areas.

(iii) The perception by Hindus and Muslims of the police during communal strife is diametrically opposed. Hindus view policemen as their friends and protectors during communal riots. Muslims, by and large, consider policemen their enemies in similar situations.

(iv) An average policeman does not shed his prejudices and predetermined beliefs at the time of his entry into the force, and this is reflected in his bias against Muslims during communal violence.

(v) The expectations of the Indian society from average policemen are communal. The policeman is believed to be a protector of the interests of his community.

(vi) The inimical relationship between the police and the Muslims makes them overreact in a confrontation-like situation.

Finally, a number of reports have been produced in connection with the major case of anti-minority violence in Gujarat in 2002 (Communalism Combat, 2002; PUCL, 2002; PUDR, 2002; Citizens' Initiative, 2002; Press Institute of India (PII) PII, 2002; Independent Fact Finding Mission, 2002; Varadarajan, 2002; CPI(M), 2002; Sondhi and Mukerji, 2002; Citizens Tribunal on Gujarat, 2002). The following analysis draws on these reports. We give detailed attention to this case as this has been the most serious such case in India since independence and also because it symbolizes in a graphic manner the basic crisis of governance, that has afflicted India following the demolition of the Baburi Masjid in 1992 (Subramanian, 1999). The recommendations of the Citizens' Tribunal on Gujarat, 2002 with regard to the role of the police in communal violence are also extremely important.

While Gujarat has had a long history of communal riots, what happened in 2002 was unique. It was not a communal riot in the conventional sense. Sixteen of Gujarat's twenty-five districts were engulfed in well-organized armed mob attacks on Muslims between 28 February and 2 March 2002, the period of the most concentrated violence. The attacks continued till mid-March. Three other districts witnessed sporadic bouts of mob violence on Muslims. Nowhere were the mobs less than two or three thousand strong, often they were more than 5,000 in number. This and the fact that the mobs were armed with lethal weapons and the fact that the manner of arson, hacking and killing of human beings were chillingly similar indicated a carefully laid out plan of action behind the attacks.

The state-wide violence, which commenced on 28 February 2002, was preceded by the mysterious arson attack on 27 February on one of the coaches of the Sabarmati Express train near the Godhra Railway Station in Panchmahal district, not far from Ahmedabad, the state capital. Nearly 60 passengers, many of them *kar sevaks* (volunteers) on their way back from the holy town of Ayodhya in Uttar Pradesh, perished in the fire. The controversy over the origin of the fire has not yet been resolved.

The lack of preparation on the part of the police and the administration to prevent the Godhra incident and the wider lack of intent to act to prevent the subsequent violence across the whole state against the minority Muslim community was clearly brought out in the reports. Some of the features of the violence in Gujarat from 28 February onwards were: (i) selective targeting of Muslims; (ii) brutality and bestiality of the attacks; (iii) unprecedented scale and degree of the violence; (iv) loot and destruction of property on an unprecedented scale; (v) military precision and planning behind the attacks; (vi) use of hate speech and hate writing; (vii) massive sexual violence against women and girls and attacks on children; (viii) colossal economic destruction; (ix) religious and cultural desecration on a massive scale; (x) largescale preparations for the violence; (xi) state complicity; (xii) serious violation of rules and regulations by the police and their active connivance and participation in the violence, and so on.

Godhra is the district capital of the Panchmahal district. Two key officials, the District Magistrate (DM) and the Superintendent of Police (SP) operate from there and are responsible for maintaining law and order throughout the district. They are connected by telephone to the state and national capitals and to all the police stations in the district. They have numerous intelligence officers reporting to them. In disturbed times such as the present, they have to coordinate steps on a day-to-day, hour-to-hour and even minute-to-minute basis. They must function as a team and provide leadership to their staff throughout the district. There is a police control room in the district which monitors developments and provides information to these functionaries. The system of district administration, created and placed in position by the British, has been the key to political stability in the country throughout the colonial and postcolonial period. In addition to these administrative arrangements, there are central government institutions such as the CRPF, the Railway Police and a major railway station, all located in Godhra. It is easy to remain in touch with these units and to get inputs to maintain law and order in the district. There is also a large central government intelligence set-up and a state government agency whose personnel are located in the district headquarters and often report to the DM and the SP.

During the last decade, Gujarat has been a major participant in the Ramjanmabhumi agitation, which has polarized society as never before. The state has contributed perhaps the largest number of *kar sevaks* for the VHP/BJP-sponsored temple construction programme at Ayodhya in Uttar Pradesh. Considering the feverish activity in that town, there has been a large volume of traffic from Godhra Railway Station to Ayodhya and back throughout the period of heightened tension related to the construction of the temple slated to commence on 15 March 2002. The *kar sevaks* were known to have been harassing Muslim vendors of tea and eatables in their journeys from Godhra to Ayodhya and back. Press reports indicate clashes between these two sections of people. Still, the district administration appears to have remained indifferent, neither collecting nor taking any action on intelligence inputs on activities which could pose a threat to law and order management in the district.

Even after the arson attack at the Godhra Railway Station, no serious steps were taken by the district administration to avert the further disasters that occurred in Godhra. No preventive arrests were made. No action under Section 144 of the CrPC was taken. In fact, the administration seems to have gone out of the way to cooperate with the wishes of the political executive in their disastrous decision to take the dead bodies in procession from the Godhra Railway Station to Ahmedabad as specifically prohibited in the detailed instructions of the Government of India directive (Mullik, 1966). Experience of district administration in India suggests that district authorities in Godhra were guilty of serious dereliction of duty.

A similar pattern of inactivity was subsequently seen in Ahmedabad where continuous anti-Muslim rioting took place for several weeks following the Godhra incident on 27 February. All known canons of administrative behaviour in relation to communal incidents established by the Government of India and regularly adopted by the administration in the country were totally ignored, except in isolated cases by a few district officials posted in a few field formations away from the state headquarters. Not only did mobs of rioters roam the streets freely attacking and destroying Muslim property and killing, raping and maiming innocent Muslim men, women and children and terrorizing them but policemen on a large-scale actively took part in the violence and facilitated it.

Official information furnished to the Election Commission of India (ECI, 2002), indicated that 20 out of 25 districts in the state were regarded as 'affected areas' for purposes of relief distribution. The Additional Director General of Police (Intelligence) of the state government further informed the ECI that 151 towns and 993 villages, covering 154 out of the 182 Assembly constituencies in the state and 284 police stations out of a total of 464, were affected by violence (ECI, 2002). The two metropolitan cities of Ahmedabad and Vadodara were among the worst affected. The failings and omissions of the administration and the delay in dealing with the violence as per existing law and procedure are clear from various reports, including those of the National Human Rights Commission (NHRC).

Apart from the Constitution of India and the UN Conventions and norms adopted by India, the criminal law and procedure to deal with violence of the kind perpetrated in Gujarat are quite detailed and clear. These are supplemented by statutory instructions and guidelines issued from time to time (Mullik, 1966). The basic law is contained in the Police Act, the Indian Penal Code, the Criminal Procedure Code and the Evidence Act. The reports of the first-ever National Police Commission (1979–81) of India summarize the experience of implementation from independence onwards.

Briefly, the Police Act 1861 delineates the structure and duties of the Indian police. These include execution of lawful orders and warrants issued by the competent authority; collection and communication of intelligence affecting public order; prevention of crime and public nuisance; bringing offenders to justice and arresting persons liable to be arrested; independent performance of duties without the need for any clearance from above; liability for departmental action and punishment for any negligence; and so on. The Criminal Procedure Code 1973 provides powers to arrest without warrant 11 categories of persons even on suspicion; use of force in effecting arrests in case of resistance; search without warrant; use of force in the dispersal of unlawful assemblies; preventive arrests; arrests on suspicion of indulging in cognizable offences or injury to public property; safeguards are provided in the Police Act, the CrPC, the IPC and in the Constitution of India. The laws existed before the adoption of the Constitution of India.

Strictly speaking, the laws were not 'constitutionalized' when the Constitution came into existence but became part of the criminal law of the land. The reports of the National Police Commission (NPC) lists the tasks of the police such as investigation, prevention and service provision; and provides that the executive cannot interfere with the investigative process though overall guidance and supervision by the executive is permitted with regard to prevention and service provisions. The NPC notes that discretionary enforcement of law in dealing with public order situations is a typical instance of the exertion of pressure on the police by politicians. Potent weapons in the hands of politicians, in this connection, are incentives for career advancement, threats of drastic punishment, penal administrative action including transfers and suspensions from duty and so on. In view of this, the NPC has recommended that the police chief of the state should be selected from a panel of officers to be prepared by a statutory commission composed of distinguished persons, including the leader of opposition in the state legislative assembly. In spite of this, the NPC notes that executive orders of doubtful validity are often passed and obeyed by pliant bureaucrats.

If a no-nonsense and non-partisan approach had been followed by the administration after the Godhra incident of 27 February and prompt arrests of potential troublemakers had been made, as the administration normally does, tension could have been contained. The chances of a vengeful and organized spree of retaliatory killings could have been pre-empted. That this did not happen suggests a lack of intent on the part of those in government to take prompt preventive measures in order to de-escalate the situation. In Godhra, there is always one State Reserve Police (SRP) Company on duty. A Railway Protection Force (RPF) contingent is posted on the Godhra Railway Station itself having 42 policemen in all. Further, two constables per reserved compartment are normally posted in a running train. The fact that *kar sevaks* were expected on this route and the fact that Godhra has a fragile communal history are sufficient to institute additional precautionary deployment of force. Besides, Godhra, as district headquarters, has sufficient police deployment, including armed police, a control room, a town police station with eight police posts, all equipped with telephones, plus a sub-divisional police station. It is also the headquarters of an SRP battalion and has a municipal fire brigade. All these factors are enough to make any responsible citizen feel that adequate preventive action was deliberately avoided before and after the Godhra arson attack.

It is clear from the evidence of the DM and SP Godhra, that on 27 February, after the Godhra attack, that though the Rapid Action Force (RAF) was called in, adequate powers were not given to it. Though curfew was imposed on the city, the RAF men were made to sit in the officers' mess, helpless, unable to do anything. Though the fire brigade is located near the railway station, where the arson attack took place, it took a while for them to reach the place of occurrence. On the day of the occurrence, there were only 3 SRP men on duty; of the over hundred GRP (Government Railway Police) officers stationed at Godhra, only 2 or 3 were on duty. While two of the GRP personnel reached the spot within minutes, it is not clear why they did not resort to firing to deter the miscreants.

The post-Godhra violence in Gujarat continued for several weeks and embraced a number of districts. A noticeable feature was the distinct and similar patterns of violence that emerged in different parts of the state. While local conditions and socio-economic factors differentiate the attacks from one place to another, detailed and extensive evidence pointed to a sinister similarity in the attacks in different places.

Some features of police behaviour in this context are the following: (i) police participation in the violence; (ii) illegal registration of FIRs; (iii) omnibus FIRs; (iv) FIRs without names of the accused; (v) deliberate obfuscation of the identity of the accused; (vi) victimization of the minority community; (vii) unprofessional investigations; (viii) real culprits not arrested; (ix) no identification parades; (x) malicious combing operations in minority community areas; (xi) no relief to rape victims; (xii) no action against errant media publishing legally actionable reports; (xiii) no action against the VHP/Bajrang Dal activists behind the violence; (xiv) non-implementation of the recommendations of the NHRC; (xv) non-implementation of the Disturbed Areas (Special Courts) Act, 1976; (xvi) non-implementation of the Prevention of Damage to Public Property Act, 1984, and so on.

B.N. Mullik's work (1966) *Civil Disturbances* is an important official document indicating the 'Powers of Magistrates and the Police to deal with Unlawful Assemblies'. Mullik was Director of the Intelligence Bureau. Extracts from Chapter IX of the volume are quoted below:

It is the duty of every Superintendent of Police to mobilise the support of all his subordinates down to the level of constables and village *chowkidars* and make them fully and genuinely understand the most serious implications of such communal disturbances, so that at the slightest sign of trouble, the entire police force may rise as one man to fight and suppress it. The mind of every police officer—whatever religion he may profess—must be clear on the point that he has taken a pledge to protect the people and it is his sacred duty to protect the weak against the strong and the minority against the majority. There can be no compromise on this issue and this should be a matter of fundamental faith with every police officer for the vindication of which he should be prepared to lay down his life. (Mullik, 1966, p. 48)

The authorities must make it clear to the people that they will act with the utmost severity. The Superintendent of Police should repeatedly speak to all his subordinates and build up their moral strength, without which preventive action at the time when disturbances take place will be lacking in strength and determination. In most cases, with such strong action taken at the start, the danger of communal disturbance would recede and then finally disappear. But so long as tension remains, very strict watch should be maintained and precautionary measures should not be relaxed. (ibid., p. 49)

If in spite of these precautions, trouble breaks out, it is then clearly the duty of the magistrate and police to act quickly, resolutely and strongly at the very outbreak of such disturbances. They must not bank on the hope that with the exercise of patience and forbearance the trouble will pass off without any serious damage. The entire experience of the past has been to the contrary. The use of force at the very beginning is essential, so that the attacking crowds may immediately realize that retribution against them would be swift and severe and the damage that will be caused to them will be much greater than what they will be able to inflict. (ibid., p. 49)

Clear instructions of the Government of India exist to the effect that executive officers will be held personally responsible if they fail to prevent communal disturbances in areas within their charge, and that they must use force at the early stages. (ibid., p. 50)

Prompt arrangements should be made to evacuate the injured to the hospital or the dead to the morgue. Their photographs should be taken unless they are identified. Dead bodies should be delivered to the next of kin at the burial or cremation grounds and should not be allowed to be taken out in processions. It is necessary to maintain a careful watch on crowds when they return to their respective localities after performing the last rites of such bodies. It is essential that the press should be taken into confidence and full accounts should be given to the correspondents. If this is not done, then the press will be forced to obtain accounts from interested people and thus publish highly exaggerated reports. In dealing with such mass uprisings, the magistrate and the police should clearly understand that these crowds have already passed into a state of mob and have been completely seized by communal frenzy and are driven by one single desire, i.e. to kill and destroy members of the minority community. Members of such crowds have lost all noble human sentiments. At such time persuasion not backed by force will be of no avail. Therefore, what is needed is swift action to make the crowd realize that if it raises its head, it will be knocked down. There is no second alternative and any attempt to temporise will lead to disastrous consequences and cause irreparable damage. (ibid., pp. 50–1)

INDIAN ADMINISTRATION: ITS HISTORICAL BACKGROUND

Police participation and facilitation of violence, along with participation of many Hindu middle class elements, including women, was a significant feature of the recent violence in Gujarat. Similarly, the failure and indifference of the state machinery in providing relief to the victims of violence and violation of constitutional protection to due process under article 21 of the Indian Constitution, along with other similar fundamental provisions of the Indian Constitution for the protection and well being of minorities, members of the scheduled castes and tribes, women and other weaker sections are often significant features of socio-political violence (Subramanian, 1992; Bandyopadhyay, 1977). Continued neglect of capacity building of administrative institutions for human development and humane governance norms reflect an underlying crisis of State in South Asia, a crisis which, in the Indian case, has been described as the 'organic crisis of the state' (Bose and Jalal, 1997).

In this context, the historical background of the inherited administrative machinery in South Asia, which is basically regulatory rather than developmental, needs to be appreciated (Potter, 1986; Arnold, 1986). Potter stresses the strength of the administrative structure in India in maintaining order, unity, integrity and stability and its relative lack of innovation, responsiveness, expertise and accountability to the people. The institutional structure of government in the states as well as the centre is highly centralized and administrative power is concentrated in the hands of small groups of elite civil servants strategically located in districts, state secretariats and the central government. A marked orientation towards order is built into the overall fabric of administration. The value of this frame to political leaders at the centre was repeatedly demonstrated after independence whenever there were political crises involving the imposition of president's rule or a national emergency (1975–7). A single group of 'political administrators' in a national frame controllable from the centre was found to be a most useful mechanism. As Potter puts it:

Indian revolutionaries perhaps tended to underestimate the strength of the state bureaucracy. Inefficient in implementing development programmes they may have been but that was never their strong point. What the bureaucratic structure of state power in India continued to hold and what the ICS tradition emphasized was maintaining order and dealing with any serious internal opposition to their rule.

Potter goes on to make a useful analysis of the fundamental contradiction between this administrative structure and some of the essential features of the Indian constitution framed in 1950. These features are: (i) the formal provision for a parliamentary system of democratic government and the consequent spread of democratic politics with politicians increasingly involved in administration at the district, state and central levels; (ii) the Directive Principles of State Policy and all the steps taken subsequently in the Five Year Plans to pursue in an active manner the economic and social development; and (iii) the federal structure of government which, in combination with the democratic feature, did set in motion forces opposed to an all-Indian Administrative Service.

Further, in the context of state violence against the rural poor in India, a former civil servant (Bandyopadhyay, 1977) has noted that historically the prime objective of district administration has been the maintenance of order and tranquility in the countryside. The general administrative procedures and traditions, criminal and civil laws, judicial pronouncements and practices are centred on the preservation of the status quo and the prevailing property structure. If a conflict occurs between the implementation of a social legislation, which might upset the social status quo, and the maintenance of law and order, the weight of administrative culture and tradition favours the latter. The Indian Penal Code and the Criminal Procedure Code contains elaborate provisions for the maintenance of public order and tranquility and more than 33 per cent of the operational provisions of the Indian Penal Code relate to offences against property. The Criminal Procedure Code was overhauled in 1973 but still contains drastic provisions for the dispersal of unlawful assemblies by force. The picture described here remains, by and large, intact. It may be useful here to explore further the historical background of the Indian police in order to understand its unchanged role in the management of social violence in India (Subramanian, 1995).

Indian scholars have often missed the political purposes behind the origin of the Indian police (Gupta, 1979; Arnold, 1986). Arnold has observed that the evolution of the Indian police during the nineteenth century was conditioned by the political needs of the British colonial regime. The distinction between political and crime control functions of the police did not in fact exist, a point missed by other writers (Gupta, 1979; Griffiths, 1971). The British Indian police, modelled on the colonial Irish police, was a centralized paramilitary force. Its chief officer was called an inspector general of police, an apt designation for the head of a colonial paramilitary police. The officer was directly responsible to the chief secretary of the government. Its availability as an armed force under civilian control and its centralized paramilitary character made it useful to the government of a restless and violent country. By the late 1850's, the basic structure of the Indian police as a partly military and partly civilian organization had become established. After the mutiny of 1857 and the transfer of governance of India to the British Crown, the Code of Civil Procedure 1859, the Code of Criminal Procedure, 1861 and Indian Penal Code, 1860 were enacted. The Police Commission of 1860 led to the formulation of the Police Act of 1861. The recommendations of the Police Commission of 1902 were intended mainly to strengthen the police more fully to take over from the army responsibility to maintain internal control and to counter the emerging nationalist opposition to British rule. Special attention was paid to the armed police and the CID, which became the growth areas claiming a larger share of the budget. The following were established features of the Indian police at the time of independence (Arnold, 1986):

- Continued strict subordination to the civilian administration, despite increase in the relative importance of the armed police and the Special Branch;
- Unaccountability to the public and their elected representatives and their express role as state servants rather than public servants;
- Coercive strength and disposition and frequent use of high levels of state violence which became a part of departmental custom and police procedure and mentality;
- Institutionalization of a paramilitary wing within the police organization combining the strength of quasi-military arms, training and discipline with the perceived advantages of a police form of organization.

The further feature of pervasive secrecy and lack of transparency in the organization must be noted as well. These features have continued to this day. It will be readily seen how useful this structure has proved to be for the Indian elite in maintaining order in India throughout the post-colonial period. Independence in 1947 saw no basic change in this police structure. What has happened subsequently is the 'massive growth of centralized police power' in the post-independence period, defying the federal logic of the Indian Constitution.

Post-independence India has witnessed no attempt to separate the political and crime control functions of the police. This is allied to the failure to separate the law and order functions from the investigative functions at the field level. A visible neglect of investigative functions at the cost of the law and order functions has grown. Further, there has been a steady increase in the numbers of armed police at all levels, especially at the central level. The increasing importance of the intelligence police is to be added to this, again especially at the central level. This police and administrative structure headed by the IAS and the IPS has pre-existed and survived the Indian Constitution and is the cause of many a malaise in India today. However, this administrative structure has played a crucial role in maintaining the post-colonial status quo in India.

The theory of public administration in India has operated on the assumption that the members of the IAS and the IPS should provide impartial and free advice to political masters and be guided by the latter only if contrary orders are given in writing to them. The IAS and the IPS are the key services involved in the maintenance of public order and development. The following features of the administrative situation in India call for adequate analysis (Subramanian, 1996):

- The role of the administration in the context of the explosive emergence of social conflicts;
- The nature of the relationship of the administration to the 'dominant proprietary classes' in India;
- The emergence of the 'massive growth of centralized police power' in the post-independence period;
- The 'relative autonomy' of the bureaucratic structure within the overall political structure of the state;
- The persistent phenomenon of 'governmental lawlessness' and 'state-sponsored violence';
- The factors behind the failure of the powerful Ail-India Services to exert a moderating influence on the political executive.

CONCLUSION

Administrative reforms for human development have never been a major issue in Indian politics. Unless far-reaching reforms are carried out, the phenomena of socio-political violence witnessed recently in Gujarat and elsewhere are likely to continue. Political will to carry out these reforms, suggested in many reports on communal and other violence, is lacking mainly because communal mobilization for political gain has become an important factor for professional politicians. It is necessary for all sections of the people to build pressure on the political class to place human development for the people above their immediate political survival.

REFERENCES

Ahmad, Aijaz, *On Communalism and Globalization: Offensives of the Far Rights*, New Delhi: Three Essays, 2002.

Ansari, Iqbal. A., *Communal Riots, The State and Law in India,* New Delhi: Institute of Objective Studies, 1997.

———, *Report on Communal Riots: Prevention and Control*, New Delhi: Minorities Council, 1999.

Ansari, Iqbal A. (ed.), *Prevention of Communal Violence: Rule of Law & Peace Initiative,* New Delhi: Minorities Council, 2002.

Arnold, David, *Police, Power and Colonial Rule: Madras, 1859–1947*, New Delhi: Oxford University Press, 1986.

Bandyopadhyay, D., *External Impediments to the Growth of Organizations of the Rural Poor,* New Delhi: National Labour Institute, 1977.

Bose, Sugata and Ayesha Jalal, *Nationalism, Development and Democracy: State and Politics in India,* New Delhi: Oxford University Press, 1997.

Brass, Paul, *Theft of an Idol and other Essays*, Princeton: Princeton University Press, 1997.

Chenoy, K.M. et al., *Gujarat Carnage: A Report to the Nation* (An Independent Fact Finding Mission), 2002.

Communalism Combat, 'Genocide: Gujarat 2002' (March–April), 2002.

Concerned Citizens Tribunal, Gujarat, *Crime Against Humanity,* vols. I and II, Mumbai: Citizens for Justice and Peace, 2002.

Coverage of Gujarat Riots Media Debates its Role, Report of the Workshop on Media Coverage on the Communal Conflict held at Maneasar (Haryana), New Delhi: Press Institute of India, 2002.

Das, V., *Communities, Riots and Survivors in South Asia*, New Delhi: Oxford University Press, 1990.

Desai, Radhika., *Slouching Towards Ayodhya,* New Delhi: Three Essays, 2002.

Engineer, Asghar Ali, *Communalism and Communal Violence in India: An Analytical Approach to Hindu-Muslim Conflict*, Bombay: Ajanta Publication, 1989.

———, *Communal Riots in Post-Independence India,* Hyderabad: Sangam Books, 1984.

———, *Communalism and Communal Violence in India,* Bombay: Ajanta Publications, 1989.

Government of India, *Reports of the National Police Commission*, New Delhi: Ministry of Home Affairs, 1979–81.

———, *Annual Report,* Ministry of Home Affairs, 1990–1.

Government of Maharashtra, *Report of the Srikrishna Commission Appointed for Inquiry into the Riots at Mumbai During December 1992 and January 1993.*

Griffiths, Percival, *To Guard My People: A History of the Indian Police,* London, 1971.

Gupta, Anandswarup, *The Police in British India, 1861–1947,* Delhi: Concept, 1979.

Gupta, Dipankar, *The Context of Ethnicity: Sikh Identity in a Comparative Perspective*, New Delhi: Oxford Univesity Press, 2002.

———, *The Limits of Tolerance: Prospects of Secularism in India After Gujarat*, 2002.

Hameed, S. et al., *How has the Gujarat Massacre Affected Minority Women?: The Survivors Speak*, Ahmedabad: Citizen's Initiative, 2002.

Manor, James, 'Collective Conflict in India' (Conflict Studies 212), Sussex: UK Institute of Development Studies, 2002.

Mullik, B.N., *Civil Disturbances*, New Delhi: Government of India Press, 1966.

Maaro! Kaapo! Baalo!: State, Society, and Communalism in Gujarat, New Delhi: Minorities Council, 2002.

Potter, David, *India's Political Administrator*, New Delhi: Oxford University Press, 1986.

Rai, Vibhuti Narain, *Combating Communal Conflicts: Perception of Police Neutrality during Hindu-Muslim Riots in India*, Allahabad: Anamika Prakashan, 1999.

Roy, Ajit, 'The Changing Role of Violence in Indian Politics', in T.V, Sathyamurthy, ed., *Class Formation and Political Transformation in Post-colonial India,* vol. 4, New Delhi: Oxford University Press, 1987.

Singh, K.S., 'An Introduction', *People of India*, vol. 1, New Delhi: Oxford University Press, 1992.

———, Ethnicity, *Caste and People: India and Soviet Union*, New Delhi: Manohar, 1992.

Sondhi, M.L. and A. Mukarji, *The Black Book of Gujarat*, New Delhi: Manak Publications, 2002.

Subramanian, K.S., 'The Graham Staines Murder Case and District Administration in India', New Delhi: *Mainstream*, 1999.

———, *Political Violence, Social Movements and State in India* (Discussion Paper 308), Sussex: Institute of Development Studies, 1992.

———, *Administration Reality in India: Some Theoretical Issues, Public Administration in India*, vol. II, in Arvind K. Sharma and V. Bhaskara Rao (eds), New Delhi: Vikas Publishing House, 1996.

———, 'Police Organisation in India: A Historical and Contemporary Assessment', *Indian Defence Review*, May 1995.

———, *At the Receiving End: Women's Experiences of Violence in Vadodara*, Vadodara: PUCL, 2002.

———., *Violence in Vadodara: A Report*, Vadodara: PUCL, 2002.

Varadarajan, Siddharth, *Gujarat: The Making of a Tragedy*, New Delhi: Penguin Books India, 2002.

Varshney, A., *Ethnic Conflict and Civic Life: Hindus and Muslims in India*, New Delhi: Oxford University Press, 2002.

CHAPTER 9

Police Prejudice against the Muslims

ARSHI KHAN

Democracy in general provides a safety valve for the minorities or the non-majority groups in particular. Democratic entitlements of the minorities guaranteed under the United Nations Charter, the UN Conventions and Rulings, make it imperative for the sovereign nation-states, bi-national and multinational states to protect their identity and to provide them safety and security in normal and emergency situations. In other words, the governmental agencies are generally expected to take the matters of minority, in particular, their protection, as a part of constitutional assignment and the rule of law. In most of the historical societies, minorities may become vulnerable to three entities, which are usually dominated by the majority community. They are the people, state agencies and civic society (political parties). Among the state agencies, the role and attitude of the police is crucial when it comes to the protection of minorities and their rights. In many plural societies, constitutions and post constitutional developments have developed various mechanisms for the protection of minorities through their direct participation in the working of law enforcement agencies and also keeping a strict control and vigilance over the actions and associations of the police personnel. Such efforts have resulted in the creation of balanced ethnic and social composition of the police force and prevented it from committing crimes against humanity.

CONTEXTUALIZING THE TEXT

It appears that the role of the police in plural societies, particularly among the minorities becomes very crucial in the maintenance of law and order in the field of state–society relationship. Owing to its background, the police system has a negative image of being an instrument of the ruling section for keeping in control the renegades as well as the ordinary citizen. Colonial history is full of evidence of the suppressive role played by the police in society. For example in India, under the British colonial rule, the police not only controlled crimes but also became an effective colonial instrument to discourage and destroy the voices for freedom and justice which rose against the British occupiers. It worked both as an instrument of administrative control over the population and also as an agency of terror in case of non-compliance. Despite being an instrument of the British colonialism, the police role was not largely seen as communal and prejudiced. The British police, mainly due to its social composition and service codes, had maintained a considerable level of impartiality in dealing with the issues of social violence and detentions.

However the majoritarian attitude of the Congress and the question of 'communal settlement' raised by the Muslim League, later on largely influenced and shaped the communal psychology of the police personnel also. This was finally witnessed by the Hindus and the Sikhs when they encountered the highly communal role played by the police in newly created Pakistan. On the other hand, the Muslims received the same treatment from the communal police in different parts of India.

Communal prejudice is now an existing reality as far as the Indian police are concerned. This has been evident in several cases of riots where the police have engineered massacres in a planned manner. Police stations turn into belligerent camps against the local Muslim population. Their disengagements or partisan role towards the Muslims, before and after the riots have proved to be catastrophic to the notion of common citizenship, equal rights and rule of law. The state reserved police forces and the CPPF have also shown their anti-Muslim bias in many violent situations in several states. So far, in the period of over five decades, no sincere effort as corrective measures of the state governments, union territories and union government have encouraged the police to shed its anti-Muslim sentiment. In general, the police perceive Muslim localities as 'criminal zones', something which is prevalent even in India's capital. Anti-Muslim role of the police in the Seelampur area of Delhi in 1993 riots is one of the examples that can be cited. The police also have in their repertoire some choice exptetives reserved for the Muslims like *katuey*, uncivilized, among others.

When we look at the Western world, we find that the police system there is comparatively better-managed and is comparatively least involved in criminal activities based on race, colour and language. The example of the United States in the field of police reform is exemplary. There is no doubt that even in the United States there are cases of police atrocities based on colour but the inclusion of the African Americans and the Hispanics in the police force as well as the strict conformity to the rule of law have resulted in the minimization of the crime against the non-white community. In some places in the US, the policemen are hired and fired by the local administration. For example the elected Deering Town Committee in the New Hampshire has achieved tremendous success in setting the agenda for security and the evaluation of the police force as they are paid by the property tax collected from the local people. The image of the police in Deering Town is verifiably an example of the efficiency and honesty of the police force vis-à-vis the local people.

Similarly, the UK government has done tremendous exercise in making the British police more comfortable with the general public particularly with the non-British settlers. Canada, Germany, Austria, Italy, France and other Scandinavian countries have set examples in having efficient police systems that are less prejudiced against the non-majority groups. There is also much to learn from the experiences of the Western world, for example in Switzerland, the identity factor is considered to be of high priority particularly in the case of the deployment and stationing of the police force in any area or locality. It is not simply Christianity, which is the dominant religion of the majority of the Swiss, but rather the language, which constitutes the actual marker of identity at the inter-community (sect) level. Therefore, it is mandatory for the communes and the cantons to recruit and deploy those police personnel who speak the language of the people there.

Unfortunately in the case of India, we have not been sincere in the recruitment, deployment and stationing of the police force in accordance with the need and choice of the people. There has been a deliberate practice of keeping the police stations full of individuals professing the Hindu faith among the Muslim majority areas. Indian Muslims except in the state of Jammu & Kashmir and Lakshadweep, are scattered across many states but do have sizeable population in many districts, towns, and parts of cities. The deployed police personnel may speak the same language as the local people in

Muslim majority area but here it is not the language but the religion which acts as the identity of the community vis-à-vis the majority Hindu community. This has resulted, in many areas, to a continuous period of tensions and suspicions among the Muslims regarding their vulnerability vis-à-vis the police. Similarly, when the Hindu dominated police deal with mobs, agitations, religious processions or educational institutions with a Muslim majority, the situation becomes worse, at least, on the psychological level.

COMMUNAL PREJUDICES

The Muslim people, being victim of the minority-psychology-fear immediately feel threatened from the presence of the police force in similar situations. Their fear has proved to be the fact whenever the police dealt with the Muslim students in the campuses of the Muslim eduational institution protesting police brutalities. It has been found in a number of cases that the police have felt more free in misusing bullets against the Muslims than Hindus in similar situations in many parts of the country. It is also found from the victims in general that the police make many unusual, abusive and anti-national slurs against individuals belonging to the Muslim community. Any police deployment or the composition of the police station with the personnel belonging to one religious community in the Muslim majority area practically turns into a communal armed force. In other words while, police seems to be corrupt in general, to the majority of the Muslims, the police force also seems to be communal. It would not be erroneous to mention that the police is in most cases inefficient and callous when the Muslims ask for their protection. But the same situation may not arise if the Hindus call them for protection against the Muslims.

It is mostly the Muslim community, which has become more vulnerable to the police than any other majority or minority community. Various aspects of the operational reality prove this fact about the role of the police vis-à-vis the Muslim minority people. This has happened due to four major factors.

One, there is an existing incongruence between the constitutional rights of the minorities (differential rights and their fundamental rights as common citizenship rights) and the powers of the police. On the one hand, the Indian constitution pledges to protect and promote the identity rights and safety of the minority. On the other, the Indian Penal Code extends the British-pattern of brutal powers to the police within the criminal justice system and criminal administrative system. Whatever the pronouncement of the constitutional values regarding the accountability of the union and the states to the well being and protection of the minorities be, it stands defeated by the over-riding powers wielded by the police. It is the police, which deal with the local people individually and collectively. Even the institutional mechanisms like the judiciary, vigilance, and complaint cells have not so far reduced either the fear or prejudice of the Muslims against them. In other words, minimum democratic entitlements of the Muslim minority community like 'fundamental rights' remain elusive or got violated on several occasions. Affirmation of the minimum rights to life and security automatically stand negated by the powers vested in the police. Therefore the 'automacity' factor needs to be taken seriously both by the academicians and the decision making elite. The police on their part can receive or reject any complaint of any sort or they can file one on their own. They can take cognizance of any crime, which either happened or was engineered. The police do all the investigations (under Sections 156–73 of the Criminal Procedure Code) in which they act arbitrarily. Despite the provisions of the check on their arbitrariness, there are so many 'riders' within the law that it diminishes the virtual effects of the 'checks' on the police. The rate of acquittal (in case of the majority community) and detention (in case of the Muslims) itself suggests the manner in which investigations are conducted by the police. Framing charges for the police is by no means a tough task.

The Muslims detained for the Godhra carnage have been denied bail whereas the thousands of murderers in the Gujarat genocide are roaming free. It was in the case of the Best Bakery trial, that one of the senior police officers openly stated that there were political instructions to hang up the wireless so to avoid recording the messages and also not to entertain complaints or rescue the Muslims. Judicial decisions depend on the investigations carried out by the police officials. The irony is that once a police report or investigation proposes or suggests name of an innocent person, the report of the investigating officer is considered good enough to hold culpability of that person prima facie. The police have ample powers to detain any person or persons merely on the ground of apprehension of breach of peace, under Section 144 of CrPC. On the pretext of maintaining law and order, the police can misuse its powers. If the police continue to misuse such draconian measures against the Muslims, which have happened almost on a regular basis in violent situations minimum values of democracy, and citizenship rights will remain merely constitutional symbols.

Two soft-pedaled Hindutva of the Congress, the leading national party for over forty years at the centre and in the states, five years of the 'hot pursuits' of the Bhartiya Janta Party and the 'indecisive attitude' of the weak coalition governments of the National Front–Left Front in 1989–90 and 1996–8 at the centre have all contributed in producing a tainted political culture all over the country. Whether it was to defeat the Congress or the 'third force', the rightist forces targeted the Muslim community in their electoral campaigns. The mainstream print and electronic media also followed the party politics in their larger interests to subtly malign the minority. They mobilized the voters on the basis of Muslim, mosque and *madrasa*.

Three, the Hindu majority community which disproportionately dominates the police force in almost all the states and union territories having a Muslim minority, has retained anti-Muslim prejudice due to majoritarian character of the Indian democracy. Muslims are least represented in various structures of power in comparison to others. Besides perpetuating the electoral and parliamentary domination by the majority community, the contemporary political culture based on ethnic and communal considerations and the social configuration of the governmental institutions and service sectors have also contributed to the communalization of the police force. Eventually, this kind of political culture strengthened the communal bias of the police force. In other words, communalism of the police officials was supplemented and complemented by the communalized political culture of the country.

Four, largely it has been a policy of deliberate and benign neglect on the part of the political parties and the people in power. Their policies, assessments, negligence and prejudice based on their political and other considerations have finally resulted in their 'doing nothing' against the communalization of the police force. The situation will remain so until there are fundamental changes made in every state government to reverse the prevalent policy of excluding the Muslims in the police force and also in other sectors.

DISLOCATING THE RULE OF LAW

The study of riots in India provides us with complete and unambiguous evidence of utter violation of the rule of law. The Indian Constitution and the governmental agencies, particularly the law and enforcement agencies are supposed to carry out this principle in pursuance of democracy and the 'social contract' expressed in the constitution making mandatory the protection of minorities and their participation in power sharing. What actually happened after Indian Muslims trusted the Indian State after 1947 is the most pertinent question today. It is not only persons belonging to the majority community but also the police who act collectively against the Muslims. In some cases, where the police followed its code of conduct in dealing with violence, it has either controlled the violence within a short span of time or prevented it from taking place. On the other hand, major riots can be easily identified as a police war against Muslims in collaboration with other local, state and central officials.

Raju from California quotes his friends from Ahmedabad that the 'state machinery has been openly complicit in attacks against Muslims and provocateurs are trying to disrupt even relief lines to riot-torn families'.[1] The Gujarat savagery has been a serendipitous international event telling the truth of India that is 'Bharat'. Leave alone the general Muslim community who are vulnerable to the police, there are examples of how the Muslim elite who are also part of the government and key players in civil society, felt threatened by the police. The Gujarat riots of 2002 have thrown up many such examples. Even some of the officials belonging to the majority community, who wanted to act according to the rule of law, were either transferred or discouraged in their duties. Ex-member of Parliament Ehsan Jafri who lived in an elite locality, was brutally killed by the rioters and his house burnt along with other houses in a very planned way. On the day of the tragedy, he made numerous calls to the high police officials many hours in advance to rescue him or to give some protection so he could shift to some other locality. But nothing happened. It was not a case of inefficiency on the part of the police but a clear case of calloussess generated by communal indoctrination and anti-Muslim syndrome. Cases like these have recurred in many riots. Justice V.R. Krishna Iyer brought out some symptomatic testimony.

Is it true that Justice Qadri, a sitting judge, had to leave his official quarters because of communal intimidation (and lack of police protection by the state) only to seek asylum in a Muslim sanctuary? Or that Baxi, a Muslim, who was the vice-president of the Central Income Tax Tribunal in Ahmedabad, had to take leave for fear of Hindutva hoodlums and flee till he got a transfer to Kolkata? Is it true that revolvers and *trishuls* are available at the VHP centres on payment of Rs. 3,050 provided you declare that you are a Hindu? Is it true that all Muslim police officials have been removed from law and order sections and normal investigation situations and put in innocuous places? Is it true that all the transfers of police officials in Gujarat are under the de facto orders of an extra constitutional authority?[2]

Communal consciousness of a person may become a menace if he or she is employed in the law and order agencies. His communal prejudice is then expressed through guns and by the manipulation of powers in his hands. If this tendency is overlooked again and again by the monitoring and other controlling agencies, then the riots not only get institutionalized but also take shape as a police war against the Muslims. The Gujarat riots are the manifestations of the communal consciousness of the police and their allied agencies, which show their complete disregard to the rule of law.[3] The extensive media coverage has exposed the blatantly partisan role played by the law enforcement system. The police not only failed to protect the lives of innocent persons but on occasions aided and abetted the rioters. Ajit Bhattacharjea observed in his investigative report on the 1969 riots in Ahmedabad, that 'the police failed to take firm action for the first three days and that this was not a matter of slackness but policy'.[4] Iqbal Ansari, who is recognized for his scholarly contributions on the understanding of riots, finds the role of police in major riots in 1980s and 1990s as partisan.[5] Justice Srikrishna observed in his report on the Mumbai riots (1992–3) that 'there was a general bias against the Muslims in the minds of average policemen which was evident in the way they dealt with the Muslims'.[6] Iqbal Ansari refers to V.N. Roy, senior police official who wrote several books on riots and police, for his views that in all the riots studied by him, the police acted more like a Hindu force. His fieldwork revealed that the negatively stereotyped image of Muslims was generally retained by Hindu policemen throughout their career.[7]

The report also says that:

[T]he response of police to appeals from desperate victims, particularly Muslims, was cynical and utterly indifferent. On occasions, the response was that they were unable to leave the appointed post; on others, the attitude

munalism has resulted in violence, terror and discrimination against minorities particularly against the largest minority. Communalization of politics has also 'postponed the shift from feudal, atavistic, emotionally charged passion-politics, which in essence is anti-democratic, to interest-cum-class-based democratic politics, resting on the recognition of individual citizens, as equal and free members of the polity without discrimination made on the basis of tribe, caste, domicile, language, gender, etc'.[20]

Communalism in India has basically implied discord, tension and conflict between its two major communities. Communalism has sought to appropriate rather arbitrarily religious tenets, traditions and values to suit their exigencies of current political life and tactical interests. Communalism exploits parts of religious dogma for expedient political pragmatism. Communalism thus is exploitation, naked and subtle, of religion, and of genuine attachment to a particular religious community. It envisages a religious community alone as the base and universe[21] of its political ambition and action.

Communalism grew stronger mainly due to the fact that the Indian establishment failed to remain a prejudice-free entity. It created the majoritarian image of the state. Rasheeduddin Khan noted in the early 1990s that communalism had 'acquired a most dangerous form and an alarming proportion'[22] which endangered India's multicultural society. He found communalism an affront to India's nationalistic identity and 'as enemy number one of our democratic polity'.[23] Now communalism has spread to many institutions in the country. This phenomenon has been supplemented by perpetuating violence, atrocities and neglect against minorities on the one hand and by providing them least space in public affairs on the other.

S.M. Murshed,[24] a senior civil servant made the following statement:

> In 1969, I was in the home department of the government of West Bengal. Jyoti Basu of the CPM was my minister and also deputy chief minsiter. One day I drew his attention to a copy of a circular issued by the centre which suggested that I should be removed from my post. It said, in effect that Muslims should not hold any sensitive post in government. There was a companion circular to the effect the Muslim applications for passports should be subjected to severe scrutiny. These were first issued in the 1950s and reiterated from time to time. The infamous circulars were obviously based on the premise that the integrity of Muslims in India was suspect. The same notion manifested itself in West Bengal in 1965 during the Indo-Pak war. Thousands of innocent Muslims were arrested and kept in detention without trial on no other ground than their religion.

There is a curious phenomenon which is little known outside the Muslim community. It is communalism vis-à-vis minorities particularly the Muslims in India which seems to raise certain valid questions for Indian democracy. Their remedy could have given a constructive dimension to identity and consciousness in Indian society. Recognition of difference could have really achieved unity in diversity. Over decades differences have increased between the majority and the minority community. Indeed, social identity theory suggests that even trivial differences between people will automatically lead to attempts to discriminate in favour of the 'in group'[25] and against the 'out group'. Imposition of one identity as dominant and permanent majority group on the excluded groups weakens democratic forces.

ETHNICIZATION OF THE ESTABLISHMENT

In the following debate over the ethnicization of the ruling institutions, various agencies of the Indian establishment have maintained the policy of 'benign neglect'. This is to recall that the rightist forces in India not only advocate the imposition of religious tenets of the majority community in the establishment and society but also fan anti-Muslim sentiments. They have remained almost unchecked under the prevalent political culture and administration. These forces affiliated with mainstream political parties have grown in numbers and their offshoots spreading into different branches including the educational and research institutions.

Moreover, there are examples of chief ministers who allowed high ranking bureaucrats to attend the daily meeting of the Rashtriya Swayamsevak Sangh, the 'cultural wing' of the Bharatiya Janata Party. In the, IAS Academy (India's highest civil servant training school) sweets were distributed by the trainees after the domolition of the Baburi Masjid and token puja (religious ceremony) was held there. There are many examples of retired civil servants including senior judges joining communal organizations. There are examples of allocation of prime urban land to religious and semi-religious organizations for building temples and trusts, ignoring the mushroom growth of temples in the residential parks built by the governments in residential and other areas, through illegal land capture. Moreover, the mainstream media has also been guilty of providing wide coverage to the interests of the communal forces on different grounds. There are numerous examples of the manifestation of the extra-legal favour and support to individuals and organizations of the majority community by the governmental agencies at the level of the union/states, and local governing bodies in larger parts of the country.

There are examples of the 'career development' (job promotions, attractive transfers and enterprising deputations) of the police personnel involved in the killings of Muslims in riots. It is not difficult to feel the impact of communal consciousness in the series of security and control management by the centre and the states of the movements of the *kar sevaks*, several politico-religious tours of the BJP–VHP leaders throughout the country, collection of the 'symbolic bricks'from every village of the country and ceremonial puja of these bricks at several places in the context Ayodhya. There were massive anti-Muslim speeches by the leaders leading to disastrous violence against the Muslims in different corners of the country. Such incidents clearly indicate and signify either the 'failure' or the 'deliberate ignorance' on the part of the governmental agencies vis-à-vis the protection and security of the Muslims. There are many examples of the state governments and some railway stations welcoming the arrival of the *kar sevaks* moving to Ayodhya and other services provided to them. All such activities, since 1986, have shown uninterrupted rise of anti-constitutional elements in the country. A question may be asked. Was it possible for any Muslim organization to hold anti-Hindu rallies even in one district of India? Perhaps not. However, its possibility in the case of the rightist forces show emerging bond of relationship or a kind of natural association between the governmental agencies, with few exceptions and the anti-Muslim forces. In other words, such phenomena gives rise to or promotes communalism within the police force as it remains the major institution alongside political actors mobilized by rightist parties. These phenomena give rise to institutional injustice to the Muslims in the country.

Partiality of judgement and the impossibility of justice seems to remain a reality in those societies where equality and justice fail to reach the marginalized section due to socio-cultural differences. In the case of India, such differences seem to be institutionalized at two levels—institutionalization of consciouness within the 'fraternity' and its institutionalization 'outside' the fraternity. The former can be equated with the caste-based differences within one religious community whereas the latter signifies differences between religious communities. But it is also important to mention that despite structural inequalities difference-based caste and communities have also examples of some commonalities and cooperations. Under the feudal system lower castes and upper castes supplemented each other's interests despite the fact that lower castes were vulnerable to the higher castes. Similarly the *Ganga-Jamuni tehzeeb* (composite culture) regarded both religious communities as two eyes of a beautiful bride and their long history witnessed 'give-and-take', at many levels.

The introduction of modern political structures and modern market system began to transform historical pattern of relationships. It did not dismantle identities based on ascriptive characteristics but rather established strong bond between dominant identities and modern polity. On the contrary, liberal democracy was a revolutionary package against this unholy alliance, which developed in this country. Such an alliance can be traced in the rise and perpetuation of those political forces, which have strengthened their foundations in the roots of caste and communal consciousness. Nirja Jayal says that '(T) he superimposition of democracy on these structures was expected to dissolve older ascriptive identities, and create in their stead the new overarching identity of the Indian citizen, equal before law and equal in political voice'.[24]

The Indian establishment, from the union to the block levels has failed to be an impartial institution in many ethnic conflicts or inter-religious feuds. Asish Nandy points out that all too frequently, the ruling party, the bureaucracy, and to an extent the judiciary gets involved in ethnic violence as partisans, a hazard common to nations the world over. These factions also, reluctantly but surely, try to take political advantage of such involvement.[27] Therefore, consolidation of an alliance of modern power structures with the difference-based country of communities provided an opportunity for the 'strong' and the majority community to exploit the sources of modern political authority particularly in the absence of any safeguards or precautionary measues to ensure equality and justice for the minorities.

Power, privileges and representation of a person or group became decisive factors to construct its identity and status. The modern political structure, which was aimed at promoting state's neutrality towards all persons as equal citizens, were overwhelmed by the domination of those privileged persons who belong to the majority community. Several incidents of riots, unemployment and marginalization affecting the Muslim minority, which were also prevalent at the time of independence, were attributed to mass poverty, rural backwardness, weakness of secularism and to the politics of some political parties. It was also attributed to the lack of inter-communal initiatives. But all such formulations of locating justice and equality failed to show positive results. Neither urbanization nor decrease in the level of poverty nor the expansion of the governmental agencies has checked politicization of ethnic and caste consciousness or balanced structural inequalities.

Scholarly works on secularism and frequent elections have proved to be a symbolic exercise of justice towards minorities. The networking for inter-ethnic civic engagements, which were proposed by Ashutosh Varshney,[28] as a solution to ethnic conflict seems to be the remedy for controlling riots. This view can be briefly substantiated by the argument that peace committees or the like may be useful and successful in some places where general masses are well connected to their representatives who can request the government officials and the respective community. These local crisis-management organizations which are formed for temporary purposes and duration, should not be studied in isolation of other realities.

Despite the fact that Muslims constitute more than 20 per cent of the electorate in 197 out of a total 545 parliamentary constituencies, including 79 constituencies with at least 40 per cent Muslim population, in the country their presence in legislatures remain insignificant. In the existing first-past-the post-system, 30 per cent of the vote is enough to win a seat in multiparty contests. Any community, particularly in the Indian situation, whose marginalized factor is self-manifested, cannot be in a position to impress upon the privileged community, on the one hand and the governmental agencies, having majoritarian bias, on the other. Melissa S. Williams' account of 'history' can also give us insight to look into historical factors that led to discrimination and inequality. T.K. Oommen looks into the sociology of affirmative action, which are denied to Muslims and Christians. The presumptions underlying the policy clearly unfold the big divide between native and alien religions.[29]

The Sangh movement has been active to describe the Muslim minority in the country in such a manner as they are a dangerous and undesirable community, who do not qualify for being equal citizens. The Sangh literature and their speeches throughout the country during the Ram Mandir movement and on other occasions clearly showed their prejudices against the Muslim minority. The Sangh movement has succeeded in widening its base even in the remote corners of the country together with their educational, cultural and institutional settings. Majoritarian consciousness is also reflected even in the government managed schools, in their history books, modes of greetings and in formal cultural programmes. It is important to note that all successive governmental authorities ranging from districts to the centre have failed to even check the Sangh Parivar.

The RSS adopted a resolution in Bangalore on 17 March 2002, which said that 'let Muslims understand that their real safety lies in the goodwill of the majority'.[30] This can be related to the idea of the Sangh ideologue, M.S. Golwalkar who said, 'Non-Hindu people in Hindustan must adopt the Hindu culture . . . must entertain no idea but glorification of the Hindu race and culture . . . they must cease to be foreigners or may stay in the country wholly subordinated to the Hindu nation, claiming nothing, deserving no privileges, far less any preferential treatment, not even citizen rights.'[31]

The historical factors also include unilateral majoritarian claim holding Muslims responsible for the creation of Pakistan without going into the details of partition politics. Iqbal Ansari's report on discrimination has included the following factors, (a) concept of exclusivist Hindu cultural nationalism; (b) chauvinist Hindu reading of medieval Indian history treating Muslims as oppressors; (c) viewing Islam as an adversary of Hindu Dharma, which allows recourse to force for political power as well as religious conversion; (d) the bitterness caused by communally divisive politics of 1940s leading to partition; (e) continous unfriendly Indo–Pak relations; (f) perception of renewed threat from the rise of Islamic fundamentalism; (g) Hindu vulnerability arising from its hierarchical-pollutional caste system which makes lower castes willing to leave the fold. They have cumulatively contributed towards developing attitudes and mindsets of large sections of power-wielding Hindus, which provide justification for treating Muslims as a suspect community (even a fifth column of Pakistan), one whose Islamic identity leaves no room for loyalty to the country.[32]

Therefore, the institutionalization of inequalities and marginalization of the Muslim minority has encouraged influential sections of the majority community which include mainly the Sangh activists and their followers as well as the governmental agencies to express their communal consciousness at the time of tensions and violence. It is also important to mention that the benign support of the officials and the provocative role of the Sangh activists succeed in mobilizing sections of the majority to take away the right to life and security. Thus structural inequalities rooted in the communal consciousness-based discrimination affect not only individuals' full participation in the electoral process, but their freedom to participate as equals in all social institutions. Kancha Ilaiah says that 'the Hindu religion, in the context of the existence of many religions in India, is not only majoritarian but has also declared itself to be above the State'.[33]

As a result, the basic purpose of introducing and maintaining many infrastructures of democracy, justice and equality has failed to justify its cause vis-à-vis the Muslim minority. Both Arend Lijphart and John C. Calhoun do not consider voting rights as the ultimate factor for democracy. Voting equality does not bring equality. It is basically the nature of the constitution and development of political culture, which determine judicious distribution of powers, rights and privileges among different sections of the multicultural society. Wherever these fundamental points have not been adhered to, democracy has only served the purpose of the absolute majority. As a result several democracies can be criticized including our own. Many people criticize some democracies for being dominated by groups or the elite that have unequal influence over decisions, while others are marginalized in the policy-making process and its outcomes.[34] Normative critical theory constructs account of these democratic ideals that articulate systematically those feelings of dissatisfaction and lack which we normally experience in actual democratic politics.[35]

Normatively, democratic polity is supposed to fulfil basic objectives such as political equality, deliberation and communication, representation, self-rule and shared-rule. In other words lack of 'equality' and 'justice' does not make a polity really 'democratic'. Structural inequalities caused by 'history of discrimination and oppression[36] deny justice in a democracy. It is also true that our democracies contain structural inequalities—for example, inequalities of wealth, social and economic power, and access to knowledge, status, work expectations. Iris M. Young says, '(T)hese inequalities are unjust to the extent that they help produce or perpetuate institutional conditions which support domination or inhibit self-development.'[37] In her opinion:

> Our democratic policy discussions do not occur under conditions free of coercion and threat, and free of the distorting influence of unequal power and control over resources. In actually existing democracies there tends to be a reinforcing circle between social and economic inequality and political inequality that enables the powerful to use formally democratic processes to perpetuate injustice or preserve privilege.[38]

Despite being quite illuminative about the repercussions of the structured inequality, injustice and discrimination, majority of the Western liberal intellectuals, however, do not provide a ready-made solution to riot related problems in India. The problem of the communalization of police in the country cannot be addressed properly without taking into account the breeding factors. They emanate from the structures of powers. Indian democracy is dominated by the majority community and its continuous approach of 'exclusion' of the Muslims in governmental and non-governmental sectors. Communal prejudice of police cannot be rooted out easily in the Indian context. On the contrary, it can be balanced or checked by the inclusion of the Muslims on the basis of the principles of proportionality. The presence of the Muslims in the police force and in many other enforcement agencies including the judiciary would check the communal element both in the society and in governmental agencies. In fact balancing of the ethnic composition of police and of other representatives and other agencies combined would reset the balance of power in Indian society and polity. Otherwise, existing situation would gradually become worse in the coming years. Declining confidence of the Muslims in the Indian State and police due to the latter's injustice would basically deny the constitutional purpose of elections, development, democracy, secularism and justice enshrined in the Indian Constitution and parliamentary-federal polity.

NOTES

1. Raju Rajagopal, 'A Letter to Chachaji About the Gujarat Riots', *The Hindu*, 26 March 2002, p. OB-1.
2. V.R. Krishna Iyer, 'The Gujarat Syndrome', *The Hindu*, 13 May 2002, p.12.
3. Arshi Khan, 'Situating Riots, Communal Consciousness and Culture of Exclusion in India's Liberal Democracy', *Social Action* (Special Issue on Communal Violence and Nation Building), vol. 52, no. 3, July–September 2002, pp. 258–72; 'Beyond Federalism and Constitutionalism: The Painful Politics and Implications of Communal Consciousness in Gujarat', *Mainstream*, vol. 40, 7 September 2002, pp. 27–9.
4. Iqbal Ansari, 'Pakistan Police', *The Times of India*, 16 April 2002, p. 12.
5. Ibid.
6. Ibid.

7. Ibid.
8. The paragraph of the Report of the Justice B.N. Srikrishna Commission on the Mumbai Riots of 1992–93 is available on http://www.sabrang.com/srikrish/antimin.htm. This website also includes similar excerpts from the justice Jaganmohan Reddy Commission (1969), Justice D.P. Madon Commission (1970), Justice Joseph Vithyathil Commission (1971) and Justice Ranganath Misra Commission on the 1984 anti-Sikh riots in Delhi.
9. Ibid.
10. Ibid.
11. Report of the Commission of Enquiry into the Communal Disturbances at Bhiwandi, Jalgaon and Mahad in May 1970 by Justice D.P. Madon, vol. III, Bombay, n.d, p. 13.
12. News Report, '39 Acquitted in Bhagalpur Riot Case', *The Hindu*, 18 March 2002, p. 5.
13. P.B. D'sa, 'Police Atrocities at Katipalla: Muslims Treated as Anti-national Enemies', *Human Rights Today*, vol. IV, no. 1, January–March 2002, New Delhi, p. 13.
14. Arshi Khan, 'Federalism and Nonterritorial Minorities in India', in G. Alan Tarr, Robert F. Williams and Josef Marko, eds., *Federalism, Subnational Constitutions and Minority Rights*, London: Praeger, 2004, pp. 199–212.
15. Paul R. Brass, 'Development of an *Institutionalised* Riot System in Meerut City 1961 to 1982', *Economic and Political Weekly*, vol. XXXIX, no. 44, 30 October–5 November 2004, pp. 48–9.
16. Arshi Khan, 'Muslims' Pogrom in Bhagalpur', 1989, unpublished paper.
17. Abdulrahim Vijapur, 'Minorities and Human Rights: A Comparative Perspective of International and Domestic Law', in D.L. Sheth and Gurpreet Mahajan, eds., *Minority Identities and the Nation-State*, New Delhi: Oxford University Press, 1999, p. 252.
18. Ibid., p. 252.
19. UN DocE/CN.4/1994/79, dated 20 January 1994.
20. Rasheeduddin Khan, *Bewildered India: Identity, Pluralism, Discord*, New Delhi: Har-Anand, 1994, p. 199.
21. Ibid., p. 204.
22. Ibid., p. 208.
23. Ibid.
24. 'Muslim Factor in India', *The Times of India*, 16 February 1993.
25. Ann Phoenix, 'Dealing with Difference: the recursive and the new', *Ethnic and Racial Studies*, vol. 21, no. 5, September 1998, p. 861.
26. Nirja Gopal Jayal, 'Introduction: Situating Indian Democracy', *Democracy in India*, New Delhi: Oxford University Press, 2001, p. 24.
27. Asish Nandy, 'The Political Culture of the Indian State', *Daedalus*, 4, Fall 1989, p. 10.

28. Ashutosh Varshney, 'Ethnic Conflict and Civil Society', *World Politics*, 3 April 2001, pp. 362–98.
29. T.K. Oommen, *State and Society in India: Studies in Nation-Building*, New Delhi: Sage, 1990, p. 213.
30. *The Hindu*, 18 March 2002, p. 1.
31. M.S. Golwalkar, *We Or Our Nationhood Defined*, Nagpur, 1947, pp. 56–7.
32. Iqbal A. Ansari, 'Report on Intolerance and Discrimination Against Muslims in India', paper presented to the NGO workshop during the World Conference Against Racism, Durban, 27 August–7 September 2001.
33. 'Major Priorities: Religion Cannot Highjack the Polity', *The Times of India*, 8 March 2002, p. 14.
34. Iris Marion Young, *Inclusion and Democracy*, New York: Oxford University Press, 2000, p. 11.
35. Ibid., *Justice and the Politics of Difference*, Princeton: Princeton University Press, 1990, pp. 5–7.
36. Melissa S. Williams, 'Memory, History and Membership: The Moral Claims of Marginalized Groups in Political Representation', in Juha Raikka, ed., *Do We Need Minority Rights? Conceptual Issues*, The Hague: Martinus Nijhoff Publishers, 1966, p. 86.
37. Iris Marion Young, *Inclusion and Democracy*, p. 34.
38. Ibid., p. 17.

CHAPTER 10

Police Partisanship during Communal Riots: Need for its Secularization and Pluralization

IQBAL A. ANSARI

Police in a law-governed democratic country like India, where citizens have been guaranteed protection of right to life, liberty and equality, cannot perform its basic duty, if it is organized as a ruler appointed body carrying out policies of the government based on cynical political calculations for consolidation of power. Unfortunately the police in India is still functioning under the 1861 Act as a policy enforcement and not as a law enforcement body, as noted by the National Police Commission (NPC) (1979–81) in its second report.[1] Rule of law and protection of life, liberty and equality of members of vulnerable sections like religious minorities get further undermined if the police personnel have biased attitudes towards minorities, making them behave in a partisan manner especially during situations of communal conflicts and violence. The situation gets further aggravated if the composition of the police and security forces is overwhelmingly majoritarian.

All these factors, i.e. subservience to the executive, communally biased attitudes and majoritarian social composition, responsible for partisan functioning of the police and security forces have been in full operation during the four decades of communal violence in India.

The three major incidents of violence against minorities in Independent India, i.e. the 1984 anti-Sikh pogroms, the 1992 demolition of Baburi Masjid and widespread violence in its wake, and the genocidal killings of Muslims in Gujarat 2002 can be attributed to the partisan role of the police which, instead of performing their duty as an impartial law enforcement force, became passive or active participants in the acts of killings, destruction of property and places of worship, arson, loot, and rape.

In May 1987 the PAC of Uttar Pradesh picked up Muslims from their homes, took them in trucks to Ganga canal near Murad Nagar, Ghaziabad, shot more than forty of them dead and threw their dead bodies into the canal. The incident was universally condemned as a kind of Nazi pogrom against the Muslim minority to terrorize them.[2]

Such partisan role of the police has been well documented. It was noted by the NPC in its Sixth Report on Communal Riots (1981), which makes the following observations[3]:

> We also heard of stringent criticism from many responsible quarters that the police do not often act with impartiality and objectivity. Several instances have been cited where police officers and men appear to have shown unmistakable bias against a particular community while dealing with communal situation. Serious allegations of highhandedness and other atrocities, including such criminal activities as arson and looting, molestation of women, etc., have been levelled against the police deployed to protect the citizens. There is evidence to suggest that in one recent riot, the police resorted to uncontrolled firing, killing many people of the congregation and later indulged in looting, and arson, when some of their colleagues were assaulted by the crowd. In another incident, it is alleged that a group of anti-social elements was able to brutally kill many persons, including women and children, while the police was present in the vicinity. In yet another recent incident it has been alleged that the force ran amuck after one of their colleagues was stabbed. All these incidents are only symptoms of the underlying malaise. The failure of leadership coupled with the low morale of the force leads to such indisciplined reaction from the force.

In 1982 N.C. Saxena, the then Joint Secretary of the National Commission For Minorities (NCM) inquired into the riots in Meerut and reported that 'the district administration perceived threat to public peace only from Muslims . . . the order from the senior officers in the district to the police could be "summarized in one phrase: 'Muslims must be taught a lesson". The PAC, and the Police faithfully implemented this policy.'[4]

In 1983 N.C. Saxena carried out a study for the NCM on the attitudes and perceptions of the magistrates and senior police officers about various communities during riots. The following are the conclusions of the study[5]:

(a) Riots take place in such districts where Muslims are either in a majority or they constitute a sizable minority.
(b) Muslims are excitable and irrational people who are guided by their religious instincts. Hindus, on the other hand, are law abiding and cooperate with the police in controlling communal violence.
(c) Riots are started by the Muslims and they invariably take the first opportunity to strike at the other community and at the police.
(d) In all other previous riots in the country before the current riot, Muslims took the upper hand which resulted in huge loss to the Hindu community. Therefore, there is moral justification if in the current riot, casualties on the Muslim's side are heavier.
(e) State Government attaches a great deal of importance in ensuring quick control of rioting. Since Muslims are aggressive, therefore, in order to control violence, it is necessary that Muslim mobs must be taught a lesson through arrests, firing and third degree methods.

The study further reports that

> the PAC treats Muslims as monsters, criminals and suspects. It has led to loss of faith among Muslims in the fairness of administration. They have started patronizing anti-social elements for their defence and in the recent riots attacks on police from the Muslim side have also increased. Police-Muslim confrontation, if not checked, may lead to terrorism just as in some countries like Philippines, Thailand, Muslim terrorism has assumed an alarming proportion.

In his dissertation on *Perception of Police Neutrality During Hindu-Muslim Riots in India,* V.N. Rai, a senior police officer, reports the following findings based on field study:[6]

(a) Police behave partially during most riots. In all the riots discussed in this study, they did not act as a neutral law enforcement agency but more as a 'Hindu' force.
(b) Perceptible discrimination was visible in the use of force, preventive arrests, enforcement of curfew, treatment of detained persons at police stations, reporting of facts and investigation, detection and prosecution of cases registered during riots. Muslims suffered in all of the above mentioned areas.

(c) An average policeman does not shed his prejudices and predetermined beliefs at the time of his entry into the force, and this is reflected in his bias against Muslims during communal violence.
(d) The inimical relationship between police and Muslims make them over-react in a confrontation-like situation.

The following extracts from two major official inquiry reports into riots of Bhiwandi, Jalgaon and Mahad (1970) by Justice D.P. Madon and that of Mumbai (1992–3) by Justice B.N. Srikrishna convincingly establish the communally partisan role of the police over a long period, which has continued till Gujarat 2002 pogrom.

Justice D.P. Madon reported the following conclusions of his inquiry[7]:

103.145: Several instances have been proved before the Commissions in which police officers and policemen either did not prevent the Hindu rioters from indulging in rioting, looting or arson or showed communal discrimination in dealing with the rioting mobs, or gave incorrect report to the Control Room or lodged incorrect FIRs, in order to make out that the persons who had rioted or were responsible for looting or arson in particular incidents were Muslim rioters and not Hindu rioters, or actively assisted the Hindu rioters in burning and looting Muslim properties.

103.148: Discrimination was also practised in making arrests and while Muslims rioters were arrested in large numbers, the police turned a blind eye to what the Hindu rioters were doing. Some innocent Muslims were, arrested knowing them to be innocent. Some innocent Muslims who went to take shelter at the Bhiwandi Town Police Station were arrested instead of being given shelter and protection.

103.65: The evidence before the Commission has established the following facts with respect to the working of the Special Investigation Squad set up to investigate all riot cases:

1. The working of the Special Investigation Squad, Bhiwandi, is a study in communal discrimination.
2. The officers of the Squad systematically set about implicating as many Muslims and exculpating as many Hindus as possible irrespective of whether they were innocent or guilty.
13. No investigation was conducted into the composition and activities of Hindu communal and allegedly communal organizations operating in Bhiwandi but only in respect of Muslim communal and allegedly communal organizations.

against police attempt to arrest a student against whom another student had lodged complaint. Both the students happened to be Muslims. The following are some of the observations of the PUCL report: [9]

'The ones (students) sporting beard had their beard pulled, while doing this the police was using filthy words, and abusing the students for following a particular faith.'

The Report's conclusion include the following:

'The taunting, tortures and humiliations of the students on the ground of faith is a serious matter. It shows increasing communalization of the Delhi Police.' The team of inquiry included Justice (Retd.) R.B. Mehrotra and Dr. Anup Saraya.

The following are some of the findings of the PUDR Report: [10]

'The police entered room after room and fell upon the students calling them ISI agents and other communal abuses and asked non-Muslim students why they were in Jamia.'

'All the students we talked to, whether Hindu and Muslim, charged the policemen with making a special target of anyone who was bearded and was wearing a kurta-pyjama. The Masjid in the compound was broken into and the Imam, himself a Ph.D. student, was beaten up.'

Other studies on police have reported biased attitudes and partisan conduct as more pervasive and reprehensible than its brutality and corruption. For example in its study on *Police-Public Interface*, 2001,[11] the Commonwealth Human Rights Initiative (CHRI) reported that the 'number of public respondents who regarded the police as partial was larger than the number who considered them as brutal or corrupt'. Its earlier study on *Police Brutality in India*, 2000, the CHRI reported that 'members of the minority communities or those belonging to lower caste have often perceived the police as a biased and partisan agency. . . .'

It sadly notes that 'the police have failed to design a system, which would prevent the entry of wrong types of people into the organisation'.[12]

Such blatantly partisan role of the police has made organized Hindutva groups feel bold to pursue their hate speech and hate crimes against Muslims, Sikhs and Christians to terrorize them into submission. Impunity enjoyed by them is the major source of persistence of violence against minorities.

It was rightly pointed out in the NCM study report (1983) by N.C. Saxena that Police–Muslim confrontation, if not checked, may lead to terrorism. The prediction came true in Bombay serial bomb blasts in March 1993, about which Justice Srikrishna Report made the observation that it was the Muslim experience of the police joining hands with rioters that made them angry and desperate, and in frustration they sought revenge.

Similarly the Coimbatore bomb blast at L.K. Advani's meeting on 14 February 1998 had its origin in the killing of 18 Muslims in an indiscriminate and undisciplined police firing on 30 November 1997 in the town. The relation between the two acts of unlawful use of force by the police and the frustrated sections of the oppressed Muslim community has been established by Justice P.R. Gokula Krishna inquiry report tabled in the Tamil Nadu Assembly on 18 May 2000. Such unlawful use of firepower by the police targeting Muslims to terrorize them started in late seventies at places like Aligarh (1978) and Moradabad (1980) which continued in the 1980s and 1990s, culminating in Gujarat 2002, which were followed by terrorist attacks on Akshardham temple and bomb blasts in Mumbai on 25 August 2003.

In spite of such a dismal record of four decades of partisan policing taking a heavy toll of life, limb and dignity and destruction of property and places of worship and in spite of non-delivery of rehabilitative justice to victims and punishment of the guilty, Indian Muslims have not joined any international terrorist outfit. This is a fact testified by observers and monitors of the scene of international terrorism including several eminent Indians. It is unfortunate that instead of giving due priority to reforming the police and other wings of law-enforcement and justice delivery system in the light of the recommendations of the NPC (1979–81), NHRC (1993/4–2002) and National Commission For Minorities (1999), for impartial, effective and humane law-enforcement for prevention and control of communal violence, the Government of India's agenda of 'good governance' makes it take recourse to draconian laws like TADA and POTA which is being indiscriminately used to terrorize Muslims. This has led to further alienation and frustration in the community.

'Good governance' primarily means rule of law and observance of human rights norms of equality and non-discrimination and guarantee of protection of life and freedom and dignity of all vulnerable sections and justice to all victims.

The following are some of the reform measures that are required to be implemented for good governance, making the police function as an instrument of rule of law in a country where communal conflicts have a long history and where the agenda of some organizations, political as well as ethno-religious, includes subverting the constitutional order, making Muslims target of hate and revenge for perceived historical wrongs.

1. The present command-control system of the Police under the 1861 Act which makes it function as a ruler-appointed state–centric subordinate body to provide maximum political satisfaction to the ruling party, should be replaced by a citizen–centric system which enables the police to function independent of political directions, making it accountable to law. It requires overall supervision of an independent statutory State Security Commission (SSC) having its branches in the districts.

The posting, transfer and promotions of police personnel and punitive actions against them to be subject to review by the SSCs.

1.1. It will also require amendment of the service rules of magistrates and police officers making them liable to legal proceedings including payment of compensation to victims in the event of their failure of omission and commission leading to communal violence (or any other inter-group disorder), established by an independent Inquiry Commission (not under the present Commission of Inquiry Act, but appointed in a manner suggested by NCM Report 1999).

2. The training of the police at the initial stage and also periodic (annual, biannual, etc.) training programmes should have strong component of human rights including the right to dignity, equality and non-discrimination of all citizens.

2.1. Special course on eradication of communal prejudices and negative-stereotypes of communities acquired by police-personal from the society.

The course should include field-work by way of inter-group interaction and communal living together for a period.

3. Numerical composition of all wings of law-enforcement system including the civil police, the paramilitary forces, the intelligence gathering agencies and authorities entrusted with investigation and prosecution should be socially diverse ensuring the presence of vulnerable minorities at all levels, not only to the extent of their share in population but adequate enough to make the police force a good mix of caste, religious, regional and gender diversity.

Such a socially diverse body will ensure neutralization of biases within the police-personnel manning the system. It will also inspire more confidence in the vulnerable sections of society like Muslims and other minorities, who will thus stop perceiving police as their enemy.

4. Training of the police in more humane, intelligent and effective methods of riot prevention and control, seeking cooperation of civil society.

4.1. Amendment of the Police Manual and riot control scheme on use of force and firepower, directing the police to use non-lethal methods of mob control. Use of firepower should be governed by UN Basic Principles on the Use of Force & Firepower by Law-enforcement Officials (1990) which requires use of firepower proportionate to the situation only when there is grave imminent threat to life (and not to property), and when all other methods have been exhausted.

The idea of State Security Commission is based on the National Police Commission's basic reform measure suggested in its second report to make police functionally independent of political policy directions and interference by the government and the ruling party. It has been endorsed, among others, by the NHRC and the NCM. In the context of communal carnages, it is important to bear in mind that the partisan role of the police cannot be attributed mainly to the communal attitudes and behaviour of the police-personnel alone. Its major source lies in the partisan political direction of the executive based on cynical political calculations. The PAC in UP, for example, used firepower against *kar sevaks* to protect the Baburi Masjid in 1990 under the government of Mulayam Singh. However the same PAC became either a passive spectator or an active facilitator of the destruction of the Masjid in 1992 under a different political dispensation of Kalyan Singh, whose consolidation of power required this policy-direction.

It is well known that the present Mulayam Singh government in UP succeeded in controlling the mob without use of firepower on and before 17 October 2003 in Ayodhya when assembly of lakhs of people posed serious threat to peace. Mulayam Singh was fortunate in having senior police officers like V.N. Rai to clinically do the job of mob control, without using excessive force. Let this serve as a model to be institutionalized.

On the issue of training of the police in secular attitudes and observance of human rights norms, there cannot be any two opinions. There is however a need to rethink components of attitudinal-behavioural training, for which good course material including audio-visual, should be developed, emphasizing non-discrimination and eradication of prejudices and stereotypes.

The issue of socially diverse composition of the police and other institutions of governance is the most neglected one in the country. Under the false plea of secularism, community-wise data are generally not published. But there is no denying the fact that Muslims are under-represented in most central and state forces at all levels and in all areas of operation.

Apart from the Durban Declaration and POA 2001, to which India is a party, which requires socially diverse composition of all institutions of governance especially state forces and the judiciary, the National Commission to Review the Working of the Constitution (NCRWC) in its Report (2002) has made strong recommendation for carrying out 'special recruitment . . . of persons belonging to the under-represented minority communities in the State police, para-military forces and armed forces'. The Commission holds the view that 'this will instill confidence among minority populations as well as help them to develop responsible attitudes towards security issues confronting the nation.'[13]

In 1983 Prime Minister's Fifteen Point Programme on Minorities emphasized the need for such special recruitment. The following were its specific recommendations:

1. In the recruitment of police personnel, state governments should be advised to give special consideration to minorities. For this purpose, the composition of selection committees should be representative.
2. The Central Government should take similar action in the recruitment of personnel to the Central Police Forces.

The NPC also felt that there is a strong case for encouraging the recruitment of members of the minority community and other weaker sections at various levels in the police force.

The following observations of the NPC need attention:[14]

47.57: We would reiterate here our views already expressed in para 19.30 of our Third Report that the composition of the personnel in the police system as a whole should reflect the general mix of communities as exists in society and thereby command the confidence of the different sections so that the system would function impartially without any slant in favour of any community. In this regard the senior officers, particularly in positions of command have an important role to play. If they act in a correct and impartial manner and also discourage emphatically any partial or biased behaviour on the part of their subordinates, they can by their example instill confidence in the minds of the people regarding the ability and impartiality of not only themselves but of the entire force.

The Home Ministry's guidelines (for governments of all states and union territories) to promote communal harmony issued on 22 October 1997 makes the following recommendations:

4.4: It has been commonly observed that the presence of minority community members in the police force deployed in communally sensitive areas goes a long way in winning the confidence of the minority communities. This is of vital importance. The following steps which were recommended from time to time, should be taken earnestly:

(1) Launching of special campaigns to recruit more members of minorities in the State Police Force.
(2) Creation of composite battalions of armed police which should include members of all religious communities including SCs/STs, for exclusive use in maintaining communal peace and amity in the sensitive areas.
(3) Starting of special training/orientation programmes for State Police Force with a view to maintaining communal harmony.

In the light of these observations there is a need to develop firm policy measures for making police force qualitatively secular in attitude and behaviour and socially diverse in composition ensuring effective presence of vulnerable minorities and weaker sections not only at the lower level but at all levels.

After making the magistracy and the police function independent of the politically motivated policy directions, they must be made accountable to law, for which there is a need to amend their service rules making them liable to penal action including payment of compensation to victims, in the event of failure to prevent and control communal (and other inter-group) violence. Such a measure was recommended by the National Integration Council in 1968. We also consider making the provisions of law more stringent for offences related to hate speech and hate crimes committed by the police.

It is well that 'good governance' has acquired wide acceptance as a matter of primary concern by the citizenry and the political class in the country. But it is not widely realized that the rule of law, transparency and accountability constitute vital components of good governance.

It is a pity that even the human rights movement is not giving the issue of reform of the system the priority that it deserves.

NOTES

1. *Second Report of the National Police Commission (NPC) 1979*, New Delhi: Ministry of Home Affairs, Govt. of India.
2. Nikhil Chakravarty compared the event with 'Nazi pogrom against the Jews, to strike terror and nothing but terror in the whole minority community'.

   The Amnesty International's Inquiry Report observed that 'there is evidence to suggest that members of the PAC have been responsible for dozens of extra-judicial killings and disappearances' (AI Index: ASA/20/06/87).
3. *Sixth Report of the NPC*, 1981.
4. N.C. Saxena, 'Report on Meerut Riots 1982', in Iqbal A. Ansari (ed.) *Communal Riots, The State & Law In Indian*, New Delhi: IOS, 1979 p. 365.
5. N.C. Saxena, ibid.
6. V.N. Rai, *'Combating Communal Conflicts: Perception of Police Neutrality During Hindu-Muslim Riots in India'*, Mussoorie: LBS National Academy of Administration, 1996.
7. *Report of the Commission of Inquiry Into Communal Disturbances At Bhiwandi, Jalgaon and Mahad (1970)* by Justice D.P. Madon, vol. VI, pts. VI & VII.
8. *Report of the Commission of Inquiry Into the Riots of Mumbai 1992–3* by Justice B.N Srikrishna, vol. I.
9. *PUCL Report: Helpless Victims Crying for Justice*, pp. 2, 6.
10. *Bloody Sunday: Brutal Attack on Jamia Students*, Delhi: PUDR, May 2002.
11. *Police-Public Interface*, 2001, CHRI, New Delhi: CHRI, 2001.
12. *Police Brutality in India*, New Delhi: CHRI, 2000.
13. *Report of the NCRWC*, Chapter 10, para 10.11.2 (d).
14. *Sixth Report of the NPC*, op. cit.

CHAPTER 11

Need for People Friendly Police

CHAMAN LAL

An honest intellectual discourse on role of the Police is a welcome change because it shows that there is hope for saner elements in the force; that everything is not lost; that the academic community is willing to talk about the police by shedding their earlier 'hands off' attitude. It establishes the fact they want to talk about it with seriousness and in an atmosphere of academic freedom and with an analytical maturity. It is common to talk about police but such a discourse would invariably concern itself with only what is wrong with them. Why has the police failed? Why has the police not been able to win the trust and confidence of the people? Why does it suffer from a poor image? Wherever the police force is discussed, it is with a view to finding answers to these questions. As a Police Officer, I welcome this. I have been an IPS Officer of the rank of DG of police who has spent a lot of time in security forces. I also volunteered for postings in 'difficult' places—Punjab, J&K, Nagaland among others.

When we talk of the role of police, it is of course the role of police in a country like ours, a country that has been described as a sovereign, democratic and socialist republic in the Constitution. How is the police supposed to function in a country like ours which has diversity of every kind—ethnic, religious, social and cultural? There is no document which can explain the expected role of police in a country like ours. The only document that is available and which forms the basis of our functioning is the archaic Police Act of 1861 which was enacted in the context of the mutiny of 1857. The sole purpose of this Act was to provide for a police which could prevent and investigate crime, maintain order and protect the overall colonial interests. The concept of a people friendly police was alien to this Act and there was no mention of the citizen in it. Even after independence, the police in India has continued to be governed by this Act. This is why the police has not been able to play a larger role in the process of social transformation. I do not want to delve into the role of police as an agent or catalyst of change, as opinion on this is divided even in police circles. However, the implementation of social legislation such as Anti-Dowry Law, Child Labour Act, etc., offers the police an opportunity to act as a positive catalyst and speed up the process of social reform. But this would be possible if the policeman goes beyond combat capabilities.

All these years, we have been thinking largely about our combat capabilities only. I hate the use of the word 'force' with police—'police force'. We should not say that. Police is not supposed to be a force. Because when we use this term, we get obsessed with militarization and that is what is exactly happening in our country. We are militarizing the police, giving them more and more sophisticated weapons, more and more training on army lines. It is true that the police is now required to deal with more difficult and challenging problems than simple crime control and maintenance of law and order. The police is involved in a big way in dealing with problems of internal security such as communalism, terrorism, insurgency, left-wing extremism. Unfortunately because of our obsession with militarization, we are tackling these problems only by treating their symptoms without analysing the root causes. When we deal with symptoms, we only get immediate results and feel elated thinking that we have done wonders. But more often than not such immediate results are scored at the cost of long-term objectives. Experience tells that whenever temporary success is achieved through expediency, a heavy price has to be paid in the long run. That is why I am of the view that the police must go beyond the concept of militarization, beyond combat capabilities and build partnership and alliances with various segments of civil society and get involved in the process of social transformation.

A reference has been made to some study on police undertaken by some university. In my view most of such studies are unrealistic and totally academic. I am a believer in the worth of small efforts which can create some change in the lives of the people. That is what Asghar Ali Engineer and Julio Rebeiro are doing in Mumbai and some other activists in Gujarat. That is what the academic community should take up.

When we talk about the role of police, we should also consider the service-role which is unfortunately not mentioned in the Police Act of

1861. In actual practice, it would mean that the police is required not only to observe but also protect and promote the human rights of citizens. The National Human Rights Commission (NHRC) has, while dealing with Gujarat incidents, evolved a new principle of human rights jurisprudence. It has clearly stated that the State is responsible for preventing the violation of human rights of citizens not only by its public servants but also the non-State players. The police are, therefore, guilty of violation of human rights not only when they indulge in such acts themselves but also when innocent lives are lost in communal riots because of their incompetence or partisanship. It is unfortunate that questions are being raised increasingly about police impartiality in the handling of communal riots in recent years.

It has become fashionable these days for every police officer to say that police needs autonomy. Let us consider this issue of police autonomy. The police is totally autonomous in matters of investigation, as no agency can issue any directions in such matters. Only in the area of preventive action which is quasi-judicial, instructions and directions can be issued by the political and administration executive. Everybody says there is political interference in police work. Yes, it is there but largely because it is sought by most police officers. I have always felt that what is called political interference is a result of an unhealthy partnership in a dirty business of over-ambitious civil servants and unscrupulous politicians. I believe that even in the present system where everything is being found wrong, it is possible to work according to your conscience if you are prepared to pay the price of being different from others. The trouble is that most people do not want to pay the price of being different. They want postings at a good place; they want this for their children and that for their wife. And it is possible only if they become part of the system. But if you want to do the right thing, it is still possible but you should have the inner strength to face any attack from unscrupulous politicians.

Now the question of making the police autonomous and giving it more powers! I am of the view that we should first reform the police before we give it any more powers or make it totally autonomous. If you make police autonomous without introducing reforms to bring it in tune with the principles of democratic jurisprudence, you will be helping in the process of their becoming law unto themselves and that is what has happened in most parts of our country.

The second point is accountability of the police and proper superintendence and control over it. Under the Police Act of 1861, the superintendence and control over the police had been given to the executive—administrative and political, i.e. the DM at the district level and the Home Minister at the state level. What is the system in the UK? In the UK, the minister has no control over the police. He only has responsibility—the responsibility to ensure that the police under him functions efficiently and effectively. We need that kind of conceptualization, where the superintendence and control over police is meant for the purpose of ensuring that it is efficient, and conforms to law. This is exactly what the National Police Commission (NPC) has recommended. They have devised a system of people's control over police called the State Security Commission (SSC) which would meet the requirements of autonomy as well as accountability.

The NPC has also recommended a change in the existing system of evaluating police performance which is statistics-oriented. The performance of a police station or an individual officer is judged on the basis of the number of cases registered, the number of cases detected, the amount of property lost, the amount of property recovered and arrests made, etc. This deters free registration of crime. It is sad but true that while earlier you needed *sifarish* to get a culprit arrested or your innocent nephew released, now you need a word from somebody influential to get your complaint registered by the police. The NPC has recommended evaluation of police perfor-mance by assessing the credibility and image of the police and its ability to establish rapport and win trust and confidence of the community. One of the tasks of the State Security Commission would be to make an annual review of the performance of police and issue suitable directives and guidelines for its improvement.

The last point which I must consider is the accountability of the police. What is the present system of police accountability? Police is accountable to political leadership, to executive leadership, to the superior in the department and to the law in the descending order. Accountability to people who are sovereign does not figure anywhere in this scheme. Since the police officers derive their powers from the people who have made them trustees of their powers, they must be made directly accountable to the people. While more than 50 years have elapsed since independence and a lot of changes have taken place on political, social, economic and cultural fronts, nothing has been done to change the basic character of police in India. It is for this reason that the NPC has recommended radical changes in the role, structure, powers and procedure of the police and emphasized its accountability to the people. Realizing that police reforms cannot be considered in isolation, the NPC recommended that the Indian Law Commission should be restructured and made the Indian Criminal Justice Law Commission with representation from all the wings of the criminal justice system.

While violence and crime are on the rise, the conviction rate of police cases has been steadily falling. Why are police cases failing in court? Why in 23 districts of the UP, conviction rate in murder cases has been zero for the last 10 year? Why is it not possible for the police to fight terrorists under the rule of law? Why are fake encounters being considered inevitable and essential? If we give a serious thought to these questions, we will come to the conclusion that law is under suspension in our country or the criminal justice system has collapsed. There is no dearth of laws to take care of any problem facing us. Are additional laws required to deal with problems like terrorism? Not only now, even 10 years back when I was involved in fighting terrorism in Punjab, I used to say 'no' to this question. I am of the view that all that is needed is strict, fair and impartial enforcement of existing laws on 365-days-a-year basis. Every law, even the municipal by-laws, must be enforced to restore people's habit to obey law. What have we done during the last five decades in dealing with violence? We have sent out the message that only violence pays. The issue of 'law and order' has been turned into 'law or order'. While dealing with problems like student agitation, labour unrest or harassment of Dalits, the police allow the law to be violated in their anxiety to maintain an order which invariably turns out to be fake or spurious.

There may be occasions when we need additional laws to deal with exceptionally difficult situations like terrorism and insurgency. But these laws are required to be periodically reviewed to judge their efficacy and ensure that safeguards and checks and balances provided in them are observed. It is also necessary to see that they are linked directly with the problem that necessitated their enactment and whether it is necessary to extend them or repeal them. It is unfortunate that special laws giving additional powers to police and security forces adopted as temporary measures to deal with exigencies of an abnormal situation ultimately become permanent pieces of legislation open to large-scale abuse. That is what was happening with TADA. I am of the view that our existing laws are adequate for dealing with our current and future problems if we re-define the role of police and its powers and make it accountable to the law and answerable to the people.

Human Rights—the rights relating to life, liberty, equality and dignity of the individual—are the very essence of the rule of law. Though evolved over the centuries through political, religious and cultural traditions of the civilized world, they were formally put in the United Nation Declaration of Human Rights (1948) and the International Covenants on Civil and Political Rights (1966) and Economic, Social and Cultural Rights (1966). They enjoy a special significance in the Indian context in that almost the entire gamut of these rights has been incorporated in the Constitution of India in the form of Fundamental Rights and the Directive Principles of State Policy.

It is a peculiarity of the Indian situation that the issue of Human Rights has come into public focus in a rather negative way. Human Rights have become a matter of public concern in view of increasing incidence of arbitrary arrests, illegal detentions, custodial violence and other abuses of power resorted to by the law enforcement agencies, especially in the states affected by terrorism and insurgency. The mis-governance reflected in the failure of the administration to ensure that the citizens enjoy the constitutionally guaranteed fundamental rights is found to be a crucial contributory factor in the growth of militancy in the country.

The entry of the human rights issue into public consciousness coincides with the growth of terrorist and separatist movements in Punjab and J&K in the mid-1980s and early 1990s. The issue has also acquired importance due to the attempts of the US and other Western powers to link the international aid to the developing nations with their human rights record on the ground that the human rights situation in any country in today's world is not a domestic matter but the legitimate concern of the international community. The proliferation of NGOs and other groups especially in the areas affected by militancy in recent years has also added to the popularity of the subject.

With the establishment of the NHRC in 1993 the police leadership in India has come under great pressure to put its house in order and sensitize the rank and file for observance of human rights. The police organizations are seen vying with each other in running special training programmes, organizing seminars and making films based on real case studies for educating and sensitizing their staff about their duty to uphold and protect the right of the citizens. This new found craze for human rights is mostly found wanting in substance and is cynically described by the human rights activists as part of the fashion of the day which may better the look of the police without improving its performance. It is also observed, on the other hand, that some human rights groups take their concerns to impracticable and absurd levels leading to misgivings in the minds of even well meaning police officers.

It is sad but true that the human rights NGOs and other groups are perceived as adversaries by the law enforcement agencies in India. Both the sides can be generally seen taking opposite and at times, extreme positions on the question of human rights giving rise to an unseemly controversy.

The NGOs hold that the law enforcement agencies should not only respect the human rights of the law-abiding citizens but also the criminals including the terrorists and insurgents and follow the due process even while dealing with serious situations of internal security. The Police, they insist, must adhere to the fundamental principles of jurisprudence that emphasize the innocence of the accused till the contrary is proved against him. They hold that even the dreaded terrorists should be allowed to enjoy all the rights that our Constitution and procedural laws grant to the accused persons. They are not willing to accept the police argument that it is compelled to exceed its brief and cross the legal boundaries because of the increasing inability of the criminal justice system to cope with the challenge of organized violence. They oppose the special laws and enactment, which give additional powers to the police and security forces to fight militancy. It is also argued that these challenges must be met by using the normal legal provisions. They brand special laws such as TADA, the Armed Forces (Special Powers) Act, the National Security Act, the Unlawful Assembly Act, the Disturbed Areas Act, etc., as draconian and black laws which violate the principles of liberal jurisprudences and natural justice and undermine the safeguards provided in the Constitution. They demand that all the domestic laws should conform to the norms and standards of the International Human Rights Instruments. They are not satisfied by the Judicial pronouncement of their validity even by the Apex Court (TADA was held constitutionally valid by the Supreme Court).

I wish to make it clear that while expressing the view point of the police and other law enforcement agencies, I am voicing the feelings of the competent and conscientious officers who respect the law, accept the limitations of their functions and powers and take every professional challenge seriously. This category excludes the vast majority of police officers who resent any restrictions on their powers and are easily given to circumventing the law to seek an easy and quick solution to their problems.

My experience in Punjab and the north-east tells me that the cause of an adversarial relationship between police and the genuine NGOs (there is no dearth of fake NGOs in any field of our public life) is not a clash of values but a lack of understanding about each other's role and difficulties. I firmly believe that it is possible for the two to bridge their differences and work unitedly for the cause of human rights. I sincerely believe that the NGOs need to give a practical orientation to their approach in the light of the contextual realities to facilitate actual realization of the basic human rights instead of striving hopelessly for an ideal situation. They would do well to shed their prejudices against the police and security forces based on a limited experience of individual cases.

Human rights violations in situations of terrorism and insurgency call for a careful handling. Though no violation, big or small should be condoned, each individual case has to be viewed in the overall operational context to find out whether the act was deliberate and malafide or it was accidental and bonafide. This would help in determining the gravity of the lapse and deciding commensurate punishment. Human right activists can very well appreciate the compulsions and constraints under which the police and security forces have to work in situations which compel use of force including fire power. It is impossible to conceive a situation where such force is used and no one gets hurt. It needs to be realized that in situations where the security forces are deliberately attacked by the militants in the thickly populated areas in order to provoke a retaliatory fire, it is impossible to ensure full protection of innocent civilians and complete avoidance of collateral damages.

The natural instinct of a soldier to fire back in the direction of the actual attack, is something that needs to be appreciated. However, the inconvenience and hardship caused has also to be appreciated. Though the inconvenience and hardship caused to the general population by anti-terrorist measures can be minimized considerably, it cannot be avoided totally. The investigation of terrorist crimes will always involve a vigorous questioning of a large number of suspects, many of whom may ultimately turn out to be innocent. The police and security forces cannot help being harsh with those who provide food and shelter to the militants even though such help may be prompted by the fear of gun rather than sympathy to the militants' cause.

The police leadership at all levels of command has to accept the fact that observance of human rights is mandated by law and under no circumstance should there by any abuse regarding it. The custodians of law cannot be allowed to become its transgressors under a mistaken belief that they are serving the larger interest of the society as a whole. It is their responsibility to ensure that the men placed in their charge entertain no doubts and misgivings on this count and they are motivated to act professionally, in conformity with the law. They are free to use all the legal powers available under the law—normal as well as special—in exercising their authority to make the enemies of public order realize that violence has no chance of succeeding. They can ask for more powers if they find the challenge to be beyond the reach of the existing laws. However, such demands will receive favourable response only if they enjoy the confidence and support of the civil society. They can earn it only by professional competence and high standards of character and integrity. They must understand that they may also be deprived of the extra powers given to them for dealing with an extraordinary situation if they are found guilty of abusing them. The withdrawal of TADA can be cited as an example in this connection.

The police should free itself of the mindset that human rights groups are adversaries acting in league with the terrorists and militants. It should acknowledge the importance and hazards of the role assumed by human rights activists by choice and show respect to their commitment and determination to an extraordinary cause. It is in the ultimate interest of the police to make itself accessible and open to human rights groups, take their views and observations with due seriousness and intimate suitable action on complaints of violations received from them. Their initiative in establishing an understanding with the human rights groups is bound to evoke a matching response and lead to the evolution of a mutually beneficial alliance for promoting the cause of human rights.

The ultimate success of police in fight against militancy depends on the scrupulous adherence of its leadership to the eternal principle that good ends can be achieved only by good means and any compromise on this point in order to make some immediate short term gains is bound to harm the long term permanent interests of the organization. It must be understood that custodial violence—the widely prevalent form of human rights violations considered as a short cut to success by police has invariably proved counterproductive. It exposes its perpetrators to legal action and punishment, which cannot be taken lightly in view of the growing trend in the judicial pronouncements to make the guilty officials liable for payment of compensation to the victims. It has a sure effect of brutalizing the rank and file, alienating the police from the public and eroding the faith of the citizens in the system. Custodial violence with its most ugly manifestation in the form of extra judicial killings in fake encounters is the greatest obstacle in the way of integrating the police system into the fabric of a democratic society.

CHAPTER 12

The Infamous Carnage of November 1984

H.S. PHOOLKA

The allegations of bias of the police against the minorities during periods of communal violence is not a new phenomenon. We have been hearing about this since the last few decades. But there are certain situations when this bias was so apparent that it surpassed all the limits of discipline which a law enforcing agency is required to maintain.

One such incident was the violence perpetrated against the Sikhs in November 1984 in Delhi. This violence was not a communal riot, as it was not one religious community versus the other but can easily be termed as a carnage. The persons attacking the Sikh community, irrespective of their religion or caste, had allegiance to one political party, i.e. the Congress, which happened to be the ruling party at that time. During this violence, the atitude of the police was so atrocious that it cannot be merely called a bias or prejudice. It was a case of openly hostile attitude of the police towards the Sikhs.

Out of the total killing of 2,733 Sikhs (official figure) during the first 3 days of November 1984, about half of them took place on 1 November itself. The police at all levels, i.e. right from the Commissioner of Police to an ordinary constable, were busy demobilizing the Sikhs. The first priority of the police officers seemed to be to disarm the Sikhs. There were innumerable instances when the police officers ordered their men to divest the Sikhs of their traditional *kirpans* and licensed fire arms. At several places, the police even arrested such Sikhs who tried to defend themselves and their families and booked them under criminal cases. The police records show that most of the arrests made by the police on 1 November 1984 were of Sikhs.

There were also instances when the police went out of their way to break up peace committees set up in some localities. The objective of the police was clearly to remove all the hurdles from the path of the marauding mobs. The few places, where the Sikhs or the peace committees refused to disperse, they succeeded in driving away the rioters and protecting their localities. This underlines the fact that the police had been as much a threat to the Sikhs as the rioters themselves.

The first FIR registered during the carnage in almost every police station was against the Sikhs. The arrest made initially were also of the Sikhs. All these were happenning despite the fact that the killings were one sided and the Sikhs were being attacked in their own houses.

The first significant attack on a Sikh in the wake of Mrs Gandhi's assassination was on none other than the first citizen of India, President Zail Singh. It happened around 5 p.m. on 31 October at AIIMS, when Zail Singh's convoy arrived there straight from the airport. A mob not only raised slogans against Sikhs, but also stoned the President's convoy in the presence of the police deployed at AIIMS. Shockingly, the mob's attack on the President took place not once but twice—once when he was going in to see Mrs Gandhi in the hospital and another time, when he came out from there. The police failed to take action on both occasions, either to stop the attack nor to apprehend the culprits. Had the police done so, it would have surely sent out a firm message deterring further attacks on Sikhs.

The President was thus attacked in the presence of the police the very day the Prime Minister was assassinated. The Police's wilful failure to take action on a matter as serious as that seems to have been a premeditated plan to give two distinct signals. One, no Sikhs are to be spared, no matter how highly-placed, two, no action will be taken on any of those who attack Sikhs to avenge Mrs Gandhi's murder.

The police's subsequent conduct and its handling of the carnage bear out the assessment that it was working to a plan—a plan that involved mass killings of Sikhs. The Police Commissioner himself went to various places and arrested the Sikhs, whereas no arrest was made of the mob/rioters. On the morning of 1 November 1984, the Police Commissioner went to a gurudwara at Desh Bandhu Gupta Road. The gurdwara was under attack from a mob and the inmates of the gurudwara were keeping the mob away by firing from inside the gurdwara in self-defence. The Police Commissioner arrived at the scene and seized the fire arms of two Sikhs who were firing and arrested them. Similarly, at the historic gurdwara, Rakab Ganj Sahib, on the same day, the Police Commissioner reached with a posse of police force on getting information that Sikhs inside the gurdwara were firing. According to the police records, two Sikhs were burnt alive by a mob at this gurdwara. In his report, the Police Commissioner has admitted that he along with the police force reached there and the mob was still outside the gurdwara. Still, no arrest was made from amongst the mob. In turn, a Sikh, who was firing in self- defence from inside the gurdwara to keep the mob away, was arrested and his fire arm seized.

An incident at Patel Nagar was even more revealing. A mob attacked the house of Group Captain M.S. Talwar, a Mahavir Chakra winner in the 1971 war. Talwar had fired in self-defence. The police records show that the Police Commissioner, S.C. Tandon, and DCP Amod Kanth, reached the spot. The police seized Talwar's gun and ammunition and arrested him on the charge of murder as two members of the mob died due to his firing. Though Talwar was admittedly firing from inside his house, he was detained in Tihar Jail as a C class prisoner for over a fortnight before he was released on bail on judicial orders. SHO Amrik Singh Bhullar admitted before the Nanavati Commission that though there was a 2,000 strong mob near Talwar's house, none of them was arrested because the police were outnumbered. The Police Commissioner, S.C. Tandon, was going to attend a meeting with the Home Minister when he received a message on the way that a Sikh was firing from his house. He then changed his plans and rushed to Patel Nagar to the house of Group Captain M.S. Talwar and arrested him. As mentioned above, no action on the mob present at the spot was taken.

Amod Kanth who received a gallantry medal for arresting a family of Sikhs from Paharganj, was very much part of the trend of police officers going after the victims rather than the miscreants. Consider such instances from Inderpuri in West Delhi: One Kirpal Singh Chawla fired from his house at a mob trying to attack his family. But the police records say that he fled from his house in Inderpuri before Kanth reached there with a large force. The house was burnt by the mob. The police still booked Chawla on the charge of murder and he was in jail for many days. In another part of Inderpuri, one Harjinder Singh fired from his house. Kanth reached there with a large force, seized his gun and took him to the police station. This is borne out by police records. But Harjinder Singh went on to tell the Nanavati Commission that he was kept in the police lockup through the night of 1 November and released the next morning only after a phone call from the Rashtrapati Bhawan, where one of his relatives was posted.

Police officers behaved even worse in East Delhi where, according to the government, 1,026 Sikhs were killed. In this district, all the 26 persons arrested were Sikhs. In the Kalyanpuri locality of East Delhi, DCP Seva Dass ordered the arrest of 25 Sikhs on 1 November, while none were arrested from amongst the mobs operating there. In Seelampur located in the same district, one Ram Singh was arrested simply because he fired in self-defence. None from the mob was touched. In Trilokpuri, Sikhs gathered in a large number at a gurdwara on 1 November. But SHO Shoorvir Singh Tyagi forced them to return to their houses. Tyagi's action paved the way for the massacre of over 300 Sikhs in Block 32 of Trilokpuri.

Similarly, in west district, which is also one of the worst affected, the same pattern was followed—only Sikhs were arrested on 1 November 1984. No one from the mob was arrested.

The posh South Delhi presented a similar pattern. Bhogal has a sizable number of Sikhs who are mostly involved in the transport business. They collected in front of their houses and were able to resist the mobs despite a lot of stone-throwing. The police communicated the situation to DCP Chandra Prakash, who ordered two platoons to be sent to the area and directed that the Sikhs be sent to their houses and, if need be, to open fire at them. The directions recorded in wireless messages were silent on the need to take action against rioters. The police opened fire in the air forcing Sikhs to return to their houses. No action was taken against miscreants who burnt over 100 trucks and buses and several houses and shops.

Similarly, in the adjoining area of Harinagar in Ashram, Sikh transporters came together and put up a stiff resistance. The police directed the Sikhs to go back to their houses. But the Sikhs did not budge even when the police opened fire at them. Chandra Prakash visited the area but did little to help the besieged Sikhs, who were left to their destiny till the evening of 2 November. Meanwhile, there were attacks by huge mobs, at times numbering 5,000, but these could not break down the defence of the Sikhs. On the evening of 2 November, the Army reached there and erected a picket to protect the Sikhs. The Army personnel told the Sikhs that they could not reach earlier because the police held them back from that area.

Nevertheless, this is an instance when the Sikhs managed to defend themselves despite efforts by the police to help the mobs.

There were similar success stories of self-defence from other places, including East Delhi. For instance, in Lakshmi Nagar area of East Delhi, about 100 Sikhs assembled near a gurdwara with *kirpans* and *lathis* on the morning of 1 November. They kept the mob at bay for over an hour while the policemen present watched passively. A riot victim Gurmeet Singh deposed before the Nanavati Commission that around 11 a.m., the local MP H.K.L. Bhagat arrived there in a convoy and was seen talking to the policemen. Some of his followers remained in that area even after Bhagat's exit. The policemen then forced the Sikhs to go inside the gurdwara. But when the mob began to attack, the Sikhs rushed out to defend their homes and families. The mob ran away in the face of a strong counter-attack.

Bachittar Singh of Lajpat Nagar came up with an instance of a Hindu–Sikh joint effort in his locality to repel all attacks by mobs. Deposing before the Commission, he said a policeman tried to separate the Hindus from the Sikhs. But the Hindus, standing by their Sikh neighbours, told the police to disperse the mob. The police pleaded helplessness saying they had no orders to control the mob.

These damaging allegations against senior police officers were also confirmed by two Sikh policemen, who are now retired and have filed affidavits before the Nanavati Commission. Harbans Singh, who was a sub-inspector in Jamunapuri Police Station during the carnage, said he was not allowed to go out of the police station during that period and neither was he assigned any duties. When he entered the wireless room, he noticed that wherever there were communications saying Sikhs were defending themselves, the police were ordered to take action against them. And where Sikhs were being killed, no direction was given to protect them. His revelations were borne out by the entries in the wireless logbooks which were produced subsequently before the Nanavati Commission. Hardhian Singh Shergil, who was ASI in CID, gave an equally revealing account of a visit he made to the wireless room of the Geeta Colony Police Station. He said he heard a number of wireless messages saying that Sikhs were being attacked and found to his surprise that none of them was being recorded. When he enquired about it, the wireless operator there told Shergil that he had orders not to record messages about the attacks on Sikhs.

And after all this, not even a single police officer has been punished.

Rather, all of them have been rewarded with promotions. The then DCP of East Delhi where, according to official figures, 1,026 Sikhs were killed, and who arrested only the Sikhs, is presently a Joint Commissioner of Police and is hoping to bag the post of Commissioner of Police.

Rewards and promotions to such police officers has sent a wrong message to the force. After 1984, a trend had started among the police to act against minorities during communal violence and get rewarded. This trend needs to be checked and it can only be done by securing punishment for guilty officials.

CHAPTER 13

Role of police in 1984 anti-Sikh Massacre, Delhi

VRINDA GROVER

From the 1961 Justice S.D. Srivastava Commission Report on the Jabalpur riots to the 1993 Justice B.N. Srikrishna Commission Report on Mumbai riots, the anti-minority bias that determines the actions, conduct, decisions and orders of the Indian police force has been repeatedly documented. However despite this and more evidence of the total abdication and dereliction of duty, till date no serious and sincere effort has been made to remedy the situation. Even the suggestions made by the National Police Commission in 1977, are yet to be implemented. The political will to overhaul the present structure of functioning and exact accountability from the police force is obviously lacking as the current arrangement suits the vested interests of those in power. In the last two decades, political parties have increasingly adopted communalism as a mode of governance. This has spawned a culture of impunity which poses a direct and grave threat to constitutional democracy.

The assassination of Prime Minister Indira Gandhi, on 31 October 1984, by her own security guards, who belonged to the Sikh community, was followed by an anti-Sikh massacre. Delhi was the epicentre of this pogrom unleashed by the ruling Congress (I) party. The first four days of November 1984 were the bloodiest in the history of Delhi since 1947. According to official figures 2,733 Sikhs were brutally murdered, burnt and slaughtered in the capital. It appeared that the State had arbitrarily and illegally suspended the operation of the Fundamental Rights enshrined in Articles 14, 15 and 21, for a section of the Indian citizenry, viz., the Sikh community. They were abandoned by the State and its agents to be lynched by the marauding mobs.

Reproduced below is an edited version of an affidavit submitted by me before the Hon'ble J. Nanavati Commission of Inquiry which was constituted to establish the truth of what happened over two decades ago. This affidavit on the basis of court decisions in cases relating to the killings in 1984, explicitly shows that the police as an institution is partisan, communal and owes allegiance not to the rule of the law but to the diabolical designs of the party in power.

(1) That I have done a research study on the responses of the legal system, i.e. the police and courts, to the massacre targeting members of the Sikh community on 31 October 1984 and thereafter in Delhi. While examining this, I have relied primarily on secondary data, viz., report of the Justice R.N. Misra Commission of Inquiry, the reports of the committees constituted by the government thereafter, citizens reports like 'Who Are the Guilty' prepared by PUDR and PUCL and judgements pertaining to cases lodged in relation to the 1984 violence and killings. For purposes of analysis, I have documented a representative sample of 137 judgements comprising of 126 trial court, 7 Delhi High Court and 4 Supreme Court judgements.

(2) That my knowledge of the events relating to the violence is based largely on the documents cited above in paragraph 2, and more specifically on the judgements documented by me. I obtained certified copies of 126 Trial Court judgements from Tis Hazari Court, Patiala House Court and Karkardooma Court.

(3) That my research, documentation and analysis will have a bearing on the following terms of reference of this Hon'ble Commission-clause (c), whether these heinous crimes could have been averted and whether there were any lapses or dereliction of duty in this regard on the part of any responsible authorities/individuals; (e) to recommend measures which may be adopted to meet the ends of justice , and (f) to consider such matters as may be found relevant in the course of the inquiry.

(4) That I have carefully read these judgements and it is clear that a combination of grave lapses of investigation, shoddy investigation, inordinate delays, insufficient collection of evidence, non-compliance with legal procedures by the police led to a majority of cases concluding in acquittals. The acquittals were to a very large extent a direct consequences of the incompetent, unprofessional and casual investigation by the police.

(5) That a large number of the judgements perused by me cited lapses in police investigation as the reason for acquittals. That in the

judgement of *State* vs. *Ram Pal Saroj* (Karkardooma Court, Delhi, S.C. No. 57/95 FIR No. 426/84), the learned ASJ remarked that, 'the police investigation in each of the riot cases filed in the court has been wanting in quality'.

He further denounced the entire process of investigation and prosecution of the violence of 1984, stating that,

> In Nov. 1984 within the first week after the assassination of Mrs. Gandhi more than 3000 Sikhs were brutally murdered on the streets of Delhi by the lumpen elements in the full view of the police force and under the very nose of the powerful Central government. The police not only failed to protect the poor and innocent persons but showed total inaction in apprehending those who were responsible for this orgy of violence. However, after much hue and cry by the victims and publicity by the national and international media, the government went on appointing commission and committees one after another. The crime had taken place in 1984. The report of the crime was with the state and its law implementing machinery in November 1984 itself. The investigation continued in these cases for about 10 years without there being any investigation being done by anybody. The trial of this case started in Nov. 1995 after 11 years of the commission of crime. The criminal law justice system in this country totally failed the justice. While the criminal law justice system moved at the snail's pace and had no calendar to keep, the death kept its calendar and Santokh Singh, whose three sons were brutally murdered by the rioters, died in May 1992. The manner in which the trial of the riot cases had proceeded is unthinkable in any civilized country. In fact, the inordinate delay in trial of the rioters had legitimized the violence and the criminality. A system which permits the legitimized violence and criminals through the instrumentalities of the state to stifle the investigation, cannot be relied upon to dispense basic justice uniformly to the people. It amounts to a total wiping out of the rule of law.

In *State* vs. *Amir Chand* (Karkardooma, Delhi, S.C. No. 39/95, FIR No. 426/84) the ASJ, who had presided over several cases relating to the violence of 1984, observed that,

> While in Nov. 1984 democratic values were slaughtered and soul of Indian constitution was burned in broad daylight by the rioters, what happened after the riots was still worse and the justice itself has been slaughtered by sheer non-investigation and total absence of concern. In the name of investigation only an eye-wash has been done. The manner in which the prosecution has proceeded and the trial in these cases has proceeded speaks volumes about the health of criminal justice system. By simply delaying the trial and delaying the investigation, aged and old witnesses have either become extinct or untraceable and the accused get benefit.

(6) That I would like to draw the attention of this Hon'ble Commission to First Information Report no. 426/84, P.S. Kalyanpuri, under Sections 188/148/302/149 IPC that was recorded by the police on the night of 2 November 1984. Trilokpuri was one of the worst affected areas in Delhi. As per official figures almost 200 people were killed and 100–150 *jhuggies* were burnt and looted in Block No. 32 of Trilokpuri, within a span of 72 hours, between 1–3 November 1984. The ASJ in *State* vs. *Kishori* (Karkardooma, Delhi S.C. No. 52/95, FIR No. 426/84) observed that,

> Despite all of these facts coming to the knowledge of police, day after day from 1.11.84 till the investigation of this case was going on the police did not investigate the murders of several persons properly and carefully nor did it register the separate cases.

The police evolved a unique method to record and investigate the criminal offences and killings, a method that is totally contrary to the Criminal Procedure Code, 1973 and the Indian Penal code, 1898, a single omnibus FIR was recorded for almost all the killings, arson and looting in Block 32 of Trilokpuri. This ensured that the investigation and the prosecution of these offences would be no more than an exercise in futility. The ASJ, commenting on the dereliction of duty by the police in failing to register the criminal offences, noted in *State* vs. *Kishori and Shabnam* (Karkardooma court, Delhi, S.C. No. 45/95, FIR No. 426/84), that,

> This FIR is FIR No. 426 of 1984 which does not mention the names of any of the rioters. It is a general and vague FIR recorded by the police deliberately. Despite the fact that several injured Sikhs were there, several victims whose husband, sons and sons-in-law were killed, were available, police did not record FIR on the basis of the statement of those victims. Rijju Singh (First Informant) although living in the area, had been able to save himself and his family. His statement is only that rioting had taken place in the area and several Sikh houses had been burnt and Sikhs had been killed. This information of several Sikh houses having been burnt and Sikh having been killed, was with the police even before Rijju Singh met (SI) Manphool Singh. In fact, the information, which was received at the police station from the Addl. Commissioner of Police Nikhil Kumar, was that cutting of Sikhs was going on in Trilokpuri and when SI Manphool Singh, SHO Shoorvir Singh Tyagi and several other senior officers reached at Block 32, they with their own eyes had seen the burning of Sikh houses, rioting was still continuing and they had also seen the dead bodies of Sikhs. 95 dead bodies were removed on that very night. This information which was available with the

police officers of their own seeing the scene of occurence was sufficient to form the basis of FIR. But despite all this, the statement of Rijju Singh was recorded to make the basis of FIR. I don't know why a FIR cannot be recorded by the police officer of his own knowledge also which he gathers from the spot or from circumstances also. If a person is found having been murdered by police officer and there is nobody to tell who murdered him, then would the police officer not get the FIR recorded simply because there was no one to say that, that man has been murdered? This kind of recording of FIR by the police simply shows that the police officers did not want to convert their own information of the riots and their own knowledge of the burning of Sikh houses which they had seen with their own eyes into the FIR itself. (pp. 4–5)

(7) The FIR was registered on the basis of the statement of one Rijju Singh and was converted into an omnibus FIR for nearly all the incidents that took place in the area. The police however recorded very brief, vague, general, cryptic and fragmented statements of riot widows separately and annexed all such statements with the main challan filed before the court in respect of FIR 426/84. Despite the recommendation made by the Justice R.N. Misra Commission and the Jain Aggarwal Committee, a single *challan* was filed in the court with respect to the killings of 200 people after almost 8–10 years. The court to which the case was assigned scrutinized the statements of riot victims and identified individual cases of murder/arson, dacoity, etc., and directed the police to file separate *challans* with respect to each such case.

(8) The investigation of this case was originally with Manphool Singh from 2 November 1984 up to 23 November 1984 but during that period neither he nor the SHO Tyagi did anything to investigate any particular murder. Thereafter, the case was handed over to the Vigilance Branch and Inspector Badan Singh was handed over the investigation of the cases FIR No. 426/84 on 4 December 1984. He too did nothing specific about any particular murder case. He prepared lists of burnt houses, burnt *jhuggis*, gurdwaras and some of the persons killed during the violence. He also got photographs taken of some of the burnt houses. According to him, about 200 persons were killed in Trilokpuri area and about 150 houses were burnt and looted. Two gurdwaras were also burnt. He recorded statements of different victims about looting, burning and killing and thereafter these statements were attached to FIR No. 426. No separate FIR was registered and no separate *challans* were filed in respect of the inci-

dent which had taken place at the houses of different victims and killings of different persons.

In *State* vs. *Kishori* (Karkardooma, Delhi, S.C. No. 42/95, FIR No. 426/84) the ASJ quoting the deposition of Inspector Badan Singh noted: 'He stated that there were oral instructions of his Senior Officers that all incidents of riots are to be clubbed together and to be dealt under FIR No. 426 of 1984 and no separate case was being registered.'

(9) In *State* vs. *Kishori and Ors.* (Karkardooma, Delhi, S.C. No. 53/95, FIR No. 426/84), the ASJ observed that:

> After the assassination of late Prime Minister Mrs. Indira Gandhi on 31 October 1984, anti-Sikh riots broke out in different areas of the capital killing thousands of Sikhs. Law and order machinery was completely paralysed because of inaction/connivance of the police. This is apparent from the fact that for hundreds of murders that took place in the area of PS Kalyanpuri, only one single FIR, i.e. FIR No. 426/84 was registered and that too did not contain any specific details regarding the names of the persons killed or the names of the rioters who took part in the killings. In the name of investigation a farce was carried out. Cryptic statements of some of the victims were recorded. No attempt was made to trace the dead bodies or to get them identified. Even the formality of preparing a site plan of the places where various incidents occurred was not completed in most of the cases. Ultimately, to show the compliance of law, an omnibus *challan* in respect of FIR No. 426/84 was submitted to the court and along with it the statements of some of the victims were also attached. It was left for the courts to sort out specific cases which could be proceeded in accordance with law. It seems the prosecution expected that the trial will be equally a farce and cases would be summarily disposed of thereby drawing a curtain on the legal drama.

(10) That when the trial of all cases falling within the omnibus FIR No. 426/84 began, the Court in *State* vs. *Abdullah Khan*, etc., (Karkardooma, Delhi S.C. No. 40/95, FIR No. 426/84), found that,

> A perusal of the *challan* revealed that police had not done justice to the investigation and had clubbed all the different incidents together. In one *challan*, totally unconnected events had been clubbed together. These events were spread over several places and were of three days. Because of this conduct of the police in investigation done by police was not up to the mark and the police had acted unlike a professional force. It was also observed that the police has wrongly clubbed several incidents into one FIR. Similar observations were made by Justice Jain–Agarwal Committee and it was suggested to the police to file separate challans incident-wise . . . This court,

after finding that the trial of several separate incidents together and trial of more than 200 accused involved in these incidents together, would not be a fair, smooth and proper trial passed an order directing the splitting up of the *challan* on the basis of incidents.

(11) That in *State* vs. *Kanak Singh* (Karkardooma, Delhi, S.C. No. 18/95, FIR No. 426/84) in relation to the role played by local level Congress leaders and the apparent reluctance of the police in investigating their role in the violence and killings, the ASJ observed that,

> It is apparent that Kanak Singh and Ram Pal Saroj were the local Congress (I) leaders. They seem to have silently encouraged the riots and perhaps they were also part of conspiracy of allowing the rioters to have free hand in the area but the police had not gone into the aspect of conspiracy. Then a conspiracy on the part of local leaders, local police and their not allowing any outside help to reach Block no. 32 and of not sending any police force there to protect the innocent persons made the task easier. But for this attitude it would not have been possible for any group of rioters to wipe out almost 200 Sikh adult male members living in Block no. 32 and to burn their houses systematically. Accused, therefore, gets benefit of police and state apathy towards 1984 riot and in showing no interest by the state in investigating the conspiracy part of riots.

(12) That the casual, perfunctory, shoddy and negligent investigation conducted by the police into the violence and killings of November 1984, undermined the very foundations of the prosecution of the accused and thus in many trials the case against the accused could not be proved beyond reasonable doubt.

In *State* vs. *Kishori and others* (Karkardooma, Delhi, S.C. No. 19/95, FIR No. 426/84) the ASJ, commenting on the manner in which investigation was conducted in cases relating to 1984, observed that,

> The investigation in this case and in other cases concerning 1984 riots, which took place in Trilokpuri, has not been proper. In fact, circumstances show that there was reluctance on the part of police on conducting the investigation of the cases. This reluctance on the part of police in conducting the investigation is abundantly clear from the testimony of the witnesses as well as from the circumstances. Mr. Agarwal, the member of Jain–Agarwal committee who appeared as PW-8, has stated that there were lots of complaints that in the riots of 1984, the police had played a dubious and passive role in the riots. Similar complaints were against the administration also of indirectly helping the rioters . . . Initially, the recommendations were made

by Justice Jain–Agarwal Committee on the basis of affidavits and police records for registration of cases against the accused persons allegedly involved in the riots. However, even in 1991 when these recommendations were being sent by Justice Jain–Agarwal Committee, the recommendations were sent back by the Administration taking various pleas and one of the pleas was that either the deponent were not in existence or they were disowning the affidavit. On seeing this kind of conduct of the Administration, Justice Jain–Agarwal Committee decided to call the deponent before it, record and the statement, and then sent back the recommendation so that the plea of deponent not available or disowning the affidavits could not be raised by the Administration. Looking into this kind of conduct of the police and the Administration, it is not difficult to imagine as to what was the attitude of the police and the Administration. The effort was to thwart all attempts of booking those who were involved in the riots. Why this attempt was being made can be understood only from the historical prospects and can be understood from the political background of those who were involved in the crime. In this background, when the police and the Administration all the tune were keen to protect the rioters, impartial and true investigation in the riots by the Administration and the police was not possible. It can easily be understood as to why there was no recording of independent FIR on the basis of statements. Why the statements of the victims were recorded after long the riots? Why time of these statements of the victims were short, brief and contained no details of the incidents and why every Investigating Officer, one after another, performed his duty in a casual manner as if he has to just push the burden to the next IO?

(13) That in many judgements in my representative sample, the issue of delay in recording of First Information Reports and statements of witnesses was discussed by the courts. It has been recorded by the Misra Commission and committees set up thereafter that very few FIRs were recorded by the police at the time of the violence and killings. It was only after the Misra Commission was set up in April 85, that the victims, on the encouragement of civil liberties groups came forward and submitted affidavits detailing the criminal offences committed against them, their family members and their properties. Thereafter, affidavits were also presented by victims to the Jain–Bannerji and Jain–Agarwal Committees on whose recommendations several FIRs were recorded and investigation initiated. Delays were inevitable in the prevailing political climate. The delays eventually ran into months and years. Commenting on the situation prevailing in Delhi at the time of the violence, the Delhi High Court in *Ashok Kumar* vs. *State of Delhi* (1995 (1) Crimes 347) noted,

But it must be remembered that at the time of the incident in question, the Sikhs community was a target and they were afraid of their lives and they were taking shelters. The police machinery was completely wrecked and in these circumstances I the witnesses did not go to the police immediately to give their statement under Section 161, as the situation was beyond control of the police and if the police did not immediately start recording of evidence and investigation after the commission of offence it could not be said that the witnesses should be disbelieved and their evidence must be discarded.

(14) During the trial of most cases, the courts considered the dates that the affidavits were filed either before the Misra Commission or the committees as the date of registration of FIR. In many cases, the delay on the part of the police in recording of FIRs and statements proved fatal and was one of the factors that supported the decision of acquittal of the accused. That in some other cases in the sample the Judge, taking cognizance of the circumstances that prevailed in November 1984 and complaints of police inaction condoned similar delays in the registration of FIRs.

(15) That in *State* vs. *Kishori and others* (Karkardooma, Delhi, S.C. No. 19/95, FIR No. 426/84), the case was filed on the basis of an affidavit of Bhakti Bai filed before the Jain–Aggarwal Committee naming the accused as members of a mob that killed her husband as well as his younger brother. Weighing the evidence, the court noted the reluctance with which the police took action during the massacre and the ASJ noted that,

But for the police apathy, the statement of Bhakti Bai and other witnesses would have been recorded immediately after the riots and those involved in the riots, would have been immediately arrested and sent for trial. There would have been no necessity for the Jain–Agarwal Committee to call Bhakti Bai in Feb. 1991 before it and to record her statement. I, therefore, consider that the plea of the counsels that the witnesses have been examined by the police and by the Committee much after the riots and this gave chance to the witnesses of embellishment and of falsely implicating the accused persons, is baseless. In fact, the witnesses have been knocking from one door to another door seeking justice but the justice is being denied to them by the police and the Administration in gross derogation of the constitutional mandate of equality before law and in gross derogation of the law of the land.

(16) That police inaction and complicity during the violence and killings as evidenced by their non-recording or delayed recording of FIRs and statements, weakened the case of the prosecution and enabled the accused to secure an acquittal.

(17) That in addition to the fact that the statements were either not recorded or were delayed due to police complicity, several judgements of my representative sample noted that statements that were recorded were brief, cryptic, bereft of details and inaccurate.

In *State* vs. *Kishori* (Karkardooma, Delhi, S.C. No. 42/95, FIR No. 426/84) the ASJ said that,

> After the rioters had done their job, the rest of the job to frustrate the investigation was done by the police. The police, during the investigation, saw to it that only inaccurate and short statements of the witnesses was recorded. In almost all the cases witnesses have stated that their statement was not correctly recorded. I, therefore, consider that there is no reason to disbelieve the woman who had seen before her own eyes her son-in-law being killed.

(18) The courts in some cases also noted the deliberate collusion of the police in enabling influential and politically powerful persons to escape criminal prosecution by omitting their names from statements made by the victims. In *State* vs. *Salim & Others* (Karkardooma, Delhi, S.C. No. 43/95, FIR No. 426/84) the ASJ noted that,

> Regarding the investigation of 1984 riots, it is well established from the findings of Justice Ranganath Misra Commission that the investigation was not done properly and in many cases the investigation was not done at all. It has also been observed by the Commission that wherever the name of some official person was there, FIR was not usually recorded and if it was recorded, the name of influential person was dropped. Several investigating officers have appeared before this court and the statements, which have been recorded by these Investigating Officers of the victims of riot, are brief and give information only to the extent who was he killed and when was he killed. All the details about the riots as to when and how the riots happened are missing. This is the reason that the witnesses, who had been appearing before this court, had been repudiating their statements u/s 161 Cr.P.C. allegedly recorded by the police.

In some cases, the judges noted that the statements were deliberately recorded inaccurately by the police, which resulted in discrepancies and inconsistencies in the statements under Section 161, Cr PC and the depositions of the witnesses before the court.

In *State* vs. *Ram Pal Saroj etc.* (Karkardooma, Delhi, S.C. No. 57/95, FIR No. 426/84) ASJ said that,

> Police had not made any other person as witness in this case. In fact, there is no investigation done by the police except recording the statements. State-

ments recorded by the police are also very sketchy and sometimes the statements are actually not made by the victims but they have been recorded by the police officials sitting in the police station and it is alleged that these statements were made by victims.

In most of the cases it is found that in order to help the accused persons police has given wrong facts in the statements. The victims of the riot cases, when they appeared in the court had given altogether different story. They named not only those accused persons who are mentioned in the *challan* but even other persons who were part of the rioting mob and the court had to amend the charge or call more accused persons to face the trial.

Similarly, in *State* vs. *Ved Prakash etc.* (Karkardooma, Delhi, S.C. No. 70/95, FIR No. 426/84), ASJ observed that,

As already observed by me in different riot cases that there was a total apathy of the police in investigating these cases and the sole attempt of the police was to help the rioters and to discredit the victims. Therefore, the statements u/s 161 Cr. P.C. recorded by the police are very brief, inaccurate and imaginary, missing most of the details mentioned by the victims and not giving several facts given by the victims. Even Justice Ranga Nath Misra Commission and Jain–Agarwal Committee had observed that true statements of the victims were not recorded. Investigation was perfunctory and unfaithful. Under these circumstances, when the police and the accused joined hands against the victims, there is no wonder that there are contradictions but I consider that truth and justice cannot be made casualty because of the vicious nexus between the police and the accused persons. I, therefore, consider that witnesses cannot be discredited because of the non-recording of accurate statements by the police. I believe that the witness must have stated to the police about the death of her husband as well as about the other circumstances of riots but police did not record the same.

(19) That in several cases, the statements recorded by the police were devoid of any details and were brief.

In *Manohar Lal alias Munna and others* vs. *The State* (*N.C.T. of Delhi*) (2000 1 AD (S.C.) 52), the Hon'ble Supreme Court noted that,

Another criticism is that she did not divulge all the details of the occurrence when she gave a statement to the police on 17 November 1984. We perused the said statement attributed to her. A reading of it makes the position clear that the police officer was not inclined to elicit from the bereaved mother any details of the horrendous episode. He felt that she was not in a mood to speak out the details as the interval of time was not sufficient enough for a mother like her to regain mental equanimity. He should have postponed questioning her to a future date. In the said statement he recorded just two sentences. It would be unfair and we may say uncharitable to her if we use that cryptic statement dated 17 November 1984 to discredit the valuable testimony of the most natural eyewitnesses of his horrendous crime.

(20) That the courts also noted that the investigation conducted by the police was no more than a farce as is noted by the ASJ in *State* vs. *Kanak Singh* (Karkardooma, Delhi, S.C. No. 18/95, FIR No. 426/84) that,

> After receiving this affidavit along with the letter of Jain-Agarwal Commission for further investigation, the police, instead of doing any investigation, translated the affidavit in Hindi into a statement of Jassi Bai. That was taken as statement u/s 161 and a separate *challan* was filed reproducing what was given in the affidavit. Practically there was no investigation done by the police. The investigation does not mean translation of an affidavit from English language to Hindi language and asking the witness to sign it. The investigation implies going into the facts and circumstances finding out the truthfulness of the allegations, collecting necessary and material evidence. As there has been all other riot cases the police was not at all interested in investigation but was interested in only hushing up the things, so the best thing for the police to do was to translate the affidavit and complete the investigation.

That as the police did only perfunctory investigation, often no effort was made to join any other witness apart from the complainant in the case. It must be mentioned here that particularly in cases related to Trilokpuri, Sultanpuri and several other localities, which were the scenes of large-scale violence and killings, the offences took place in full view of the public and the houses, were often of 25 sq. mt.

(21) That according to some judgements in the representative sample, the witnesses accurately identified the accused, in court, even after a lapse of 10–12 years. However, as no Test Identification Parade (TIP) as required by law had been conducted by the police at the time of investigation, the identification of the accused for the first time in court was held to be of no value. The failure of the police to conduct TIP gravely affected the verdict in several cases, some of which are cited below.

(22) That another lapse on the part of the police in investigating the cases relating to the violence and killing of November 1984, that finds mention in some of the judgements in the representative sample, was the illegal method adopted by the police in recovering looted property. The police announced that looted property should be deposited on the road or at the police stations and that no action would be taken against them. This enabled the rioters to escape prosecution

altogether. This is borne out by the statement of the accused himself in *State* vs. *Ved Prakash etc.* (Karkardooma, Delhi, S.C. No. 70/95, FIR No. 426/84) where the ASJ noted that,

> In his statement u/s 313 Cr. P.C. accused Kishori had stated that police made pronouncements in the area that those who have looted the houses of Sikhs, they should put out looted articles on the road. These statements were made by Inspector Rathi who was from Special Staff. These announcements were made after police had come to Block no. 32. . . . Thus, from this statement of accused u/s 313 Cr. P.C. it is clear that the police was in league with the accused persons and the riot was a consequence of this league.

Again, in *State* vs. *Kishori and Shabnam* (Karkardooma, Delhi, S.C. No. 45/95, FIR No. 426/84) the ASJ noted that no effort was also made by the police to recover weapons or looted property, the recovery of which would have strengthened the case of the prosecution.

> It is submitted by the counsel for accused that no recovery of any arm has been made by the police. The alleged *khanjar* or any arm from the rioters has not been recovered. True this is exactly (what the) police has done to help the rioters. The police did not recover either looted property or arms and how could the police recover all these things? All along during the riots the police of Trilokpuri had been tacitly encouraging the rioters and after the riot, it had been announcing that the looted property should be deposited on the road and police will take it away. The role of the police all along the riots was that of tacitly helping the rioters by not implementing the law and remaining absent from the spot most of the time. Non-recovery of the instruments of crime is therefore of no consequence in this case.

(23) That the casual and shoddy manner in which the police had deliberately conducted the investigation tainted every aspect of the prosecution evidence, including the non-preparation of site plans, the non collection of corroborative evidence, failure to conduct postmortems to ascertain cause of death with a clear view to scuttle the cases.

In *State* vs. *Babu Lal and Others*. (Karkardooma, Delhi, S.C. Nos 21/95, 29/95, 2/97, 3/97, 5/97, FIR No. 426/84) ASJ noted the statement of the investigating officer:

> PW-14 SI Badan Singh was entrusted with the investigation of this case on 20 April 1993 after the receipt of recommendation from Jain–Agarwal Committee . . . In cross examination, he admitted that he did not prepare any site plan of the spot nor applied for holding TIP of accused persons.

In *State* vs. *Shayam Vir* (Karkardooma, Delhi, S.C. No. 34/95, FIR No. 426/84) the ASJ noted that,

> It is not only that police did not do its duty of investigating the crime properly but it is that police deliberately did not collect the evidence against the accused persons who were involved in this fiendish act of murder of more than 200 persons in one Block. The record filed with the court shows that the police was a party in protecting the accused persons and in wiping out the evidence against the accused persons. If it is believed that up to 3.11.84 . . . the situation was such that it was beyond the control of the police . . . ; then the subsequent investigation of these crimes would have been done honestly by the police and the criminals and rioters, would have been brought to book. But the subsequent conduct of the police, in saving the rioters and in destroying the evidence would compel any court to draw an adverse inference against police and the investigating agency being hand in glove with the rioters and acting under the directions of those unseen powerful persons who were behind all this.

(24) That the intentional reluctance of the police as the investigating agency to examine avenues such as the law of conspiracy to tackle the complexity and scale of the crimes committed in November 1984 enabled those who had engineered and master-minded this orgy of violence to escape judicial scrutiny. In *State* vs. *Mangal* (Karkardooma, Delhi, S.C. No. 51/95 FIR No. 426/84) the ASJ noted that,

> The riots in Delhi had followed a definite pattern which indicated that there was some planning and prior conspiracy but the conspiracy angle was totally overlooked during investigation. Thus, the 'eye of the storm' remained elusive. Even after the riots were over, no serious effort was made to book the guilty with an honest intention of getting them punished through a Court verdict. The dead bodies were not identified, no inquests were held. The statements of victims were not properly recorded/catalogued. Even the formalities of preparing a site plan of the scene of occurrence was not observed . . . The Courts have shown full sympathy for the victims but within limits, constraints prescribed by law. The Court cannot pronounce a verdict of guilty against any one when the proof is not of the requisite standard.

(25) That upon a careful consideration of all the 137 judgments in the representative sample, it is clear that the lapses in investigation detailed in the preceding paragraphs are indicative of the police functioning not as an agent of the rule of law but as an agent of the ruling party. That undoubtedly the Delhi Police force displayed an institu-

tional bias against the Sikh community in the investigation of these cases. Similar partisan behaviour of the police force against minority communities has been documented in detail in the Justice Srikrishna Report on the Bombay riots of 1992–3 and can was repeated once again in the violence unleashed in Gujarat, 2002. It is pertinent to note that the Police Commissioner of Ahmedabad, P.C. Pandey when questioned on police inaction in controlling the violence, has stated on record, that the police are not immune from communal sentiments.

(26) That in their quest for justice, hundreds of victims have been appearing before the courts in Delhi. However, the machinations of the police to please their political masters, compounded by the inordinate delays in the trials, ensured that justice eluded most of the victims of the violence and killings.

In *State* vs. *Shayam Vir* (Karkardooma, Delhi, S.C. No. 34/95, FIR No. 426/84) ASJ noted that,

> It is tragic that criminal justice administration has been administered differently for different persons. It has been nothing but a paper tiger against anti-social combinations, against rich and influential offenders, and it has proved to be a paper bonanza for socially oppressed and suppressed victims. 49 years after independence, our guilt by default or dubiety on the charge of ineffectiveness of criminal justice system against [the] rich, [the] influential or those who wield political power has been proved beyond reasonable doubt as the cases against these either do not reach to the courts and when they reach . . . are seldom finalized and the blood, tears and cries of victims go unheard.

(27) That it is imperative that the police force, which is increasingly becoming a threat to the democratic institutions of the country, is insulated from political interference and made accountable to law and effective steps taken to ensure that delinquent police officers no longer enjoy immunity.

(28) That if the confidence of the citizens and communities is to be restored in democratic governance and the legal system, justice must necessarily be a precursor to reconciliation.

POST SCRIPT

In early 2005, Justice Nanavati submitted his Report to the Union Govt. led by the Congress(I). The Govt. after six months of deliberation placed the Action Taken Report (ATR) before the Parliament in

August 2005. After considerable public outcry both within and outside the Parliament the Prime Minister apologised to the Sikh community albeit 21 years too late. However, admission of moral responsibility does not grant amnesty from legal culpability, prosecution or punishment. The Report of Justice Nanavati and the ATR have confirmed the nations worst fears that in situations of State and institutional complicity the quest for justice is elusive.

CHAPTER 14

National Policy for Police

AJAY K. MEHRA

The need for police reforms has never been greater in India than today. On the one hand, the police continue to remain the most abused instrument of the Indian state, on the other, the Indian state needs it more than ever before for internal security purposes. Without going into the oft-repeated charges of brutality, highhandedness and corruption against the police, which have persisted since 1861 and ironically perpetuated since independence, I would like to highlight some specific events and circumstances that call for introspection regarding the law and order machinery in India.

First, the instances of a disjuncture between the political authority, if not the state, and the police, which surely affects the morale, efficiency and neutrality of the highly politicized law and order machinery in the country, have grown in number if not become starker, to put it mildly. This disjuncture was reflected in the then Union Home Minister L.K. Advani giving a clean chit to Bajrang Dal even before the police began its investigation in the Staines murder case. He also publicly cast aspersion on the CBI. And, later in the context of the Gujarat riots, partisanship displayed by the highest quarters of the union government, the Prime Minister and the Deputy Prime Minister, has clearly sent a wrong, if not dangerous, message to the law and order machinery across the country. Another example of this trend was visible in Siwan in Bihar where the private army of the infamous RJD MP Shahabuddin fought bloody battles with Bihar police on 16 March 2001. Not only the Bihar government defended the MP with criminal antecedents, who had threatened the SP of the district with dire consequences, it also transferred the officers of the entire district administration.[1]

The second important event was the transfers effected at the highest levels in the police force to wreak vengeance on former Chief Minister

Karunanidhi. Even the union government played a partisan role in this affairs when it sought transfer of the 'guilty' officers to New Delhi, which the Tamil Nadu CM refused. In the next act of this drama, the Police Commissioner of Chennai, who carried out the orders of the 'midnight knock' at Karunanidhi's door, was replaced on 9 December 2001. The events reflected the extent to which the police had become part of partisan party politics at the highest level of national politics.[2]

Third, the role of the police in counter-terrorism has always been understated in India. It has lately been highlighted in four contexts. The spurt in Naxal violence for the past few years, the call for amnesty to police officers engaged in counter-terrorist operations, the promulgation of POTA and India's effort to project itself as a victim of cross-border terrorism since 9/11. Each of these contexts has provoked fierce but relevant debate on the police role in democratic India. The debate is useful in dispassionately analysing not only police powers, but also police accountability.[3]

Fourth, the Gujarat riots have highlighted the dangerous portents of a highly partisan and sectarian state structure politicizing police operations in a volatile communal situation and consequently brutalizing the police as never before. As stated earlier, its perilous consequences are heightened when the two topmost leaders of the ruling party and the government defend the chain of events completely ignoring the provocative political campaign of their own party.

Finally, though sporadic and much smaller in scale, the resurfacing of police agitations in recent times. Indeed, the spectre of countrywide police agitations of 1979 scale does not seem to surface, but even in 1979 no one could imagine that a slap by one Akali MLA in Patiala would spark such a massive police unrest.

Obviously, two decades since the first National Police Commission (NPC) of independent India submitted its report, the need for police reform has become even more urgent. The review of the functioning of the police by the NPC, if not the whole set of recommendations it made, is still a sound basis on which to begin the process of police reform.

DISCOURSE ON POLICE REFORMS

The fact that most states since the mid-1950s began reviewing the functioning of the Police by appointing Police Commissions clearly shows that that the need for police reforms was not missed by the leaders since independence. Obviously, by the time the recommendations of the State Police Commissions were received the colonial culture of the police in India was found to be useful and, therefore, perpetuated rather than replaced by a more democratic culture. As a result, useful reports produced by these Commissions at substantial public cost were consigned to cold storage.

The notable point, however, is that from the very beginning the political class at the helm of affairs was aware that the police in India needed reorientation and reforms. It is not very difficult to guess that the main reason for not effecting reforms in the police administration is that by the sixties the euphoria of bringing democratic transformations in the polity, political institutions and administrative apparatus had given way to the reality of coping with the political problems and retaining political power. Obviously, and it can be said more firmly with the hindsight, the police as it was inherited and as it existed, was considered useful in the power game.[4]

Since law and order and the police were placed in the State List in the Constitution of India, the union government perhaps did not consider it prudent to direct the state governments to implement the recommendations of their respective Police Commissions, neither did it develop a national perspective on police reforms. Yet, the centre did not completely ignore the issue of police reforms. The Administrative Reforms Commission (ARC) appointed by the union government reviewed the question of reforms in the police administration as well. It constituted a Working Group on Police Administration, which submitted its report to the ARC in 1970.[5] But police reforms was not the ARC's main focus. The ARC, therefore, looked at it only as a part of larger administrative reforms. Again in 1971, the Government of India appointed a Committee on Police Training headed by the celebrated sociologist M.S. Gore. The Committee's report was widely welcomed, but again its recommendations were not implemented comprehensively.[6]

The first ever National Police Commission (NPC) in independent India was appointed by the first non-Congress government at the Centre on 15 November 1977. The Janata Party government led by Morarji Desai, which was swept to power 26 March 1977 the aftermath of the eighteen months of internal Emergency imposed by Indira Gandhi in June 1975, felt that 'there has been no comprehensive review at the national level of the police system after Independence despite radical changes in the political, social and economic situation in the country. A fresh examination', the new government felt, of the role and performance of the Police is necessary—both as a law enforcement agency, and as an institution to protect the rights of the citizens enshrined in the Constitution'.[7]

However, by the time the NPC chaired by Dharma Vira, a former Governor of West Bengal, submitted its first report on 7 February 1979, the Desai government was in crisis. By the time it submitted its final report in May 1981, the clock had turned full circle. Mrs Gandhi had come back to power on 14 January 1980. Though she did not disband the Commission on assuming office, she did not act on its report either. Ever since then the report of the NPC has been laying in bureaucratic cold storage. It is only appropriate that in the new millennium the role and functions of an institutions as important as the police was assessed. For, not merely during the years preceding the NPC, but also during the years when the NPC was putting together the report, weaknesses and problems afflicting the law and order administration have been exposed in a number of cases all over the country.

The NPC: Context, Terms of Reference and Recommendations

The political context of the appointment of the NPC has already been mentioned. The police was used not merely as an instrument of the state, or the government in power, but of politicians who had lost the legitimacy to rule. The parties and politicians who came to power in 1977 had borne the brunt of this misuse. Jayaprakash Narayan's call to the police to disobey illegal orders of their bosses during his movement against corruption preceding the emergency, too was a pertinent question in the context of redefining the role of the police in India.

The countrywide police agitation beginning in May–June 1979 might not be important as a context for the appointment of the NPC. But it was certainly crucial in exposing to the NPC the extent of the rot in the police. The NPC took account of it in its second report, 'In May–June 1979, the country witnessed the spectacle of policemen's unrest and agitation in some states in regard to their living and working conditions.'[8] It exposed the stark fact of political interference and the arrogance of the political class. The agitation was ignited by the slapping of a policeman in Punjab by an Akali Dal legislator,[9] the party which had held power only for a brief period in the late sixties prior to 1977. The event also exposed to the NPC the reality that their recommendations could be ignored by the Government of India. Dharma Vira's letter of 16 August 1979 accompanying the second report of the NPC to Y.B. Chavan, Deputy Prime Minister and Home Minister,[10] stated:

> When we gave the First Report to your predecessor on 7th February, we had the assurance that the Government would expeditiously examine our recommendations for very early implementation. Contrary to our hopes, the First Report has not yet been placed before the Parliament and consequently not yet released for general publication. We understand it was confidentially circulated to State Governments, on the eve of Chief Minister's Conference on 6 June 1979 which was convened as an emergent meeting in the context of policemen's unrest and agitation that erupted in some States in May–June 1979. Our recommendations in the First Report included several measures for the redressal of policemen's grievances relating to their living and working conditions. In retrospect we cannot help feeling that if our First Report had been duly published and it was made known that the recommendations were under active consideration of the Government, perhaps the subsequent stir by policemen could have been avoided.[11]

The NPC was appointed with wide ranging terms of reference. Aside from redefining the role, duties, powers and responsibilities of the police in prevention and control of crime and maintenance of public order, the NPC's responsibilities also included 'the principles underlying the present policing system'; 'the existing method of administration, disciplinary control and accountability'; 'the system of investigation and prosecution'; 'method of crime record and statistics'; rural and urban policing; 'steps . . . for modernising law enforcement'; 'the special responsibilities of the police towards the weaker sections of the community'. The Commission was asked to recommend measures and institutional arrangements 'to prevent misuse of powers by the police', by administrative or executive instructions' and for public complaints against the police and grievances of the police personnel. It was asked to review police community relations, police training and career development of the police personnel, and above all, to assess the future challenges to be faced by the Indian police.[12]

The NPC was given wide-ranging terms of reference for two reasons. First, the way the police was misused during the Emergency had shaken everybody, creating the feeling that the police needed a comprehensive reform if it were to become an agency insulated from politics. The second, there was also the feeling that piecemeal reforms may not restore public confidence in the police. For, reform in several aspects of the law and order administration may not be complete unless reforms have been effected in all connected aspects.

As stated earlier, the recommendations of the NPC are very comprehensive. It is not possible to review the entire range of recommendations contained in the eight volumes of the report. While all the recommendations are important and crucial for police reforms, recommendations related to issues such as 'welfare measures for police families','gram nyayalayas', 'maintenance of crime records and statistics' and so on are not being taken into consideration in this paper for reasons of economy of space. However, if possible, towards the end of the paper some of these may be linked with the main recom-mendations.

The NPC rightly attempted to take off from where the Police Commission of 1902, the last Police Commission at the All India level, had left.[13] Reviewing the developments of 72 years since then and new challenges before the police in India, it said:

> Apart from the tremendous increase in the sheer volume of crime work as such, there has also been a distinct change in the quality of police tasks under the compulsions of the fast developing society. In its efforts to bring about the social changes envisaged in the constitution. Government has been systematically adding new laws, rules and regulations through social legislation year after year. . . . Police involvement in the handling of social and economic offences as also traffic violations has meant increased confrontation with a wholly different class of offenders–different from the normal professional property criminal or the rustic, violent goonda. A police force which is used to rough and tough methods has to change its style while dealing with this new class of offenders and every situation connected with them has to be handled with tact and finesse, with due regard for the requirements of law.[14]

The NPC's concluding report discussed accountability, indeed a critical issue in the performance of a public agency like the police and attempted 'to discover what the police organization has to do *now* and *from now on*, to adequately discharge its responsibility in about AD 2000'. Since the NPC had identified the Police Act passed in 1861 by the British Parliament as the main problem with the police in India, it presented a draft for a new Police Act in the eighth report.[15] We shall discuss the recommendations of the NPC issue wise.

THE CONSTABULARY

The first report of the Commission, submitted in the form of a preliminary report for initiating the process of reform, therefore, focused on pivotal issues that might bring immediate improvements in the standard of policing. The issues affecting the constabulary, are better service conditions, pay structure, housing, supply of essential commodities, orderly system, machinery for redressal of grievances[16] and welfare measures for police families, recruitment, training and career planning for improving the efficacy of the police department, and finally enforcement of accountability modalities for inquiry into complaints against the police itself. Hence, the lament of the NPC at the government's inaction in the matter of the eruption of police unrest was not misplaced.

Where else could the process of changing the 'rough and tough methods' with a style full of 'tact and finesse' begin but from the constabulary which in the present day have 'moved far from the predominantly mechanical role assigned to him by the 1902 Commission and has now to interact with the public in larger numbers in a variety of situations where he has to apply his mind, exercise his judgement, use his powers of persuasion and appeal and enforce law with public understanding and cooperation'.[17] The NPC rightly disagreed with the 1902 Commission that the head constables and constables should not be utilized for duties requiring the exercise of discretion and judgement, such as the investigation of offences. An analysis of the existing duties of the constabulary by the NPC clearly indicated that the duties in which a constable is expected to apply his/her mind, exercise judgement and discretion and take initiatives far exceeded the duties which are purely mechanical. In fact, only fourteen per cent of the duties were found to be purely mechanical. Naturally, the constable was recommended to have better qualification, better status, better promotional avenues and a highly improved role performance.

POLICE ROLE AND MISUSE OF POLICE

Maintenance of law and order is actually maintenance of order in accordance with the law. 'After laws are made in the legislative bodies . . . Police come (in) . . . as the primary law enforcement agency available to the State. Enforcement by police is primarily an exercise of taking due notice of an infraction of law as soon as it occurs and ascertaining the connected facts thereof including the identity of the offender.'[18] Despite multifarious functions assigned to the police, as society and civilization acquire greater complexity, they basically remain an agency entrusted with maintaining order in society. Even though the NPC identified the police 'as the principal law enforcement agency of the State',[19] it rightly recognized its larger role as a part of the criminal justice system. Naturally, larger problems of the criminal justice system need to be attended to in order to make the police its efficacious limb.

Any part of the administration, particularly the police, will have its functions enlarged and role redefined once the context of administration changes from colonial to democratic, for people from being the ruled to becoming the focus of governance.[20] The change of context is apparent from the 'mission accomplished' statement of the Indian Police Commission of 1860,

> . . . we have arranged for this force being in all respects subordinate to the Civil Executive Government and we have paid due consideration to the Dispatch from the Majesty's Government of the 6 July on the constitution of the Police.

Obviously, the British government was absolutely unambiguous about the nature of the police force it wanted in India, and the role it was expected to perform. 'This position is very clearly reflected in the manner in which police role, duties, powers and responsibilities have been spelt out in the Police Act of 1861,' noted the NPC.[21] It recommended that the redefined role, duties, powers and responsibilities of the Police be spelled out, and the report lists twelve of them in the new Act. This comprehensive list along with the objective outlined for the police organization that 'every member of the organization renders service due and not service that is demanded, extracted or purchased' sets out the goal of people-oriented policing.

The misuse of the police has several dimensions to it. Criminalization of politics, politics of agitation, politicization of the police and violation of legal and administrative powers by the police themselves are some of the dimensions of misuse of the police. The politics of agitation and increasing politicization of society has taken its toll. 'Police have been increasingly drawn into the resultant law and order situations and are expected by the ruling party to deal with all such situations with a political eye. Putting down political dissent has become a tacitly accepted objective of the police system.'[22] The NPC analysed in great detail each dimension of the misuse of the police as an instrument. It also criticized the tendency of some of the state governments to issue instructions that contravened law. The long-term impact of such acts on the police cannot be underrated. While endorsing the general superintendence of the Police by the respective state governments, the NPC suggested measures like tenured office of the Chief of Police, selected from a panel drawn by a committee consisting of the Chairman of the Union Public Service Commission (Chair), the Union Home Secretary, the senior-most amongst the Heads of Central Police Organizations, the Chief Secretary of the state and the existing Police Chief of the state. Another important measure suggested by the NPC was the constitution of a statutory State Security Commission, constituted for a term of three years with State Minister for Home as the ex-officio Chairman and six other members. Its functions included, among other things, evaluation and review of the performance of the police on an annual basis.

RECRUITMENT AND TRAINING

One of the welcome recommendations of the NPC was that going beyond the existing structure, it suggested that the future recruitment in police should be only at two levels—Constable and the IPS. In other words, one opening at the state and the other at the centre, as against five openings currently, with slight variations from state to state in regard to the quantum of recruitment at different levels.[23] The suggestion is sound from the perspective of career planning and motivation as it would impel the police personnel to excel in the job to achieve promotion, as it opens up much greater promotional avenues at the lower level. It would also mean raising the quality of recruits substantially at the lowest level, which would automatically improve the standard of policing.

The basic flaw, however, in the NPC's recommendations on recruitment is that it does not foresee the implications of the suggested radical change in recruitment and organizational policy on the police leadership. First, the recommended phase-wise change does not mention even a tentative periodization. For, unless such a recommendation is put forth in a very concrete form, it may not be implemented ever. Of course, in the intervening period steps need to be taken to improve recruitment at the existing level and the NPC rightly made suggestions regarding that. Second, the basic flaw of the leadership of the Indian police is that it is an imposed one. It does not evolve from within. Due to the colonial heritage and the existing police culture, the IPS descends on the organization as a demi-god. This does not necessarily mean that a constable must rise to be the police chief. It is nonetheless important that the leadership must have the first hand experience of functioning at the basic unit of policing, at a police station in the Indian case, for a reasonable period. Even though the Indian Police (IP) cadre was the supercop during the British period, the officers' journey to the top was at a relatively slower pace, giving the officer a better feel of the lower levels because he spent greater time at the sub-district and district levels. The significant fact, however, is that it was important for the colonial administration to maintain the insularity of the leadership from the ranks, even from the supervisory levels, it need not be so in a democratic India. Whatever the point of entry for the leadership, it must begin its work at the police station level and function at that level for a minimum of five to seven years.

The NPC, however, must be complemented for suggesting that not more than 50 per cent of the requirements of the IPS be filled in by direct recruitment, the rest on promotion from the states.[24] It would, in fact, be much better if the central government creates a national pool from amongst the state level police officers who have put in five to ten years of service. Obviously, the issue of leadership requires greater and more intense debate.

Training in the police is naturally linked to the organizational structure and recruitment policy. If the organizational structure of the Indian police is altered as radically as suggested by the NPC with reduced entry points and greater avenues of promotion, the training programme would also need to be tailored accordingly. If the constable is to rise at least to the supervisory ranks, and ideally to the level of leadership, educational qualification of the recruits must be raised to the bachelor's degree. A better quality training, which is implied, would not be meaningful otherwise. In fact, to return for a while to recruitment policy, the recruitment tests would also have to be of a different kind to find candidates with the right kind of aptitude for the police force. Lamenting that the implementation of the recommendations of the Committee on Police Training has been half-hearted and tardy, the NPC stressed on its implementation and prescribed training programmes at each level. It rightly emphasized the teaching of modern management techniques and organizational behaviour to the leadership. In fact, some of it must be included in the training curricula at the supervisory level.[25]

ORGANIZATION AND STRUCTURE OF POLICE

The NPC literally put the nail on the head when it said:

> The hierarchical structure of the Indian Police was evolved in 1861 in the shadow of the Mutiny of 1857 with the main objective of ensuring imperial rule. This objective is no longer valid now. At that time exacting standards of efficiency were not required of the police and there was not even any sense of accountability to the people. Independence, a democratic Constitution and the flux of social change in this century have changed the picture entirely.[26]

The NPC went into the organization and structure of the police in sufficient detail. The basic thrust of their recommendations was fourfold: institutional, organizational, structural and operational. Contrary to the prevalent tendency to lay stress on district in talking of police reform, the NPC has rightly focused on the police station, which indeed is the basic and the most important unit of 'all police work and policing', and yet the most neglected one. Here too it rightly went into every aspect of police station–delimitation of its area, including the number of outposts supporting it, allocation of staff, the rank and status of the Station House Officer (SHO),[27] infrastructure at police stations—particularly communication and transport, and so on.

While the NPC was not in favour of putting the investigation and law and order duties in watertight compartments, it regretted 'The deployment of police personnel in law and order duties at the expense of investigation work in Police Station', which it admitted 'arises primarily from inadequacies of manpower resources at the Police Station'. The suggestion of the NPC to make the SHO the sole in charge of police station with full control over all the personnel at his/her disposal is indeed sound, yet there is room for greater specialization and professionalization in police work. It may be argued that the NPC has recommended greater professionalization through better training and in-service refresher courses. The recommendation is well taken, but in the age of narrow specialization, the need for specialists in different aspects of policing is growing. Fields like investigation, law and order, traffic control, crowd management, etc., are acquiring high degree of specialization due to the advancement of technology, and particularly when criminals are making increasing use of high technology equipments. Naturally, this area requires special attention.

The NPC under this section has made elaborate suggestions regarding the organizational structure of the police department—from police station, as discussed earlier, to police chief. It is difficult to go into details of all the suggestions made in this brief paper. It should, however, be mentioned that the NPC, irrespective of the merits of the suggestions made, many of which are indeed sound and some debatable (yet useful because they can generate public debate), has done a very comprehensive job of analysing various dimensions of police work and making elaborate suggestions. Without going into the details, we would like to emphasize the need for a public debate.

Though the NPC has dealt with the magisterial control over district police separately, we would like to bring it in under reorganization, for in a sense it is a question of reorganization of the district police. It is unfortunate that the district police has continued under an 'operational control exercised by the Chief Executive of the district', i.e. District Magistrate (DS), even five decades after the decolonization of the Indian State. It was designed to suit the objectives of the colonial rule, which needed to maintain 'a tight control over the people of this country so that the stability and growth of British rule was not threatened'. The Police Act of 1861 placed the police under 'general control and direction' of the DM, the phrase which is still ambiguous in law. The impact, however, is that 'the only areas in which the DM is not expected to control the activities of the Superintendent of Police (SP) are drill, arms and armaments and discipline. The DM has come to acquire considerable authority to interfere with the internal management of the district police organization'.[28] The NPC has rightly not recommended mechanisms, if any, for coordination with the DM. It has proposed amendments in section 4 of the Police Act, 1861 vesting in the SP administration of the police throughout a district, or part thereof.[29] Without rectifying this anomaly, reorganization of police in India will not be complete.

CONCLUSION

This paper has touched upon some of the critical issues reviewed by the NPC and briefly discussed its recommendations on them. The report of the NPC, as mentioned earlier, is indeed comprehensive. It is possible to disagree with several of the NPC's recommendations, but only because for the first time since independence, a comprehensive look at police reforms from the national perspective has been undertaken. In a small research paper like this one it is not sufficient to review or comment upon the entire range of questions the NPC has raised in eight of its reports.

The need for police reforms in India is getting urgent by the day. Unfortunately, no government since the submission of the NPC report has taken it seriously. We are lucky that police unrest has not raised its head on a countrywide scale since 1979, but disaffection in police organization in different states has surfaced from time to time, the last one in Bihar in 2001. The NPC has recommended an elaborate machinery for grievance redressal. No thought has so far been given to a matter as important as that. The report of the Fifth Pay Commission, which lowers the status of the constabulary and places the IPS at a disadvantage, is a veritable time bomb. The Fifth Pay Commission, which has exceeded its terms of reference in every respect, did not care to look into the NPC report while recommending changes in the position and status of the police personnel.

In a democracy, public-police relations is an important dimension of police work. The NPC has not ignored that. Though we do not discuss its recommendations on this issue, its importance cannot be underrated. It is a matter on which the police are in a position to take initiative autonomously. And they must do it forthwith.

The recommendations of the NPC are not dated, while some parts of it may need updating. It was not able to go into a number of issues which have acquired importance since. For example, terrorism, intelligence work, the role of the CBI and so on, which can be looked into. In fact, there have been attempts to put the issue of police reforms on the centre stage during the past few years. In 1996, two retired Directors General of Police filed a civil petition in the Supreme Court, praying for the issue of orders to the government to implement the recommendations of the NPC. In 1997, the then Union Home Minister Indrajit Gupta wrote to all the Chief Ministers to initiate measures on police reforms. In pursuance of the Supreme Court's directions issued in the context of the above mentioned writ petition, the Ministry of Home Affairs, Government of India constituted a committee headed by J.F. Rebeiro in 1998. However, police reforms have still eluded the country. A debate on the report of the NPC could well be the beginning to bring the issue in the mainstream of national agenda.

NOTES

1. For a detailed discussion and analysis of these event see my 'Chinks in the Armour', *The Hindu*, 10 January 2001 and 'Bizarre in Bihar', *The Hindu*, 17 May 2001.
2. For a discussion on this see my 'An Ambivalent Police', *Mainstream*, 13 October 2001.
3. See my 'Police Accountability', *The Hindu*, 28 May 2001.
4. 'The greatest obstacle to efficient police adminisitration flows from the domination of party politics under the state administration' (The Kerala Police Reorganization Committee, 1959). 'The evidence presented before the Commission has disclosed that members of political parties, particularly of the ruling party, whether in the Legislature or outside, interfere considerably in the working of the police for unlawful ends' (The Punjab Police Commission, 1961–2). 'We have little doubt that such (political) interference takes place, although it is difficult to say to what extent they are prevalent' (The West Bengal Police Commission, 1960–1). 'The problem of political interference is not a new one. . . . It has grown over the years, during the term of office of a number of different Ministers' (The Tamilnadu Police Commission, 1971). 'There have been instances where governments have been accused of using the police machinery for political ends. There are also instances of individual politicians interfering with the administration and the work of the police' (The Committee on Police Training, 1972). 'We would also like to point out . . . the danger of political infiltration into the police system. It is conceivable that some political parties adopt a deliberate strategy of injecting into the police system, through channels of recruitment at different levels, young men who are strongly committed to the ideologies of the political party and could be expected to influence, from within, the functioning of the police system to conform to these ideologies' (The National Police Commission, 1979).
5. Government of India, *Report of the Working Group on Police Administration*, Administrative Reforms Commission, Nasik; Government of India Press, 1970.
6. Government of India, *Report of the Committee on Police Training*, New Delhi: Ministry of Home Affairs, 1972.
7. Government of India, Ministry of Home Affairs, Resolution No. VI. 24021/36/77-GPA. I dated 15 November 1977. See Government of India, *First Report of the National Police Commission*, New Delhi: Ministry of Home Affairs, February 1979, pp. 1–2 for the full text of the resolution.
8. Government of India, *Second Report of the National Police Commission*, Ministry of Home Affairs, New Delhi: Government of India Press, August 1979, p. 1.

9. For an analysis see Ajay K. Mehra, 'Dealing with Police Unrest', *Mainstream*, 20 November 1982.
10. Charan Singh was Home Minister when the NPC was appointed. H.M. Patel was Home Minister when its first report was submitted. Y.B. Chavan, leading the breakaway Congress, was Deputy Prime Minister and Home Minister in the short-lived Charan Singh government when the next report was presented. The rest of the reports were presented ironically to the Indira Gandhi government, the excesses of whose government during the Emergency had motivated the Janata Party government to appoint the NPC.
11. Government of India, February 1979, op. cit., p. iii.
12. Ibid., pp. 1–2.
13. It is widely known that the present structure of the police administration in India was designed and created by the British soon after the fateful events of 1857. The design was based on the recommendations of the Police Commission appointed in 1860 by Her Majesty's Government. The commission submitted its report in 1861 and in the same year the new police force came into existence. By the beginning of this century the colonial administration felt the need to review the functioning of the police force. Hence the Commission of 1902 was appointed. We shall come back to some of the comments of the Police Commission of 1902 later in the paper in appropriate contexts. For details of historical background see Ajay K. Mehra, *Police in Changing India*, New Delhi: Usha, 1985.
14. Government of India, February 1979, op. cit., p. 11.
15. Government of India, *Eighth and Concluding Report of the National Police Commission*, May 1981, pp. 13–26 and 43–89.
16. As stated earlier, the first report of the NPC was submitted to the MHA in February 1979. The NPC had already considered and recommended a grievance redressal machinery, which became a much talked about issue three months later in the wake of police unrest. Unfortunately, even today most states do not have an effective grievance redressal machinery for police personnel.
17. Government of India, February 1979, op. cit., p. 11.
18. Ibid., August 1979, op. cit., p. 5.
19. Ibid., p. 10.
20. Making a distinction between role and functions may amount to indulging in semantics, but it is a worthwhile exercise to understand the impact of change from colonial rule to democratic governance for the police. For a detailed discussion on the subject see Ajay K. Mehra, 'Functions and Role of Police: An Analysis of Police Behaviour in Colonial and Democratic India', in S.K. Chaturvedi (ed.), *Police and Emerging Challenges*, Delhi: B.R. Publishing Corporation, 1988, pp. 1–30.

21. Government of India, August 1979, op. cit., p. 11.
22. Ibid., p. 21.
23. Government of India, *Fifth Report of the National Police Commission*, New Delhi: Ministry of Home Affairs, November 1980, pp. 1–2.
24. Ibid., *Sixth Report of the National Police Commission*, New Delhi: Ministry of Home Affairs, March 1981, p. 7.
25. See Government of India, November 1980 and March 1981, op. cit.
26. Ibid., *Seventh Report of the National Police Commission*, New Delhi: Ministry of Home Affairs, May 1981, p. 1.
27. While in some parts of the country the Officer-in-Charge of a police station is known as SHO, in many parts the former nomenclature is used. The police manuals too refer to the officer as Officer-in-Charge. The NPC is clearly in favour of designating the presiding officer of police stations as SHO. See Government of India, May 1981, ibid., p. 2.
28. Government of India, November 1980, op. cit., pp. 33–4.
29. Ibid., p. 44.

Contributors

AMARJIT S. NARANG is Professor of Political Science and coordinator, Human Rights Education at Indira Gandhi National Open University, New Delhi. He has participated in UN Human Rights Commission sessions for several years and writes extensively on issues related to Indian Politics, Human Rights and Ethnicity.

ASGHAR ALI ENGINEER is Chairman, Centre for study of Society and Secularism, Mumbai and Director, Institute of Islamic Studies. He is recipient of several awards including Right Livelihood Honorary Award and a renowned Human Rights activist and social reformer.

KIRPAL SINGH DHILLON is a former Director General of Police, Vice-Chancellor and Fellow of Indian Institute of Advanced Study, Shimla. He writes extensively on criminal justice, human rights and social issues. Two of his books on Indian police history and police and politics in India have been well-received in India and abroad.

R.K. RAGHAVAN retired as Director, Central Bureau of Investigation. He is the author of *Indian Police: Problems, Planning and Perspectives* (Manohar, 1989) and *Policing a Democracy: A Comparative Study of India and the US* (Manohar, 1999).

PRAKASH LOUIS is the Executive Director of the Indian Social Institute New Delhi. He contributes to journals like *Economic and Political Weekly, Mainstream and Social Change.* He also contributes regularly to many national dailies. Two of his major publications are *People Power: The Naxalite Movement in Central Bihar* and *Political Sociology of Dalit Assertion.*

PREM DHAR MALAVIYA is a retired member of the Indian Police Service. He has been the Director-General, Madhya Pradesh, Police and Director of the National Police Academy. He was the recipient of UNDP Human Rights Fellowship and has had long and varied experience of civil police, police research, training and anti-insurgency operations.

ABDULRAHIM VIJAPUR is Professor of Political Science at Aligarh Muslim University. He is currently working as Professor, Ford Foundation Endowed Chair in Dalit Studies at the Academy of Third World Studies, Jamia Millia Islamia, New Delhi.

MD. MOHIBUL HAQUE is Lecturer in Political Science at Aligarh Muslim University, Aligarh.

K.S. SUBRAMANIAN is former Director General of Police, Professor of Public Administration, Indian Institute of Public Administration and Director General of the State Institute of Public Administration and Rural Development, Tripura.

ARSHI KHAN is Senior Lecturer in the Centre for Federal Studies, Hamdard University. He has written several papers on federalism, minority rights and conflict resolution and edited books and journals in India, USA, UAE and Northern Cyprus.

IQBAL A. ANSARI served the Aligarh Muslim University from 1962 to 1995. He was Visiting Professor at Jamia Hamdard (2001–3) and Jamia Millia Islamia (2003–4). His publications include three volumes on Minorities and one on communal riots, the *State and Law in India* (1997). He is founder Secretary General of the Minorities Council and is closely associated with Human Rights Movement. He edits the quarterly *Human Rights Today.*

CHAMAN LAL honoured with the national award of Padamshri is a Police Officer with wide field experience of working in Madhya Pradesh, Punjab, Nagaland, BSF, ITBP and the Prime Minister's Security. Since his retirement from the IPS in 1996, he has been associated with the National Human Rights Commission dealing with important issues such as Jails, Child Labour, Bonded Labour and Mental Health, etc.

HARVINDER SINGH PHOOLKA is a Senior Advocate practicing in Supreme Court of India. He has been Additional Advocate General for State of Punjab, Senior Standing Counsel for Central Government, Senior Standing Counsel for Election Commission of India, Advisor to Chief Minister of Delhi. He has been Convener of Citizen's Committee. Phoolka was the main counsel for victims before Misra Commission of Inquiry as well as Nanavati Commission of Inquiry.

VRINDA GROVER is a Senior Advocate and a human rights activist.

AJAY K. MEHRA is Director, Centre for Public Affairs. He writes extensively on Indian Polity and policy affairs and has edited a number of books on these subjects.